Jesus Christ Today

JESUS CHRIST TODAY

A COMMENTARY ON
The Book of Hebrews

Neil R. Lightfoot

1976

BAKER BOOK HOUSE
Grand Rapids, Michigan

Library of Congress
Catalog Card Number: 76-45239
ISBN: 0-8010-5563-6

Printed in the United States of America

TO

Dad and Mother

and in memory of
William D. Lightfoot, Jr.

"Jesus Christ is the same yesterday and today and for ever."
(13:8)

"Today, when you hear his voice, do not harden your hearts. . . ."
(3:7-8; cf. 3:15; 4:7)

"But exhort one another every day, as long as it is called 'today,' that none of you may be hardened by the deceitfulness of sin."
(3:13)

"I appeal to you, brethren, bear with my word of exhortation. . . ."
(13:22)

Preface

In the sacred writings the word "today" often has special meaning. When Jesus returned to His hometown of Nazareth and went into the synagogue, He opened the Scriptures, read from Isaiah, and said, "Today this scripture has been fulfilled in your hearing" (Lk. 4:21). If the hearers were to understand Scripture, they were to see its fulfilment in Jesus "today." Early apostolic preaching characteristically referred to Psalm 2—"Thou art my Son, today I have begotten thee"—and saw its fulfilment in Jesus (Acts 13:33). "Today" expresses realization of long held anticipations and hopes. "Today" is a word of fulfilment and a word of opportunity. It corresponds to the "now" of the Gospel of John (Jn. 4:23; 5:25) and explains the urgency of Paul's "now" in his exhortations to Christian living (Col. 3:8; Rom. 6:19).

The author of Hebrews especially connects "today" with Jesus. As William Manson expressed it, "It is ... the 'today' of the Christian revelation as centered in the Incarnation which forms the core and all-essential substance of the writer's presentation." Hebrews 1–2 portray Jesus' grand enthronement which takes place "today" (1:5; cf. 5:5). Hebrews 3–4 take up the "today" of Psalm 95:7-11 and by repetition impress it on the minds of the readers. "Today" they are to respond to the exhortation of Scripture. Hebrews 13, as it warns against strange teachings, seeks to bind the readers to Jesus Christ, who is "yesterday and today the same and for ever" (13:8).[1] *Jesus Christ Today* is chosen as a title for Hebrews because Jesus Christ is its main subject and because "today" emphasizes particularly what the Epistle emphasizes— Jesus is now enthroned with the Father and as High Priest intercedes for His own. "Yesterday" He lived on earth as man, died, and rose again; "today" He lives in God's presence and "holds his priesthood

---

1. The quotation here follows the Greek word order.

permanently, because he continues for ever" (7:24). "Today" as a descriptive title for Hebrews asserts that this masterful, first-century exhortation is also a contemporary exhortation.

Many would dispute that Hebrews is in any sense contemporary. It deals in symbolism and many of its symbols—blood, priesthood, sacrifice—pertain to a distant age. Much of its argumentation has to do with a bygone, Levitical ritual. Modern readers find this difficult, and too often lay Hebrews aside as boring and wearisome. It is regrettable that many readers never go far enough into and through the sacrificial language to see that Hebrews is the greatest piece of exhortation found in the New Testament. Chapter after chapter urges the Christian to hang on to his faith in Christ, to hang on no matter what the odds or circumstances. The exhortation throughout is for Christians to pay attention to the Word, ever living and active, that spoke not only in the past but also speaks to the present. In times of meaninglessness and drift, Hebrews, although outwardly archaic, is a modern book with a modern message.

There are commentaries on the Biblical text, and there are commentaries. Perhaps I should explain what this work attempts to be.

I have written this as a commentary for college-university level work and for serious students of the Bible. This accounts for some explanations given that would be superfluous for specialists. I have tried to refer to articles and books that would be helpful and accessible to English students, although at times it has been necessary to cite publications in other languages. The summaries given at appropriate places are for students and at the ends of chapters additional notes are given for further study. These notes are put in special sections, unless they fit better with the body of the text. Then they are included in footnotes. This commentary seeks to be both exegetical and theological —exegetical always as to its method and theological, I hope, in stressing the message of Hebrews. Above all, I have tried to produce a work that is interesting and not tedious or obscure for the general reader. The text of the Revised Standard Version has been used as a basis for comments. The Revised Standard is a very readable translation and a good one, despite criticism to the contrary. My convictions are based on my doctoral dissertation on the RSV New Testament.

I would add that the present work has been an independent research project. Nevertheless, I have profited immeasurably from others: from F. F. Bruce, from James Moffatt, and from A. B. Bruce, who incomparably exposes the soul of Hebrews. Their works are indispensable and should be consulted for discussions of many points that I could not include.

It has now been some years since I began. The bulk of this work was done before 1970, but until now I have been unable to bring it to a close. There have been delays, distractions, and interruptions innumerable. I have soared and stumbled on Hebrews, sometimes within the same hour. But I delight in knowing that I have somewhat traversed the territory. It has been a faith-building journey.

To my friends who have encouraged me, I say, "Thank you." May God bless all who read Hebrews and discover in it *Jesus Christ Today*.

March, 1975
Abilene Christian College

Contents

Abbreviations

Alford	Henry Alford. *The Greek Testament*. 4 vols. Second ed. London, 1861.
Arndt-Gingrich	William F. Arndt and F. Wilbur Gingrich. *A Greek-English Lexicon of the New Testament and Other Early Christian Literature*. Chicago, 1957.
ASV	American Standard Version
ATR	*Anglican Theological Review*
Barclay	William Barclay. *The Letter to the Hebrews*. Edinburgh, 1955.
Barclay	————. *A New Testament Wordbook*. London, 1955.
BASOR	*Bulletin of the American Schools of Oriental Research*
Beare	F. W. Beare. *The First Epistle of Peter*. Oxford, 1947.
BibSac	*Bibliotheca Sacra*
Blass-Debrunner-Funk	F. Blass and A. Debrunner. *A Greek Grammar of the New Testament and Other Early Christian Literature*. Translated by Robert W. Funk. Chicago, 1961.
A. B. Bruce	A. B. Bruce. "The Epistle to Hebrews," *A Dictionary of the Bible*, II. Edited by James Hastings. New York, 1899.
A. B. Bruce	————. *The Epistle to the Hebrews: The First Apology for Christianity*. Edinburgh, 1899.
F. F. Bruce	F. F. Bruce. *Biblical Exegesis in the Qumran Texts*. Grand Rapids, 1959.
F. F. Bruce	————. *The Epistle to the Hebrews*. Grand Rapids, 1964.
F. F. Bruce	————. (ed.). *Promise and Fulfillment*. Edinburgh, 1963.

Buchanan	George Wesley Buchanan. *To the Hebrews*. Garden City, N.Y., 1972.
Burton	Ernest De Witt Burton. *A Critical and Exegetical Commentary on the Epistle to the Galatians*. New York, 1920.
CBQ	*Catholic Biblical Quarterly*
CJT	*Canadian Journal of Theology*
CTM	*Concordia Theological Monthly*
Davidson	A. B. Davidson. *The Epistle to the Hebrews*. Edinburgh, 1882.
DCG	*A Dictionary of Christ and the Gospels*. Edited by James Hastings. 2 vols. New York, 1906-08.
Deissmann	Adolf Deissmann. *Bible Studies*. Translated by Alexander Grieve. Edinburgh, 1901.
Deissmann	———. *Light from the Ancient East*. Translated by Lionel R. M. Strachan. New York, 1927.
Deissmann	———. *Paul, A Study in Social and Religious History*. Translated by William E. Wilson. Second ed., 1927. New York, 1957 reprint.
Dibelius	Martin Dibelius. *A Fresh Approach to the New Testament and Early Christian Literature*. New York, 1936.
Dods	Marcus Dods. *The Epistle to the Hebrews*. London, 1910.
EB	*Encyclopedia Biblica*. Edited by T. K. Cheyne and J. S. Black. 4 vols. New York, 1899-1903.
ERV	English Revised Version
ExpTimes	*Expository Times*
Feine-Behm-Kümmel	Paul Feine, Johannes Behm, and Werner G. Kümmel. *Introduction to the New Testament*. Translated by A. J. Matill, Jr. Nashville, 1966.
Fuller	Reginald H. Fuller. *A Critical Introduction to the New Testament*. London, 1966.
Gregory	Caspar René Gregory. *Canon and Text of the New Testament*. Edinburgh, 1907.
Guthrie	Donald Guthrie. *New Testament Introduction*. London, 1961-65.
Harnack	Adolf Harnack. *The Mission and Expansion of Christianity in the First Three Centuries*. 2 vols. Translated and edited by James Moffatt. New York, 1962 reprint.

Harrison	Everett F. Harrison. "The Theology of the Epistle to the Hebrews," *Bibliotheca Sacra* 121 (1964), 333-340.
HDB	*A Dictionary of the Bible*. Edited by James Hastings. 5 vols. New York, 1899-1904.
Héring	Jean Héring. *The Epistle to the Hebrews*. Translated by A. W. Heathcote and P. J. Allcock. London, 1970.
Hewitt	Thomas Hewitt. *The Epistle to the Hebrews*. London, 1960.
Higgins	A. J. B. Higgins. "The Old Testament and Some Aspects of New Testament Christology," *Promise and Fulfillment*. Edited by F. F. Bruce. Edinburgh, 1963.
HTR	*Harvard Theological Review*
IDB	*The Interpreter's Dictionary of the Bible*. Edited by George A. Buttrick. 4 vols. New York, 1962.
JBL	*Journal of Biblical Literature*
Jeremias	J. Jeremias. *Jerusalem in the Time of Jesus*. Translated by F. H. and C. H. Cave. Philadelphia, 1969.
JTS	*Journal of Theological Studies*
Kistemaker	Simon Kistemaker. *The Psalm Citations in the Epistle to the Hebrews*. Amsterdam, 1961.
KJV	King James Version
Leonard	William Leonard. *Authorship of the Epistle to the Hebrews*. Vatican City, 1939.
Liddell-Scott-Jones	*A Greek-English Lexicon*. Edition revised by Sir H. S. Jones. Oxford, 1925-1940.
Lindars	Barnabas Lindars. *New Testament Apologetic: The Doctrinal Significance of the Old Testament Quotations*. Philadelphia, 1961.
LXX	Septuagint
T. W. Manson	T. W. Manson. *Studies in the Gospels and Epistles*. Edited by Matthew Black. Manchester, 1962.
William Manson	William Manson. *The Epistle to the Hebrews*. London, 1951.
Metzger	Bruce M. Metzger. *A Textual Commentary on the Greek New Testament*. London, 1971.
Michel	Otto Michel. *Der Brief an die Hebräer*. Twelfth ed. Göttingen, 1966.
MOF	James Moffatt. *A New Translation of the Bible*.
Moffatt	————. *A Critical and Exegetical Commentary on the Epistle to the Hebrews*. Edinburgh, 1924.

Moffatt	———. *An Introduction to the Literature of the New Testament.* Third ed. Edinburgh, 1918.
Montefiore	Hugh Montefiore. *A Commentary on the Epistle to the Hebrews.* London, 1964.
Moulton- Howard- Turner	James Hope Moulton, W. F. Howard, and Nigel Turner. *A Grammar of New Testament Greek.* 3 vols. Edinburgh, 1908, 1929, 1963.
Moulton- Milligan	James Hope Moulton and George Milligan. *The Vocabulary of the Greek Testament.* London, 1930.
MS, MSS	Manuscript, Manuscripts
MT	Masoretic Text
Nairne	Alexander Nairne. *The Epistle of Priesthood.* Edinburgh, 1913.
Nairne	———. *The Epistle to the Hebrews.* Cambridge, 1922.
NEB	New English Bible
NovTest	*Novum Testamentum*
NTS	*New Testament Studies*
Peake	A. S. Peake. *The Epistle to the Hebrews.* Edinburgh, 1914.
Peake	———. *Heroes and Martyrs of Faith.* Edinburgh, 1910.
Ramsay	Sir William Ramsay. *The Letters to the Seven Churches of Asia.* London, 1904.
Ramsay	———. *The Teaching of Paul in Terms of the Present Day.* London, 1914.
Richardson	Alan Richardson (ed.). *A Theological Word Book of the Bible.* New York, 1951.
Robinson	Theodore H. Robinson. *The Epistle to the Hebrews.* New York, n.d.
Ropes	James Hardy Ropes. *The Epistle of St. James.* Edinburgh, 1916.
RSV	Revised Standard Version
Selwyn	E. G. Selwyn. *The First Epistle of St. Peter.* London, 1946.
SJT	*Scottish Journal of Theology*
Souter	Alexander Souter. *The Text and Canon of the New Testament.* Edited by C. S. C. Williams. London, 1954.
Sowers	S. G. Sowers. *The Hermeneutics of Philo and Hebrews.* Richmond, 1965.
Spicq	C. Spicq. *L'Épître aux Hébreux.* 2 vols. Paris, 1953.
StEv	*Studia Evangelica*

StPaul	*Studiorum Paulinorum Congressus Internationalis 1961.* 2 vols. *(Analecta Biblica* 17-18). Rome, 1963.
Stuart	Moses Stuart. *Commentary on the Epistle to the Hebrews.* Second ed. Andover, 1833.
Tasker	R. V. G. Tasker. *The Gospel in the Epistle to the Hebrews.* London, 1950.
Tasker	————. *The Greek Testament: Being the Text Translated in the New English Bible 1961.* Oxford, 1964.
Tasker	————. *The Old Testament in the New Testament.* London, 1954.
TDNT	*Theological Dictionary of the New Testament.* Edited by G. Kittel and G. Friedrich. Translated and edited by G. W. Bromiley. 9 vols. Grand Rapids, 1964-74.
TEV	*Good News for Modern Man. The New Testament in Today's English Version.*
Thayer	J. H. Thayer. *A Greek-English Lexicon of the New Testament.* New York, 1886.
Thyen	Hartwig Thyen. *Der Stil der Jüdisch-Hellenistische Homilie.* Göttingen, 1955.
Vaux	Roland de Vaux. *Ancient Israel: Its Life and Institutions.* Translated by John McHugh. New York, 1961.
Weiss	Johannes Weiss. *Earliest Christianity,* II. Translation edited by Frederick C. Grant. New York, 1957 reprint.
Westcott	Brooke Foss Westcott. *The Epistle to the Hebrews.* Third ed. London, 1903.
Wikenhauser	Alfred Wikenhauser. *New Testament Introduction.* Translated by Joseph Cunningham. New York, 1960.
Zahn	Theodor Zahn. *Introduction to the New Testament,* II. Translated by John Moore Trout and others. Edinburgh, 1909.
ZNW	*Zeitschrift für die Neutestamentliche Wissenschaft*
Zuntz	G. Zuntz. *The Text of the Epistles: A Disquisition upon the Corpus Paulinum.* London, 1953.

An Introduction
to
HEBREWS

Of all the precious writings that speak of the Christian faith, it is doubtful if any makes a more distinctive contribution than the Epistle to the Hebrews. It describes in an elevated, incomparable way the true nature and value of the Christian religion. For the author of the Epistle, Christianity is the *better* and the *best* of all possible religions. Beside it, there is none other.

Yet the Epistle through the centuries has been surrounded with mystery. Like the Melchizedek of whom it speaks, it seems to make its appearance in history "without father or mother or genealogy." Who was the author that produced it? What were the time, the place, and the circumstances that brought it forth? To whom was it originally addressed? And, indeed, is it even permissible to speak of it as an epistle? There have been many answers suggested to these questions, but no last word has been spoken on any of them. The Epistle, not inappropriately, has been termed "the great riddle of the New Testament."

Authorship

A major reason why the Epistle is such a riddle is that its authorship is altogether unknown. Why did the author write anonymously? Only guesses can be made. The simple fact is that the author did not choose to give his name. Although he was certainly not unfamiliar to his readers, within a generation or so, and for some unexplained reason, exact knowledge of who the author was passed out of existence. In the second century A.D., the most learned men were in the dark on this question. True, there were opinions and conjectures, and there have been many conjectures since that time. Some of the main conjectures are as follows:

Paul

The oldest extant evidence on authorship of the Epistle comes

19

from Clement of Alexandria, near the close of the second century. Clement said that it was written by Paul for Hebrews in the Hebrew language, and that it was translated into Greek by Luke for the Greeks.[1] A generation later Clement's successor, the learned Origen, was willing to follow in the steps of his teacher up to a point: the thoughts of the Epistle, he said, were Paul's, but the style and composition were the work of someone else.[2] After the time of Origen, the opinion spread gradually that the anonymous Epistle was from the hand of Paul. In an early papyrus manuscript from Egypt, the Chester Beatty manuscript abbreviated as P[46], the Epistle to the Hebrews appears in a collection of the Pauline letters in the order of Romans, Hebrews, 1 and 2 Corinthians, Galatians, etc. So at that time (early third century) and in that area it was the firm belief that Paul the Apostle was the author of the Epistle. This opinion, which came to be dominant in the East, spread gradually to the West and eventually prevailed in the church from the fifth century to the time of the Reformation.

The reasons given for Pauline authorship have been many.[3]

1. The circumstances presented in the closing verses of Hebrews 13 are similar to those in the acknowledged Pauline letters.

    a. "You should understand that our brother Timothy has been released, with whom I shall see you if he comes soon" (13:23). Paul and Timothy were, of course, close associates for many years.

    b. "Pray for us, for we are sure that we have a clear conscience..." (13:18). Paul asks his readers to pray for him (Rom. 15:30; 2 Cor. 1:11) and often refers to a good or clean conscience (Acts 23:1; 24:16; 2 Cor. 1:12; 1 Tim. 3:9; 2 Tim. 1:3).

    c. "I urge you the more earnestly to do this in order that I may be restored to you the sooner" (13:19). Paul wrote in the same manner to Philemon and to the Philippians, expressing his hope that he might see them soon (Phm. 22; Phil. 1:24-25).

    d. Expressions like "the God of peace" (13:20) and "grace be with all of you" (13:25) appear similarly in the writings of Paul (cf. Rom. 15:33; 1 Thess. 5:28; 2 Thess. 3:18).

2. The ideas presented in Hebrews are similar to those found in the Pauline letters.

---

1. Eusebius, *Ecclesiastical History* 6.14.

2. Ibid., 6.25.

3. In the nineteenth century Moses Stuart devoted more than a hundred pages of his commentary to a defense of the Pauline view (Stuart, pp. 120-253); for a twentieth century defense of Pauline authorship, see Leonard, pp. 3-43.

a. Christology. In Hebrews and in Paul Christ is represented as the image of God (1:3; cf. Col. 1:15); the agent and sustainer of all creation (1:2-3, 10-12; cf. Col. 1:16-17; 1 Cor. 8:6); humbled as man and exalted above the angels (2:14-17; 1:4-14; cf. Phil. 2:5-11; Eph. 1:20-23); the very One whose death was a sacrifice for all (1:3; 2:9; 9:26; 10:12; cf. 1 Tim. 2:6; Eph. 5:2; 1 Cor. 15:3).

b. The Two Covenants. The old covenant was only a shadow of good things in the new (10:1; cf. Col. 2:16-17), just as events and arrangements in the old were typical of the new (8:1-6; 4:1-2, 11; cf. 1 Cor. 10:11). The old covenant, because of its weakness (7:18; cf. Rom. 8:3), had to look to something beyond itself (8:8-13) and be superseded by the establishment of the new covenant (7:19; 8:13; cf. 2 Cor. 3:9-11).

3. A number of the terms and phrases in Hebrews are similar to those found in the Pauline letters. The following is a list of some of the parallels as given by Moses Stuart.[4]

a. Hebrews 1:5: "Thou art my Son, today I have begotten thee." Acts 13:33: "Thou art my Son, today I have begotten thee." The quotation is used by Paul and applied in both passages (but nowhere else in the New Testament) to Christ.

b. Hebrews 2:4: ". . . by signs and wonders and various miracles and by gifts of the Holy Spirit."
1 Corinthians 12:4: "Now there are varieties of gifts, but the same Spirit."
1 Corinthians 12:11: "All these are inspired by one and the same Spirit, who apportions to each one individually as he wills."
Romans 12:6: "Having gifts that differ according to the grace given to us. . . ."
All of these passages speak of the miraculous yet differing gifts distributed by the Spirit.

c. Hebrews 2:10: ". . . for whom and by whom all things exist."
Romans 11:36: "For from him and through him and to him are all things."
Colossians 1:16: "All things were created through him and for him."

---

4. See Stuart, pp. 147-51. One sometimes wonders if such parallels have really been looked at by scholars of recent years. It is necessary to caution, however, that no conclusions about such parallels should be drawn without careful study of the parallels in the Greek text. The Greek phrases are often *similar*, not necessarily *identical*. See Stuart, where the parallels in Greek are listed.

       1 Corinthians 8:6: "...one God...from whom are all things and for whom we exist."

       In all these passages God is spoken of as author and possessor of all things.

  d. Hebrews 2:16: "...the descendants of Abraham."

       Galatians 3:29: "And if you are Christ's, then you are Abraham's offspring."

       Galatians 3:7: "...men of faith who are the sons of Abraham."

       Romans 4:16: "...Abraham, for he is the father of us all."

       The designation of the family of faith as descendants or sons of Abraham is found only in Paul and in Hebrews.

  e. Hebrews 4:12: "For the word of God is living and...sharper than any two-edged sword."

       Ephesians 6:17: "...the sword of the Spirit, which is the word of God."

       The comparison of the word of God to a sword is found only in Paul and in Hebrews.

  f. Hebrews 6:3: "...if God permits."

       1 Corinthians 16:7: "...if the Lord permits."

       This is a phrase nowhere else employed.

  g. Hebrews 10:19: "...since we have confidence to enter the sanctuary by the blood of Jesus."

       Romans 5:2: "Through him we have obtained access to this grace in which we stand."

       Ephesians 2:18: "...for through him we both have access ...to the Father."

       Ephesians 3:12: "...in whom we have boldness and confidence of access through our faith in him."

       The idea of access is designated in this way only in Paul and in Hebrews.

These are some of the main parallels that have been noted in the past in defense of the theory of Pauline authorship of Hebrews.

It is true, however, that in recent decades Pauline authorship of the Epistle has been generally rejected. Famous Reformers like Luther, Melanchthon, Calvin, and Beza led the way in the rejection; many leading scholars especially of the nineteenth century joined in, until at last the long-held Pauline view was forced to give way. Today it is argued that Paul could not have written Hebrews, the line of reasoning being something like the following.

  1. The historical support for Pauline authorship is practically nil. The evidence from Clement of Alexandria, referred to earlier, is late

and in certain respects admittedly inaccurate. The Epistle clearly was not first written in Hebrew; for the smoothness and artistic polish of the Greek, regarded as the finest in the New Testament, argue for its being an original composition. This being so, the reference to Luke as a translator is likewise in error. The witness of Origen lends even less support to the Pauline view. Origen thought that the ideas of the Epistle belonged to Paul, but would not commit himself on the question of actual authorship. "But who wrote the epistle, God only knows certainly."[5] So it seems that in the area where Pauline authorship was first accepted, even there considerable confusion existed concerning it. Added to this is the negative character of other evidences from the second and third centuries. The Muratorian Canon,[6] Irenaeus, Hippolytus, and Gaius of Rome did not regard the Epistle as Pauline.[7] It is evident, then, that there is little historical evidence to show that the Apostle Paul was in the real sense the author of Hebrews.

2. The style and language of the Epistle differ considerably from the letters known to have been written by Paul. Wikenhauser points out that 168 words in Hebrews do not occur elsewhere in the New Testament, and an additional 124 do not appear in Paul.[8] The polished style of the Epistle, characterized by its precise syntax and its masterful use of rhetorical devices, is very unlike the often rough, abrupt style of Paul. Hebrews reads like a careful composition, not as an occasional letter whose semi-rambling process of dictation at times interrupts and obscures the main line of thought.

3. The thoughts of the Epistle and other of its aspects are likewise dissimilar to Paul. Noticeably absent from Hebrews, except for a few instances (2:3; 10:10; 13:8, 21), are the typical Pauline terms "Jesus Christ," "Our Lord Jesus Christ," "Christ Jesus" and "the Lord" (for Christ)—expressions used by Paul more than 600 times. Remarkable also is the fact that Paul never mentions the high-priesthood of Christ, a subject that the author of Hebrews explores in depth. The method of argumentation pursued in the Epistle is different from Paul's. Paul regularly quotes from the Old Testament, using such formulas as "it is written" or "the Scripture says"; while the author of Hebrews introduces his citations with such formulas as "God says" or "the Holy Spirit says" or "it has been testified somewhere." In its use of Scripture

---

5. Eusebius, *Ecclesiastical History* 6.25.
6. This is an early list of New Testament books, drawn up at Rome in the last part of the second century. It ascribes to "the blessed Apostle Paul" thirteen letters addressed to seven churches and to three individuals, thus excluding Hebrews. See Gregory, p. 132.
7. See Zahn, pp. 301-02, 309-10.
8. Wikenhauser, p. 467.

Hebrews quotes from the Septuagint translation. This is not always the case with Paul. And does it not seem strange that Paul, who so much insisted on his independent authority (Gal. 1:11-12), would have written that the great salvation "was attested to us by those who heard him" (2:3)?

But these points, though often made, do not prove that Paul could not have been the author. Who can say what kind of vocabulary or method of reasoning Paul would have used had he addressed himself to the subject of the Epistle? As R. V. G. Tasker has said, "Had St. Paul been concerned to develop the contrast between the sacrificial death of Christ and the Levitical system of sacrifice, just as he had in Romans contrasted law and grace, we cannot say that he could not have done so along the lines of this Epistle...."[9] Although the arguments against Pauline authorship are weighty, at best they show only the improbability that Hebrews was written by Paul.

Barnabas

Another early view of authorship, current in some parts of Africa as is indicated by Tertullian,[10] named Barnabas as the author of the Epistle. The identification was made most likely because it was thought that Barnabas, as a Levite from Cyprus (Acts 4:36), was eminently qualified to write on the Levitical regulations of the law. There was, further, a possible connection between Barnabas as a "son of exhortation" (Acts 4:36) and the "word of exhortation" (13:22) given by the author of Hebrews. But if Barnabas were the author, why was it not more generally known in ancient times? Being an early disciple and a companion of Paul, Barnabas himself was well known. And is it likely that Barnabas, one of the early disciples in Jerusalem, would have written 2:3? It is probable that Barnabas as author was simply an ancient hypothesis advanced in the absence of any real knowledge on the question. Certainly there is nothing in the Epistle to indicate that Barnabas wrote it.

Luke or Clement of Rome

Origen, as he discussed the problem of authorship, mentioned that some believed that the Epistle was the work of Luke, and others that it was the work of Clement of Rome.[11] From a literary standpoint, perhaps there is some basis for associating the Epistle with the author of Luke and Acts; but it would be precarious to claim Lucan authorship

9. Tasker, *Gospel,* pp. 9-10.
10. Tertullian, *On Modesty* 20.
11. Eusebius, *Ecclesiastical History* 6.25.

solely on the grounds of stylistic similarities.[12] As for Clement, it is indeed true that striking parallels exist between his letter to the Corinthians (1 Clement) and Hebrews. These parallels, however, indicate no more than that at Rome Clement knew and made use of the Epistle. But there are significant differences between 1 Clement and Hebrews, as Westcott has shown.[13] Montefiore has summed up the matter well: "The Epistle to the Hebrews is written by someone with a first-rate mind, an economical style and a great command of language. Clement's Epistle to the Corinthians is written in discursive vein by someone with a second-rate mind and an imitative style."[14] So Clement can hardly be considered a serious candidate for authorship.

Apollos

In the modern era other names have been put forward. Martin Luther, in denying Pauline authorship, seems to have originated the idea that Apollos was the author of the Epistle. Since Luther this idea, which some have called a brilliant guess, has gained many followers, including such recent expositors as T. W. Manson[15] and W. F. Howard.[16] C. Spicq in his encyclopedic commentary has collected the chief arguments in behalf of Apollos' authorship.[17] These have been followed and made available for English readers by Hugh Montefiore.[18] A number of these arguments, briefly given below, are based on Acts 18:24-28.

1. Apollos was an Alexandrian Jew. It seems unquestionable that the author of Hebrews was a Jew, and many hold that his thought shows distinct marks of Alexandrian influence.[19]

---

12. For similarities of language in Luke and Hebrews, see Moffatt, *Introduction*, pp. 435-37. Moffatt, after an exacting study of the similarities, concludes that "community of atmosphere" and not Lucan authorship is the best hypothesis to account for these similarities. For a considerable study of the similarities of Hebrews and the Lucan writings, see C. M. P. Jones, "The Epistle to the Hebrews and the Lucan Writings," *Studies in the Gospels: Essays in Memory of R. H. Lightfoot*, ed. D. E. Nineham (Oxford, 1955), pp. 113-43. Jones does not seek to establish Lucan authorship, but only that the writings of Luke and Hebrews have a "common family likeness."

13. Westcott, p. lxxvii.

14. Montefiore, p. 2.

15. T. W. Manson, "The Problem of the Epistle to the Hebrews," *Studies in the Gospels and Epistles*, ed. Matthew Black (Philadelphia, 1962), p. 242ff.

16. W. F. Howard, "The Epistle to the Hebrews," *Interpretation* 5 (1951), 80ff.

17. Spicq, I, pp. 209-19. See also F. Lo Bue, "The Historical Background of the Epistle to the Hebrews," JBL 75 (1956), 52-57.

18. Montefiore, p. 9ff.

19. For a brief summary of the Alexandrian background of the Epistle, see Guthrie, pp. 45-47. See also Sowers, pp. 64-88. On the possible connection between the Epistle and Philo, see especially Ronald Williamson, *Philo and the Epistle to the Hebrews* (Leiden, 1970).

2. Apollos was an eloquent man. The term for eloquent is *logios,* which may also be translated "learned" or "cultured." The term would apply well to the author of Hebrews. No writer in the New Testament shows more learning, for the author's literary style is smooth, rhythmical, and entirely without flaw.

3. Apollos was powerful in his use of the Scriptures (at that time the Old Testament). This too applies to the author of Hebrews. Adducing proofs from a variety of passages, the author displays a masterful grasp of the Old Testament and its institutions.

4. Apollos "spoke and taught accurately the things concerning Jesus." This accords with the subject of the Epistle. It is worth noticing that in this Epistle the name *Jesus* is used more than in any other of the epistles. This Epistle also is unquestionably a work that was written "accurately." Its tenses and its terms are precise. Again and again it uses the exact word to convey its meaning.

5. Apollos was "fervent in spirit," a man characterized by boldness of speech. Certainly the author of Hebrews was this type of person. He exhorts his readers passionately, and one important word that he uses in his writing is the word "boldness" *(parrēsia).*

6. Apollos was a man of high reputation in the early church. Undoubtedly he had made a great impression on Luke, as is seen in Acts 18. Paul, when speaking of Apollos, places him in the category of Peter and himself (1 Cor. 1:12). Apollos' contacts with Paul might explain certain traces of Pauline influence in Hebrews and would account for such references as that to Timothy in Hebrews 13:23.

The suggestion of Apollos as the author is not without appeal. He is the kind of person required to produce such a work. On the other hand, it must not be assumed that Apollos was the only man or the only Alexandrian in the apostolic period who could fit Luke's description as one "eloquent . . . well versed in the scriptures." There is the further difficulty that Apollos' authorship is supported by no ancient tradition. So far as is known, Apollos did not write anything. The hypothesis of Apollos as author has received wide acceptance; but without doubt much of this can be accounted for on the ground that in the search for a positive solution, there seems to be no other place to go.

Others

Many other possibilities on the authorship of Hebrews have been thought of. Peter, Stephen, Philip, Silas, Priscilla and Aquila, Aristion, and even Jude have had their advocates. Of these, Silas (or Silvanus) perhaps has received more consideration because of his close association with the apostle Paul and because of his known writing activities

(1 Thess. 1:1; 2 Thess. 1:1; 1 Pet. 5:12).[20] But a similar case can be made for almost any New Testament person, especially if that person left no other writings which by comparison would disprove his authorship of the Epistle.

Conclusion

Aside from what is not known on the question of authorship, it is good to keep in mind that certain definite things are known about the author. It is clear, for example, that the author was familiar with his readers (5:12; 6:9; 13:18-19, 23-24). It is also clear that the author was acquainted with Timothy (13:23). As to whether he was a Jew or Gentile, his knowledge of the Levitical ritual, and the application that he makes of it, argue strongly for his being a Jew. The literary character of the Epistle would go so far as to argue that the author was probably a Jew with distinctive Greek training as well—that is, that he was a Hellenistic Jew. His writing style, so skillful and penetrating, marks him as a great spiritual power among a generation of giants. Still, his name is unknown. Although modern pride resents it, on the matter of authorship it is best to conclude, as Origen did seventeen centuries ago, that "God only knows certainly."

A. B. Bruce has beautifully summarized the whole matter. "We must be content to remain in ignorance as to the writer of this remarkable work. Nor should we find this difficult. Some of the greatest books of the Bible . . . are anonymous writings. It is meet that this one should belong to the number, for it bears witness in its opening sentence to One who speaks God's final word to men. In presence of the Son, what does it matter who points the way to Him? The witness-bearer does not desire to be known. He bids us listen to Jesus and then retires into the background."[21]

Position and Use

Among the different manuscripts and versions, Hebrews appears in various positions. William H. P. Hatch has shown that, among the numerous New Testament manuscripts, Hebrews occupies three different positions: (1) among the epistles addressed to churches—after Romans or after 2 Corinthians, or very rarely after Galatians, Ephesians, Colossians, and Titus; (2) after 2 Thessalonians, that is, after the epistles

---

20. See Hewitt, pp. 26-29. Selwyn, in his erudite work on 1 Peter, argues that Silas shared in the writing of the circular letter sent out from Jerusalem (Acts 15) and also that Silas was joint author of 1 and 2 Thessalonians. See Selwyn, pp. 9-17.
21. A. B. Bruce, "Epistle to Hebrews," HDB, II, 338.

written to churches; (3) after Philemon, that is, after the epistles written to individuals and at the end of the Pauline group.[22]

The varying position of the Epistle reflects the different opinions about Hebrews that were held at different times. As has been noticed previously, in the second and third centuries there was considerable uncertainty about the authorship of the Epistle; and in the West there was the firm denial of Pauline authorship. In the fourth century Eusebius plainly attests to hesitation on the part of some with reference to Hebrews. "The fourteen letters of Paul are well-known and undisputed, yet it is not right to ignore that some dispute the Epistle to the Hebrews, saying that it was rejected by the church of Rome as not being by Paul...."[23]

It was particularly in the West, then, where doubts existed about the Epistle. Yet it should be remembered that it was in this very region where Hebrews is first known to have been used. Clement of Rome in the last part of the first century (c. A.D. 95) wrote a letter in behalf of the church at Rome to the church at Corinth. In this letter he not infrequently quotes from or alludes to the Epistle. The references are unmistakable and the parallels are obvious and clear. This can be seen in the following table, which presents a number of parallels between Hebrews and the First Epistle of Clement.

Hebrews	1 Clement
He reflects the glory of God.... When he had made purification for sins, he sat down at the right hand of the Majesty on high, having become as much superior to angels as the name he has obtained is more excellent than theirs. For to what angel did God ever say, "Thou art my Son, today I have begotten thee"?... Of the angels he says, "Who makes his angels winds, and his servants flames of fire.".... But to what angel has he ever said, "Sit at my right hand, till I make thy enemies a stool for thy feet"? (1:3-5, 7, 13).	"...who being the reflection of his Majesty is by so much greater than angels as he has obtained a more excellent name." For it is written thus, "Who makes his angels winds, and his servants flames of fire." But of his son the Master said thus, "Thou art my Son, today I have begotten thee. Ask of me, and I will give thee the heathen for thy inheritance, and the ends of the earth for thy possession." And again he says to him, "Sit thou on my right hand until I make thy enemies a stool for thy feet" (36:2-5).

22. For a full discussion see Hatch, "The Position of Hebrews in the Canon of the New Testament," HTR 29 (1936), 133-51. Two things in particular should be noted with reference to Hatch's article. On one hand, Hebrews is linked somehow with the acknowledged epistles of Paul; on the other hand, no epistle ascribed to Paul has been so variously arranged in the canon as Hebrews.

23. Eusebius, *Ecclesiastical History* 3.3.

... he is able to help those who are tempted. Therefore ... consider Jesus, the apostle and high priest of our confession (2:18; 3:1).

This is the way, beloved, in which we found our salvation, Jesus Christ, the high priest of our offerings, the defender and helper of our weakness (36:1).

... as Moses also was faithful in God's house.... Now Moses was faithful in all God's house as a servant ... (3:2, 5).

Moses was called faithful in all his house.... Since the blessed Moses also "a faithful servant in all his house ..." (17:5; 43:1).

... discerning the thoughts and intentions of the heart (4:12).

For he is a searcher of intentions and thoughts (21:9).

... in which it is impossible that God should prove false ...(6:18).

For nothing is impossible with God except to prove false (27:2).

By faith Enoch was taken up so that he should not see death; and he was not found, because God had taken him (11:5).

Let us take Enoch, who being found righteous in obedience was taken up, and death did not find him (9:3).

By faith Noah, being warned by God concerning events as yet unseen, took heed ... (11:7).

Noah was found faithful in his service ... (9:4).

By faith Abraham obeyed when he was called to go out to a place which he was to receive as an inheritance; and he went out ... (11:8).

Abraham ... was found faithful in his obedience to the words of God ... (10:11).

By faith Rahab the harlot did not perish with those who were disobedient, because she had given friendly welcome to the spies (11:31).

For by her faith and hospitality Rahab the harlot was saved. For when the spies were sent to Jericho by Joshua ... the hospitable Rahab took them in ... (12:1-3).

They went about in skins of sheep and goats ... (11:37).

Let us also be imitators of those who went about in the skins of goats and sheep ... (17:1).

Therefore, since we are surrounded by so great a cloud of witnesses ... let us run with perseverance the race that is set before us, looking to Jesus ... (12:1-2).

Seeing then that we have received a share in many great and glorious deeds, let us hasten on to the goal of peace, which was given us from the beginning, and let us look to the Father and Creator of the whole world ... (19:2).

"For the Lord disciplines whom he loves, and chastises every son whom he receives." ... but he disciplines us for our good, that we may share his holiness (12:6, 10).

The admonition which we made one to another is good and helpful beyond measure, for it unites us to the will of God. For the holy word says thus ... "for the Lord disciplines him whom he loves, and chastises every son whom he receives." ... You see, beloved, how great is the protection given to those who are disciplined by the Master, for he is a good father and disciplines us that we may obtain mercy through his holy discipline (56:2-3, 16).

This rather extensive and early use of the Epistle by Clement shows that in that time Hebrews was known and its ideas were being dispersed with some measure of respect and authority.[24] It seems certain that Clement, as he refers to Hebrews, is not introducing a novel document. It would appear that the church at Corinth knows something of the Epistle, for why would Clement employ its language again and again if it were completely unfamiliar to them? It may well be that Hebrews was better known and more frequently used in the first century than has often been allowed. In the second and third centuries, circulating anonymously as it did, doubts were bound to be raised concerning it. By that time many in the church had become conscious of rival, hybrid writings and of the need to mark clearly the limits of the accepted writings. The chief mark of delimitation was apostolicity; and as Hebrews did not bear the name of an apostle, this quite naturally brought it under scrutiny and sometimes led to its rejection. Nevertheless, it should be kept in mind that Hebrews was widely accepted even in this period of scrutiny. Ultimately its intrinsic worth secured its proper place in the canon.

Readers

Who exactly the author was, so long as he gave expression to a divine wisdom within him, does not really affect the interpretation of the Epistle. To whom the Epistle was addressed, however, if it can be

---

24. Other parallels might be cited, not only from Clement but also from the Shepherd of Hermas, the Epistle of Barnabas, and the works of Ignatius and Polycarp. Stuart (p. 73ff.) gives a tentative list for examination. Recently, Buchanan (pp. 261-62) notes the use of Hebrews by Irenaeus and Clement of Alexandria and concludes that "Hebrews seems early to have been recognized as some kind of wisdom literature and used as a valid authority."

discovered, does directly bear on the message conveyed by the author. And, fortunately, the Epistle gives some hints here. On the basis of what the author says, it seems that—

Community of believers

The readers formed a definite community of believers. One thing seems to be evident about the Epistle: it was not a "general epistle" directed to Christians at large, but rather it was sent to a specific group to meet a specific need. This being so, it is correct to speak of it as an Epistle, though it lacks in its opening the typical form of address. As indicated previously, there is a direct connection between author and readers. The author expects to be united with the readers (13:23), as he had been in the past (13:19). He knows about their early history and exhorts them to remember their "former days" when they had been called upon to endure "a hard struggle with sufferings" (10:32). They had been exposed to public shame; they had joyfully accepted the plundering of their goods, knowing that they had "a better possession and an abiding one" (10:33-34). Yet in those days it had not been necessary for them to resist sin to the point of shedding their blood (12:4). They had indeed conducted themselves as true Christians, showing love and compassion for those that were abused (6:10; 10:34). But all was not well with them. They had lived for some time as Christians, but they were "babes" instead of "teachers" (5:11-14); and there were unmistakable signs that they were about to drift away (2:1; 10:25). The latter may indicate that the Epistle was directed to a group smaller than that of the larger congregation of Christians which met at a given place. This indication is strengthened by the author's request at the close: "greet all your leaders and all the saints" (13:24).

Jewish Christians

The readers were Jewish Christians. In the oldest extant manuscripts (the Chester Beatty papyrus, the Vatican, the Sinaitic, and the Alexandrian) the title of the Epistle reads simply "To Hebrews" (*Pros Hebraious*). Although later added as a heading to the original writing, the title undoubtedly reflects an early tradition. And this tradition is indeed borne out by the contents of the Epistle. Its first readers appear to have been people of Jewish background. Although linguistically and culturally they may well have been Hellenists,[25] still their thoughts and aspirations were centered in the religion of the old covenant. The author, therefore, appeals to them on the basis of what they knew and loved the best—the Old Testament, with its elaborate ceremonies, its

---

25. See F. F. Bruce, " 'To the Hebrews' or 'To the Essenes'?", NTS 9 (1962-63), 232. For further reference on the Old Testament background of the readers, see F. F. Bruce, *Hebrews,* p. xxiiiff.

types and shadows, and its great historic figures like Moses and Aaron. His finely-wrought argument runs thus: you will grant the dignity of Moses and Aaron, and the authority of the old covenant. But Christ is supreme over all; His dignity and authority cannot be compared with others; therefore, you should honor and hold only to Him. So the main drift of the argument in the Epistle, more than anything else, shows that its original readers had grown up with the religion of Israel as their background and way of life.

On the other hand, a few scholars, the most noteworthy being James Moffatt,[26] have taken an entirely different point of view. They say that the Epistle was first written to Gentiles. They argue that the title "To Hebrews" was tacked on by some later scribe who was in no better position to know the facts than men are today. They further argue that the Old Testament was "Scripture" for Gentile Christians as much as for Jewish Christians, since on their entering the church they acknowledged both that God is and that He has spoken through the prophets. The author, it is said, is not contending against a possible relapse into Judaism, but a relapse of a more pervasive character—a general "neglect" (2:3), a "dullness of hearing" (5:11), a "falling away from the living God" (3:12). But these arguments, although ingeniously contrived, fall short of the mark. A warning against "falling away from the living God," for example, could apply equally to those who were Jewish or Gentile by birth; for certainly in the author's mind a return to Judaism would amount to a complete apostasy. Moreover, although the Old Testament was meaningful for Gentiles, it is nevertheless true that an extended discussion of the weaknesses and inabilities of the old system contrasted with the new would make a greater impression on someone who had always acknowledged the excellence of the old. Why the author would try to dissuade a Gentile from leaving Christ by using an argument based on the old Jewish ritual is an unexplainable mystery. A. B. Bruce ably summarizes the point at issue: "If the readers were indeed Gentiles, they were Gentiles so completely disguised in Jewish dress . . . that the true nationality has been successfully hidden for nineteen centuries, and even now, after learned critics have done their best to show us the Gentile behind the Jew, we shake our heads in honest insurmountable doubt, and feel constrained to agree with Westcott when he pronounces the argument . . . 'an ingenious paradox.' "[27]

Other views on the readers

In addition to the above on the Epistle's original readers, other recent views should be noted. F. C. Synge follows Stather-Hunt in

---

26. Moffatt, *Hebrews*, p. xvif. Cf. E. F. Scott, *The Epistle to the Hebrews* (Edinburgh, 1922), pp. 14-21.
27. A. B. Bruce, "Epistle to Hebrews," HDB, II, 337.

holding that *Pros Hebraious* means against Hebrews or Jews, and that the primary object of the Epistle was to set forth the thesis that the Jewish law had been superseded by the law of Christ.[28] In this sense the Epistle was against Judaism and was addressed to Jews who were on the verge of accepting Christianity but who had not taken the final step.[29]

The publication and study of a number of ancient documents, usually known as the Dead Sea Scrolls, have been responsible for several proposals connecting Hebrews and Qumran. Qumran, adjacent to the original discovery site of the scrolls, was a community of Essenes that existed in the first century A.D. Hans Kosmala argues that Hebrews was written specifically to an Essene group to prepare them to accept Jesus.[30] Other views, such as those of Yigael Yadin[31] and C. Spicq,[32] associate Hebrews and Qumran by asserting that the Epistle was addressed to a group of Christians who had either come out of the Qumran community or had been greatly influenced by Essene culture. A more moderate position had been advocated in 1957 by Otto Michel.[33] It is Michel's position that, although no direct historical connection between Hebrews and Qumran can be demonstrated, still certain linguistic and conceptual similarities point to a common background for Hebrews and Qumran. In 1963, F. F. Bruce published a significant article in *New Testament Studies* entitled " 'To the Hebrews' or 'To the Essenes'?"[34] In his article Bruce examines the parallels between Hebrews and Qumran that have received so much attention from recent scholars. He concludes that the differences between the materials considerably outweigh the similarities and that "it would be outstripping the evidence to call them [the readers of the Epistle] Essenes or spiritual brethren to the men of Qumran."[35] New theories, which directly link Hebrews and Qumran, have not been forthcoming since the work of Bruce.

---

28. F. C. Synge, *Hebrews and the Scriptures* (London, 1959), p. 44.

29. Ibid., p. 51.

30. Hans Kosmala, *Hebräer–Essener–Christen* (Leiden, 1959), p. 44ff.

31. Yigael Yadin, "The Dead Sea Scrolls and the Epistle to the Hebrews," *Scripta Hierosolymitana* 4 (1958), 36-55.

32. C. Spicq, "L'Épître aux Hébreux: Apollos, Jean-Baptiste, les Hellénistes et Qumran," *Révue de Qumran* 1 (1958-59), 365ff.

33. In the tenth edition of his commentary, *Der Brief an die Hebräer*, pp. 151-52, 376-78, etc.

34. In NTS 9 (1962-63), 217-32. This is not to overlook the independent work of Joseph Coppens, *Les affinités qumrâniennes de l'Épître aux Hébreux* (Louvain, 1962), who about the same time reached conclusions similar to those of Bruce.

35. F. F. Bruce, " 'To the Hebrews' or 'To the Essenes'?", 232. In addition to Bruce's article, for a good summary of various viewpoints in recent years, see Irvin W. Batdorf, "Hebrews and Qumran: Old Methods and New Directions," *Festschrift to Honor F. Wilbur Gingrich*, ed. Eugene Howard Barth and Ronald Edwin Cocroft (Leiden, 1972), pp. 16-35.

Destination and Date

Where did the first readers of the Epistle live? This question also remains unresolved. Some places have been put forward due to certain theories on authorship: Antioch, assuming that Barnabas was the writer; Caesarea, along with the view of Lucan authorship; and Alexandria, on the supposition that Apollos expressed his ideas in Alexandrian form. Other localities such as Colossae, Ephesus, and Corinth have been suggested recently.[36] But for one reason or another these views have had difficulty gaining an audience. After other possibilities have been considered, discussions on the destination have over the years narrowed down to two views, Jerusalem and Rome.

Jerusalem has had its advocates from early times.[37] The choice is a natural one if "To Hebrews" is considered an authentic title. But there are weighty objections against a Jerusalem destination. The language of the Epistle, for one thing, presents a barrier; for it is not likely that Greek, especially in this form and with these ideas, would have been written to Aramaic-speaking Jews at Jerusalem. Nor can it be said that the Jerusalem church had not resisted sin to the point of shedding blood (12:4), for Jerusalem was the place where Christian martyrdom began (Acts 7:54–8:3). And would the author address a Jerusalem group as though none of them had personally heard the Lord (2:3)?

Rome lately has received much attention, mainly along the lines that the Epistle was addressed not to the whole church but to a small circle or house-church in the capital.[38] According to the available information, it was at Rome where the Epistle was first attested by Clement's use of it about A.D. 95. Of course, this in itself would not prove a Roman destination, for by this time Christian writings were circulating rather freely. There is, further, the statement "they of Italy salute you" (13:24). While admittedly ambiguous, it implies that either the author or the readers were in Italy; and some would argue that it is more plausible to think of Italians away from home sending greetings back to Italy by means of the author's note. On this, however, as on the whole question, there is room for considerable difference of opinion. Other arguments can be given for a Roman destination—the eminence of the

---

36. For Corinth, see Montefiore, p. 18ff.; for Ephesus, see W. F. Howard, "The Epistle to the Hebrews," *Interpretation* 5 (1951), 80ff.; for Colossae, see T. W. Manson, *Studies in the Gospels and Epistles* (Manchester, 1962), p. 252ff.

37. To the long list of older commentaries holding this view should now be added the new work of Buchanan. Buchanan (p. 256) takes expressions such as "you have come to Mount Zion" (Heb. 12:22) literally and finds in them evidence that the Epistle was written to a certain group of people (he suggests a communal, monastic sect) who were residing in Jerusalem.

38. So Zahn (p. 345ff.), Peake *(Hebrews,* p. 26ff.), William Manson (p. 11ff.), etc.

group's past leaders (13:7), the conditions of persecution depicted, the connection with Timothy (13:23), all fit in with what is known of the church at Rome; but the apparent strength of such arguments is due simply to the fact that no better solution to the problem has been offered.

The date of the Epistle can be fixed within broad limits. Recognized at Rome in the last part of the first century, it surely must have been written at least several years earlier. Was it written, say, prior to the destruction of Jerusalem in A.D. 70? There are good reasons for thinking so. Present tenses are used by the author as though the temple is still standing and Levitical offerings are still being made (7:8; 9:6-10; 13: 10). It is true that the Epistle makes no direct reference to the temple cultus; but it is also true that the author's argument, developed from the written Old Testament, applies as much to the temple ritual as to that of the tabernacle. When it is said that "the priests go continually into the outer tent, performing their ritual ..." (9:6), the author no doubt is using the form of the present tense (called "historical present") that speaks of a past event with present vividness. Still the author's use of the present, as Bruce says, "would be more pointed if this state of affairs were still going on."[39]

Yet of greater significance in reaching an approximate date is the tone of the whole Epistle. Assuming that it was written to Jewish Christians whose allegiance was wavering, and that after A.D. 70, it is unthinkable that there would be no reference to the Jerusalem catastrophe. This would have been the author's clinching argument—not that the old system was about to disappear (8:13), but that the old system had already, physically and violently, passed away. Thus the Epistle seems to place itself in the period before the destruction of Jerusalem. This is in keeping with other details in the Epistle. The people addressed have been in Christ for some time. Their first leaders are now dead. They have known the glories of former days, but now they are experiencing a different danger. Although other dates have been given, it seems reasonable to assign the Epistle to a time near A.D. 65.[40]

Purpose and Contents

Any understanding of the purpose of Hebrews must take into account what the author says at the close of his Epistle: "I appeal to you, brethren, bear with my word of exhortation, for I have written to

---

39. F. F. Bruce, *Hebrews*, p. xliii.

40. With this C. F. D. Moule is in general agreement. Moule likes A. Nairne's view that the Epistle was written before A.D. 70, "when, with the outbreak of the Jewish War, a wave of patriotic nationalism may well have swept from Palestine over the whole of diaspora Judaism, constituting a sore temptation to Christian Jews to revert to Judaism." See Moule, "Sanctuary and Sacrifice in the Church of the New Testament," JTS 1 (1950), 37.

you briefly" (13:22). The author himself says, then, that he wrote in order to exhort. Thus it is to be kept in mind that, no matter how lofty and exalted his presentation is, his purpose all the way through is a supremely practical one. He did not have in mind an abstract treatise. His brothers in Christ needed encouragement. In the first flush of Christian enthusiasm they had joyfully accepted the loss of all things. But the years had taken their toll. That first enthusiasm had died out. Hope itself was fading from view. Some of them were neglecting the public assembly (10:25). There were signs not only of slipping but of complete and irrevocable apostasy (6:1-6; 10:26-31).

So the author's heartfelt appeal is that his readers be worthy of their past. But with men born under and nurtured by the law, this was not as easy as it might seem. From almost the first day that they heard the gospel, Jewish Christians had been under fire. For them, in a special way, Christ had brought not peace but a sword. Were Christianity and Christ Himself really as important as they had been led to believe? And there was more: as time wore on it became clearer and clearer that the Jews as a whole would not accept Christ. Theoretically, this might tend to show that God's promises to them in the Old Testament had been broken. Had God cast away His people? Practically, it did mean that a choice had to be made once and for all between the synagogue and the church.

The author's method of dealing with these difficulties is to lay before his readers the inner, permanent significance of Christianity.[41] His theme is the absoluteness of the Christian religion. To him there could never be any other religion. Noticeably, as he develops his thoughts, he does not so much as allude to the heathen religions; rather he confines his attention to the two religions which rest historically on divine revelation—Judaism and Christianity. In comparing the two, he cannot but compare the two covenants. With the old covenant (8:13) there go certain characteristic words: "daily" (*kath' hēmeran*, 7:27; 10:11) or "repeatedly" (*pollakis*, 9:25, 26; 10:11; cf. 6:7); "shadow" (*skia*, 8:5; 10:1), or "copy" (*hupodeigma*, 8:5; 9:23); "first" (*prōtos*, 8:7, 13; 9:1, 2, 6, 8, 15, 18; 10:9); "earthly" (*kosmikos*, 9:1); "made with hands" (*cheiropoiētos*, 9:11, 24).

But the new covenant is vastly different, and this is evident from

---

41. It is doubtful if a better analysis of the contents of Hebrews has been written than that of A. B. Bruce, whose exposition to some extent is followed here. See his treatment of the subject in his article "Epistle to Hebrews," HDB, II, 327ff. Bruce's article was written some time ago; but in 1951 W. F. Howard could say of it, "After more than 50 years the present writer can still feel the thrill with which he first read that article..." (Howard, "The Epistle to the Hebrews," *Interpretation* 5 (1951), 81. Bruce's article contains an excellent digest of his book, *The Epistle to the Hebrews: The First Apology for Christianity* (Edinburgh, 1899).

certain key terms. With the new covenant go the terms "once" *(hapax)* and "once for all" *(ephapax)*. Again and again the author underscores the uniqueness of Christ and Christianity with these terms *(hapax,* 6:4; 9:7, 26, 27, 28; 10:2; 12:26, 27; *ephapax,* 7:27; 9:12; 10:10). In place of the many sacrifices of the old, there is the once for all sacrifice of Jesus. There is also the term "true" *(alēthinos)*. It is not used often in Hebrews but it is significant. It means "real" or "genuine" and stands in contrast to whatever is marked by shadows and imitation. So Christ is the "minister in the sanctuary and the true tent which is set up not by man but by the Lord" (8:2; cf. 9:24; 10:22). There is the word "heart" *(kardia)*. The new covenant is a matter of the heart and faithfulness to God is primarily a condition of the heart (3:8, 10, 12, 15; 4:7, 12; 8:10; 10:16, 22; 13:9).

Two terms in Hebrews, however, are especially important and show that the religion of the new covenant far excels that described in the books of Moses. The terms are "better" *(kreittōn)* and "eternal" *(aiōnios)*. Hebrews speaks of "eternal salvation" (5:9), "eternal judgment" (6:2), "eternal redemption" (9:12), "the eternal Spirit" (9:14), "the promised eternal inheritance" (9:15), and "the eternal covenant" (13:20). The author's tone is absolute and final. And this is the case with his word "better." Jesus is represented as being "so much better than the angels" (1:4); He is the mediator and guarantee of a "better covenant" which offers "better promises" and a "better hope" (7:19, 22; 8:6). Not only so, but inherent in the better covenant are "better sacrifices" (9:23), a "better possession" (10:34), a "better country" (11:16), a "better life" (11:35), and the blood of Jesus that has "better things to tell than the blood of Abel" (12:24, NEB; cf. 6:9; 7:7; 11:40). With such precisely chosen terms the author argues that Christianity is better than anything that had previously been made known to man. And, as Bruce remarks, it is not difficult "to read between the lines, and to see behind the apologetic *better* the dogmatic *best.*"[42]

The comparison of the two religions and of the two covenants, therefore, is the burden of the Epistle and covers the bulk of it (1:1– 10:18). The remainder of the Epistle consists of encouragements to faithfulness and warnings against apostasy (10:19–13:25). In the first and larger section of his work, the one grand truth that the author sets out to prove is the priesthood of Christ and its eternal consequences. For the author this subject—and this is the only book in the New Testament that presents it—is crucial. What good is a religion that cannot cleanse the conscience? What good is there in a religion that always keeps man outside, that cannot because of its very nature establish

---

42. A. B. Bruce, "Epistle to Hebrews," HDB, II, 327.

intimate relations between God and man? This was the result, the one tragic failure of Leviticalism. But the very failure of the old system is the strength of the new: Jesus Christ is that access by which men can now draw near to God (7:19; 10:21-22).

Although this is the sum and substance of what he wants to say, the author begins elsewhere. He does not launch immediately into his real subject. First he lays the necessary foundation and then he moves steadily, imperceptibly toward his goal. From the Old Testament he selects as his starting point the *agents of revelation,* and from there he goes on to the *agents of redemption.* Under the first category the author speaks of the prophets and the angels, while in the second category he lists Moses, Joshua, and Aaron. He contrasts these agents with Christ, each in their turn: (1) Christ and the prophets (1:1-3); (2) Christ and the angels (1:4—2:18); (3) Christ and Moses (3:1-19); (4) Christ and Joshua (4:1-13); and (5) Christ and Aaron (4:14—10:18).

Christ and the prophets

This contrast appears only in the Epistle's opening words and is not worked out. God has indeed spoken in the past through the prophets, but this ancient revelation was fragmentary and came in varied forms. At the end of the age, however, God has spoken through one who has the rank of a son; and the word spoken through Him is complete and final.

Christ and the angels

The angels are dealt with directly in 1:4-14, and then in the following verses they gradually fade into the background. The subject of the angels was one of importance for any Jew. He thought of the angels as the highest beings in God's creation. They were the divinely appointed intermediaries between God and man; through the angels Moses received the law and delivered it to the people (2:2; Acts 7:53; Gal. 3:19). But the angels, as selected passages from the Old Testament show, are no rivals to Christ. Christ is superior to the angels as a son is different from servants, as a king is over his subjects, as a creator is above his creation. The angels—even the highest archangel—exist to serve God, to serve Christ, and to serve Christians, who are to inherit salvation (1:14). The conclusion must also be, then, that the revelation mediated by the angels was far inferior to that which came through Christ.

Christ and Moses

The author approaches Moses with extreme care, knowing how highly the ancient lawgiver was esteemed by every Jew. He does not speak of Moses at length, but holds him up as one who proved faithful in God's house. Yet in the same house, where Moses was faithful as a servant, Christ was faithful as a son. Even though he praises Moses, the author puts him in a different category than the Son.

Christ and Joshua

The superiority of Christ to Joshua is brought about in a rather incidental manner. In speaking of Moses, the author recalls the tragic failure of the Israelites in the wilderness. They failed to reach the land of their hopes; and likewise the readers are exhorted to hold on to their faith lest they also fall short of their goal. Moses could lead the children of Israel out, but he could not lead them in. But what of Joshua who came after him? Yes, Joshua led the people across the Jordan, but the land into which he led them could not really give rest. The implication is that Christ is a greater Savior than Joshua, for He is able to bring His people to final rest.

Christ and Aaron

Here the author comes to the heart of his subject. All the elaborate ritual on which Judaism was founded, the ceremonial purifications, the daily sacrifices, and even the annual Day of Atonement, seemed to him to be much ado about nothing. In these functions the ordinary Levitical priests and the great high priest were, of course, indispensable. Aaron was the first high priest of Judaism. As a historical figure in the Old Testament he was not so important, but as a figure representative of the high priestly office he was all-important. To prove, therefore, how meaningless the old system was, the author compares the priesthood of Christ with that of the Aaronic order (4:14–7:28) and the priestly work of Christ with that of the line of priests that had gone before (8:1–10:18).

Christ as high priest, therefore, becomes the main thesis of the Epistle. Ten times the author calls Jesus "high priest" (2:17; 3:1; 4:14, 15; 5:5, 10; 6:20; 7:26; 8:1; 9:11), and several times more he refers to Jesus as "priest" (7:11, 15, 21; 8:4; 10:21). At different points, as he recapitulates his argument, the priesthood of Christ is what he stresses:

> Since then we have a great high priest who has passed through the heavens, Jesus, the Son of God, let us hold fast our confession (4:14).
> Now the point in what we are saying is this: we have such a high priest, one who is seated at the right hand of the throne of the Majesty in heaven . . . (8:1).
> Therefore, brethren, since we have confidence to enter the sanctuary by the blood of Jesus . . . and since we have a great priest over the house of God, let us draw near with a true heart in full assurance of faith . . . (10:19, 21-22).

Christ is not only high priest but He is superior to the Aaronic priests. This principle is developed in numerous ways. One essential requirement for a high priest is that he be a man among men, a person who is capable of genuine compassion and understanding. Another requirement is that he be appointed to his office by God. Now Jesus Christ in a wonderful way fulfills these basic requirements, being sympathetic with men without being sinful and receiving a divine call to serve without taking the honor upon himself (5:1-10). To prove the latter point the author cites two passages from Scripture, one of which describes Christ as "a priest for ever, after the order of Melchizedek." In the same quotation the author finds support for his argument on the nature of Christ's priesthood. It might be objected that because Christ did not belong to the tribe of Levi, He could not be a priest. But, says the author, His priesthood is of a different kind, of an ancient order going back to the time of Abraham—a priesthood like Melchizedek's, not based on genealogical descent, a priesthood to which one might even say that Levi paid tribute. Added to this is the fact that Christ's priesthood is based on an unchangeable, eternal divine oath (7:1-14, 20-22).

The superiority of Christ's priestly work also receives much attention. As by its nature the priesthood of Christ is far superior to that of Aaron, so the blessings His priesthood brings are far greater. "Christ has obtained a ministry which is as much more excellent than the old as the covenant he mediates is better" (8:6). The excellency of His priestly ministry is demonstrated by three main points of contrast with the Aaronic priesthood: the sacrifice, the sanctuary, and the service.[43]

1. *Sacrifice.* It is necessary that every high priest have something to offer (8:3). In this respect Jesus adequately meets the requirement; for, as the author has already indicated, He made His sacrifice when He offered up Himself (7:27). And what a sacrifice that was! It was no token sacrifice of a dumb animal, but a voluntary offering of Himself to God (9:13-14). Nor was it a sacrifice that had to be offered again and again. It was a once for all sacrifice. Offered by the eternal and pre-existent Son, it covered sins of the past (9:15) as well as the future, and was so perfect that when accomplished nothing remained but to sit down at the right hand of God (7:27; 9:12, 28; 10:10-12).

2. *Sanctuary.* The old covenant, with its regulations for worship, provided a sanctuary with two compartments, the Holy Place and the Holy of Holies (9:1-5). But the very presence of these compartments

---

43. C. F. D. Moule sees these as central in early Christian apologetics: such ideas as sacrifice and sanctuary "were designed to meet the objections of Jews and also pagans who expressed a sense of outrage that Christians should have no sacrificial system" (Moule, "Sanctuary and Sacrifice in the Church of the New Testament," JTS 1 (1950), 29. Moule suggests that the whole Epistle can "be epitomized in two resounding *echomens:* we *have* a high priest, we *have* an altar: sanctuary and sacrifice are ours: 8:1; 13:10" (p. 37).

indicated the inadequacy of the Jewish system: the common people could not enter into the sanctuary; the priests could not enter into the Holy of Holies; the high priest could enter in only once a year—all of which meant that there could be no real access into heaven as long as the old covenant stood (9:6-10). Besides, this sanctuary was an earthly one (9:1). On the other hand, the one in which Christ officiates is described as "the greater and more perfect tent, not made with hands" (9:11). It does not belong to the physical creation, to the world of sense and sight; it is not constructed of material things, of gold or wood or cloth, which, no matter how precious, are destined to vanish away.

3. *Service.* The one grand service of the high priest took place each year on the Day of Atonement, and it is this annual service that engrosses the author's mind (5:3; 6:19-20; 7:27; 9:7, 11-14, 23-28; 10:1-22). At that time the high priest alone entered into the Holy of Holies to offer blood and to stand in God's presence for the sins of the people. In this, above all things, can be seen the incomparable power of the priestly ministry of Christ. The blood of bulls and goats could never take away sin (10:4). At best those unending sacrifices could only cancel men's mistakes for a short time, and after that time they were remembered again. Never fully and never finally could they deal with sin. But not so with Jesus' sacrifice. He went to the cross and then with His own blood entered into heaven itself, thus securing eternal redemption from sin (9:12). Further comparison of the two priesthoods becomes futile. The priesthood of Aaron was merely a tedious ritual. Jesus Christ, having completed the one perfect sacrifice, sits at God's right hand and always lives to make intercession for men (7:25).

The lengthy comparative study of the two religions based on the two covenants concludes with 10:18. The rest of the Epistle is given to a series of impressive exhortations to constancy. The author's first appeal is that his readers have confidence in God, that they draw near to Him, that they not be of those who shrink back and lose faith (10:19-31). This prompts him to treat the subject of faith, and this he does by eloquently picturing the great heroes of faith that have lived in the past (11:1-40). Above all Jesus as the perfecter of faith must be looked to. He suffered and endured, as indeed all of God's children must bear suffering (12:1-11). There follows, then, one last vibrant appeal to the readers: that they lift up their drooping hands and strengthen their weak knees, making sure that they do not fail to obtain the grace of God. Their privileges, he says, in contrast to those that lived in Moses' day, are wonderful and innumerable. Therefore, he pleads that they do not refuse Him who is speaking, that they receive an unshakable kingdom, and worship God with reverence and awe (12:12-29). Appended is a final chapter which includes various notes on ethical duties, warnings, and concluding personal remarks.

Literary Form and Structure

The New Testament writers were Christians primarily and writers secondarily. Their concern—even obsession—was to announce the good news of salvation in Jesus. They absorbed themselves in the stringent, practical needs of the church. They wrote, therefore, not as "literary" men to an elite readership but as men communicating Christian truths to a wider audience of fellow Christians.

Literary forms in the New Testament

The various writings of the New Testament exhibit, however, certain similarities with other ancient literary forms.

1. The *dialogue* had long been in use by the Greeks. By 400 B.C. Plato had perfected the dialogue form and had made it his principal literary medium. He expounded his ideas by putting them in conversational form between two or more persons; the Greek word for conversation is *dialogos*. In the New Testament the closest analogy to this is Jesus' talking with His disciples and other interested inquirers. Much of the Gospel of John is in dialogue form.

2. The *diatribe* was the most popular form for philosophical writing in the New Testament period. The diatribe was a dialogue converted into a monologue. In a diatribe there is an imaginary opponent who raises questions and objections. The author composes his writing, anticipating these objections and giving response to them. Paul, and other Jews, were accustomed to the question-answer method of teaching in the synagogues. They could rather easily adapt this to the diatribe form of writing. The Epistle of James and some parts of Paul's letters read very much like a diatribe. Examples of questions raised by an imaginary objector are found in such passages as James 2:18, Romans 3:1, 4:1, 6:1.[44]

3. The *epistle* was the literary form taken by the large majority of New Testament writings. The epistolary form came to be used when a person desired to direct to an audience a work less formal than a treatise. The philosopher Epicurus wrote letters to other philosophers and individuals on such subjects as natural philosophy and astronomy.[45] Unlike ordinary letters they were intended for a wide circle of readers. Seneca wrote letters addressed to Lucilius, but the actual audience intended was the Roman world at large. So the epistolary form was

---

44. For a discussion of the diatribe and its characteristics, see Ropes, pp. 10-18.
45. To Epicurus could be added other famous epistle writers such as Aristotle, Plutarch, Cato, Seneca, and Pliny.

employed in the Graeco-Roman world to present dissertations on criticism, science, morals, and on many other subjects.

A distinction is sometimes made between an epistle and a letter, the former being a literary work designed for publication, the latter being non-literary, informal, and more or less private. This careful distinction was made by Adolf Deissmann, following others before him, who argued that it is inappropriate to apply the word *literature* to many of the Biblical writings.[46] He maintained that Paul, for example, was a letter writer, not an epistolographer. On the other hand, he held that most of the general epistles were true epistles and not letters. The Epistle of James, for instance, addressed "to the twelve tribes in the Dispersion," envisaged a wider audience and was intended for publication; it was, in fact, an undeliverable letter.

The form of Hebrews

What, then, is the literary form of Hebrews? Thus far it has been referred to as an epistle. Is it really an epistle? Or would it be more correct to refer to it as a letter? Or is it more like an oral address, a sermon or homily?

The literary problem of Hebrews is unique in the New Testament for two reasons: (1) Hebrews has no opening address, and (2) it has at the end personal notes characteristic of a letter. Concerning the former point, it is not likely that an original introduction was accidentally lost in the wear and tear of some manuscript. Evidence for this among epistolary papyrus rolls, with the inner address missing, is entirely lacking. Nor is it likely that the address was deleted either on the grounds that it was written by a non-apostolic person or that it was directed to an insignificant church. Indeed, there is no compelling reason why the writing could not have begun as it appears in all extant manuscripts.

It is often said that Hebrews begins like a treatise, continues like a sermon, and concludes like a letter. The sermon or homily hypothesis has received considerable recent support.[47] Perhaps the strongest case for the homily view has been made by Hartwig Thyen.[48] According to Thyen, Hebrews is much like a number of Jewish and Christian writings which go back to about the first century A.D., all of which have the common form of the Jewish-Hellenistic homily. Hebrews, Thyen believes,

---

46. See Deissmann, *Bible Studies,* pp. 3-59; *Light,* pp. 146-251; *Paul,* p. 8ff.

47. Some of its advocates are Moffatt (*Introduction,* p. 429), Michel (p. 20ff.), Wikenhauser (p. 461), Feine-Behm-Kümmel (p. 278f.), Fuller (p. 146f.), Buchanan (p. 246).

48. Thyen, p. 17ff. Thyen's work is digested for the English reader in James Swetnam's article, "On the Literary Genre of the 'Epistle' to the Hebrews," NovTest 11 (1969), 261ff.

is a well-constructed homily of the type delivered in a Diaspora synagogue. Thyen gives many reasons for his views: the author's use of the Septuagint and his manner of citing the Old Testament;[49] the author's change from "we" to "you" to "I," which is a mark of the preacher; and the author's strengthening his exhortation to faith by the listing of outstanding examples from the past, which is likewise a characteristic of the Hellenistic homily.

It is the opinion of most scholars, however, that much more needs to be known both of Hellenistic- and Palestinian-type homilies before Thyen's thesis is established.[50] It is nevertheless true that Hebrews frequently sounds like a sermon and, further, that the author himself describes his writing as a "message of exhortation" (13:22).[51] This expression is also found in Acts 13:15, when Paul and Barnabas are invited to address the synagogue at Pisidian Antioch.

The suggestion that Hebrews is a treatise that develops one central theme—the high priesthood of Christ—has little in its favor. The author did not sit down to write a dissertation of doctrine. Although he systematically treats the subjects of priesthood and sacrifice, still this is in line with his practical purpose to renew and reinvigorate the loyalty of his readers.

Because of the inherent difficulties of these views, Hebrews is still generally referred to as an epistle. As has been noticed, Deissmann distinguished between an epistle and a letter. He maintained that, though epistle and letter are similar in appearance, they are quite different in literary intent. And to Deissmann it was clear that Hebrews, with its more calculated literary style and more theological subject matter, "is historically the earliest example of Christian artistic literature."[52]

Deissmann's distinction between epistle and letter can stand today, with modifications.[53] Deissmann went too far and was guilty of oversimplification: the lines of difference between epistle and letter are often difficult to draw. This means, too, that he extolled the literary qualities of Hebrews to the neglect of such qualities in the letters of Paul.[54] Nor does it seem that Deissmann gave sufficient consideration

---

49. Specifically, the manner in which quotations are introduced: "he says" (1:6, 7; 10:5); "and again" (1:6; 2:13; 4:5; 10:30); etc.

50. See Swetnam, "Literary Genre," p. 265ff.

51. Greek, *ho logos tēs paraklēseōs*, as in Acts 13:15. But does this refer to a homily that would typically be given in a Hellenistic synagogue or does it denote a special kind of homily that consisted mainly of exhortation and consolation?

52. Deissmann, *Light*, p. 244.

53. For criticism of Deissmann's conclusions, see Ramsay, *Seven Churches*, pp. 23-31; *Teaching of Paul*, pp. 312-444; also see Moffatt, *Introduction*, pp. 47-50; Dibelius, p. 137ff.

54. For examples of Paul's "artistry of expression," see Weiss, p. 406ff.

to the genuine letter-elements in Hebrews. As has been seen,[55] the author of Hebrews wrote to definite readers with a definite situation in mind (5:11ff.; 6:9f.; 10:25, 32ff.; 12:4). The last part of his writing especially reads like a letter, and there is no good reason for thinking that it was not integral to the original work.[56] While Hebrews may be correctly referred to as an "epistle," it is not an epistle in fictitious dress. It is a letter directly from the author's heart, who, with fervor and flame, with sincere pastoral care, instructs and admonishes in the tones of a preacher. In this sense, at least, it is correct to refer to Hebrews as an epistolary homily.

The style of Hebrews

If it is the mark of the preacher to be eloquent, certainly the author of Hebrews hits the mark. One has to reckon here with the "literary consciousness of an educated man."[57] The author's vocabulary is distinctive. According to Spicq, there are 152 words in Hebrews found nowhere else in the New Testament.[58] The author, though undoubtedly a Jew, was versatile in his reading. His language-world was not only that of the Septuagint but it was also that of the Greek philosophical writings.[59] He chooses his words with care for their sounds. This cannot be observed unless one looks at the original Greek text. His opening lines (1:1) read, *Polumerōs kai polutropōs palai ho theos lalēsas tois patrasin en tois prophētais* ("In many and various ways God spoke of old to our fathers by the prophets"); the alliteration of *pol-*, *pol-*, *pal-*, *pat-*, and *pro-* is remarkably effective. When he describes Melchizedek as "without father or mother or genealogy" (7:3), he uses three words *(apatōr, amētōr, agenealogētos)* that begin with alpha.[60] The author's familiar statement, "as it is appointed for men to die once" (9:27), is written beautifully, with almost every word beginning with alpha—*apokeitai tois anthrōpois (h)apax apothanein.*

The author is equally impressive when he pours forth long sentences (1:1-4; 5:7-10; 7:1-3; 10:19-25; 12:18-24) and when he abbreviates his thoughts (2:18; 10:18). He makes effective use of oratorical imperatives:

---

55. P. 31ff.

56. See p. 245ff.

57. The words are those of James Hope Moulton as he speaks of Hebrews and also of the writings of Luke and Paul (Moulton-Howard-Turner, I, p. 232).

58. Spicq, I, p. 353. Words that are found only once in the New Testament are called *hapax legomena* ("once said"). The number of 152 in Hebrews compares with 113 in Romans, 110 in 1 Corinthians, and 99 in 2 Corinthians. Spicq's number of *hapax legomena* in Hebrews varies somewhat from Wikenhauser's (see p. 23).

59. See Moffatt *(Hebrews,* p. lxi) for illustrations.

60. Such words are called alpha-privatives. Moffatt *(Hebrews,* p. lx) counts twenty-four alpha-privative adjectives in the Epistle and notes that, according to Aristotle, the use of alpha-privatives was a mark of elevated style.

"Therefore, holy brethren ... consider Jesus" (3:1); "Take care, brethren, lest there be in any of you an evil, unbelieving heart" (3:12); "But recall the former days ..." (10:32; cf. 7:4; 12:5; 13:7). His interrogative turns are characteristic of the Epistle, whether in the simple form (2:3-4; 7:11; 9:13-14; 10:29; 11:32; 12:25) or the double form (1:5, 13, 14; 12:5-7) or even the triple form (3:16-18).[61]

The author makes skillful use of paradox. Abel died but speaks (11:4). Moses preferred the reproach of Christ above the riches of Egypt (11:26). Moses saw the invisible (11:27). Jesus went to the cross with joy (12:2). There is in the author also a love of antitheses. As noticed earlier,[62] the doctrinal elements of the Epistle take the form of a series of contrasts. There are two covenants, two sanctuaries, two priesthoods, two forms of worship. Among persons there are the contrasts of prophets and Son and angels (1:1-13); Jesus and Moses (3:1-6); infants and adults (5:11-14); Abel and Cain (11:4); Noah and the world (11:7); legitimate and illegitimate children (12:7-11). Among things there are the contrasts of blessing and cursing (6:7-8); the many priests and the one priesthood (7:23-24); the daily sacrifices and the one-time sacrifice (7:27); type and antitype (9:24); shadow and reality (10:1); the tent and the city (11:9-10); Sinai and Zion (12:18-24).

Paronomasia, which is a play on words of similar sounds, is characteristic of the author's literary touch. Frequently such wordplay is untranslatable, as in the collocation *echomen ... ex ... echousin exousian*, the full translation of the clause being, "We have an altar from which those who serve the tent have no right to eat" (13:10). In 5:8 the striking wordplay, *emathen ... epathen* ("he learned ... he suffered"), strengthens the pathos of the passage. But if the author's wording is rendered more literally, as in 2:10 ("for whom all things and through whom all things") and in 5:11 ("concerning which much to us the saying and difficult to say"), the intended wordplay is more discernible.

So the author constantly alters his literary devices. He writes now with threats, now in tenderness. Always he writes picturesquely, at times brilliantly. "We have an anchor of the soul," he says (6:19). "It is a terrible thing to fall into the hands of the living God" (10:31). "Let us run with perseverance the set-before-us race" (12:1). "Jesus Christ, yesterday and today the same, and for ever" (13:8).

Special Stylistic Devices

Several stylistic devices exhibit the careful structure of Hebrews.

1. *Chiasm.* Chiasm, or chiasmus, is associated with the Greek letter *chi* which has the shape of an X. Thus chiasm refers to the cross-

---

61. These passages are listed by Spicq (I, p. 358).
62. P. 38.

wise arrangement of words and of ideas. It is the use of inverted order, often in the form of ABBA or ABCCBA. A good illustration of this is in Jesus' words, "So the last will be first, and the first last" (Mt. 20:16).[63] In Hebrews a good illustration of chiasm is in 1:5, 6, 7, 8. The X form can be clearly seen:

Son   angels

angels   Son.

Another illustration is in 4:16:

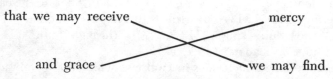

that we may receive   mercy

and grace   we may find.

The author's use of inverted order is evident in other ways. When he announces two ideas that will be discussed, he often treats the last mentioned first. In 2:17, Jesus is described as "a merciful and faithful high priest." In the material that follows, Jesus is shown to be faithful (3:1-6) and then merciful (4:15–5:10). In 5:1ff. the author enumerates several qualifications of the high priest: the high priest must be a man of compassion toward his fellow men and he must be called by God. When these qualifications are applied to Jesus in 5:5-10, they are applied to Him in inverted order.

2. *Inclusion.* An inclusion is a method of arrangement that marks off a literary unit by restatement at the end of what was said at the beginning. In the case of a paragraph, the last line of the paragraph contains the same idea as the opening of the paragraph. Jesus' saying, "the last will be first, and the first last" (Mt. 20:16), is not only a chiasm but it is also part of an inclusion; for it is a repetition of the thought, "many that are first will be last, and the last first" (Mt. 19:30). Thus the section begins and ends with the same idea.

Hebrews contains numerous inclusions by use of which the author sought to bring his reader back from the end of the passage to the beginning. Many of these inclusions are short, as in 4:12-13. Here the

63. Many illustrations of chiasm in the word order of the Greek could be given: Mt. 10:28: body–soul–soul–body (ABBA); Mt. 9:17: old–burst–skins–skins–destroyed–new (ABCCBA). For illustrations in Matthew, see J. C. Fenton, "Inclusio and Chiasmus in Matthew," StEv I (1959), 174-79; for Paul, see J. Jeremias, "Chiasmus in den Paulusbriefen," ZNW 49 (1958), 145-56; also J. J. Collins, "Chiasmus, the 'ABA' Pattern and the Text of Paul," StPaul II, p. 575ff.; cf. Moulton-Howard-Turner, III, pp. 345-47.

inclusion is not obvious to the English reader. The unit begins, "For the word of God," and concludes, "with whom we have to do." The latter expression literally reads, "toward whom to us the word [or, reckoning]." The unit thus begins and ends with "word" (Greek, *ho logos*). The paragraph of 5:5-10 begins by saying that "Christ did not exalt himself to be made a high priest" and ends with the statement "being designated by God a high priest...." Other examples are "look" and "unbelief" (3:12, 19); "enter" and "rest" (4:1, 5); "enter" and "disobedience" (4:6, 11); "priest" (7:1, 3); "Abraham" (7:4, 9); "perfection" and "law" (7:11, 19); "oath" (7:20, 28); "first" (8:7, 13); "regulations" (9:1, 10); "Christ" (9:11, 14); "covenant" or "will" (9:15, 17); "without blood" (9:18, 22); "Christ" (9:24, 28); "year after year" (10:1, 3); "offering" (10:11, 18); "fearful" (10:27, 31); "not seen" (11:1, 7); "not ... afraid" and "king" (11:23, 27); "through faith" (11:33, 39); "sons" (12:5, 8); "leaders" (13:7, 17).

There are longer inclusions in Hebrews which often embrace shorter ones. These, as sometimes with the shorter ones, do not always have the key words of the inclusion precisely at the beginning or precisely at the end of the unit. The reason for this variation is that often the author has a connecting sentence at the end of his section or sometimes at the beginning. This can be seen in the larger unit of 1:5-14. The key words of the inclusion are "to which ... angels ... ever say" (1:5), repeated in 1:13. Verse 14 then serves as a connection with what follows. Another larger inclusion is found in 3:1–4:14. This is a section mostly given to exhortation. The section begins with such terms as "heavenly," "Jesus," "high priest," and "confession" and concludes with practically the same words, "high priest," "heavens," "Jesus," and "confession." Other examples of longer inclusions are "for not ... angels" (2:5-16); "high priest" (5:1-10); "sluggards" (5:11–6:12); "Melchizedek" and "met" (7:1-10); and "peace" (12:14–13:20). All of these examples should be studied carefully. They show not only what the author wanted to emphasize and how he did it, but they supply real clues for an understanding of the structure of the Epistle.

3. *Hook words.* With regard to the structure, it is also important to see that the author uses certain words to link or hook his units together.[64] He does this by repeating at the beginning of his paragraph a word or words used near the end of the preceding paragraph. For example, "angels" in 1:4 is the hook word leading into the section on the Son and the angels beginning in 1:5. In this case, as has been seen, "angels" is a key word in the inclusion (1:5-13) as well as a hook word.

64. L. Vaganay ("Le Plan de l'Épître aux Hébreux," in *Memorial Lagrange* [Paris, 1940], pp. 269-77) maintained that the clue to the composition of the Epistle is to be found in the hook words.

Hook words often help the reader recognize subjects the author is about to discuss. The following chart lists the main hook words in Hebrews, a close study of which with open Bible will prove to be invaluable.

1:4 —"angels"	"angels"—1:5
2:13—"children" . . .	"children"—2:14
2:17—"faithful"	"faithful"—3:2
2:17—"high priest" . .	"high priest"—3:1
3:19—"enter"	"entering"—4:1
4:5 —"enter"	"enter"—4:6
4:14—"have"	"have"—4:15
6:12—"promises" . . .	"promise"—6:13
8:13—"the first" . . .	"the first"—9:1
9:23—"heavenly" . . .	"heaven"—9:24
10:39—"faith"	"faith"—11:1
11:7 —"heir"	"inheritance"—11:8
11:39—"attested" (having been witnessed to) . .	"witnesses"—12:1
11:40—"us"	"us"—12:1
12:24—"speaking" . . .	"speaking"—12:25

4. *Announcements.* The structure of Hebrews also includes on the author's part anticipations and announcements of subjects that are to be treated. In 1:3 he mentions purification for sins; he touches this again in 2:17 but does not develop the theme until chapters 9–10. Christ as high priest is stated generally in 2:17, more specifically in 5:1ff., but is not fully treated until 7:1ff. The heavenly priesthood is suggested in 1:3, it is affirmed in 4:14 and 6:19-20, but it is not expounded until chapter 9.

As the author makes anticipations, he seems also to make announcements to his readers of the main subjects to be treated. In 1:4 he announces that Christ has a better name than the angels, and he explores this theme through chapter 2. In 2:17 he states that Christ is a merciful and faithful high priest; he then deals with this topic through 5:10. In 5:10 he says that Christ is a priest like Melchizedek, and this becomes his subject for several chapters. In 10:39 he speaks of men of faith and well illustrates who men of faith are in chapter 11. In 12:11 he mentions "the peaceful fruit of righteousness" and follows by urging his readers to live at peace with one another.

The plan of Hebrews

These announcements are given by Albert Vanhoye in his important contribution to the study of the structure of Hebrews.[65] Vanhoye believes that he is able to discern the principal divisions of Hebrews from the author's own brief announcements of his subjects. He, therefore, outlines the Epistle in five main divisions, the five verses listed above announcing those five divisions.

Vanhoye's work has much in its favor and is due more attention than it has received. Some of his divisions, however, do not seem any less arbitrary than other outlines proposed for the Epistle. Further, because the author makes anticipations and announcements, it does not follow that his outline must strictly coincide with his announcements. Vanhoye's outline of the Epistle, with slight modifications, is attached below (Alternative Outline). It merits further study. The present work, however, follows a more conventional outline form (see Outline of Epistle) and employs a number of subdivisions in the hope of helping the reader grasp the meaning of Hebrews.

Alternative Outline (Vanhoye)

		1:1–4	Introduction
I		1:5–2:18	A name different from the angels
II	A	3:1–4:14	Jesus, faithful
	B	4:15–5:10	Jesus, compassionate high priest
		5:11–6:20	Preliminary exhortation
	A	7:1–28	Jesus, high priest like Melchizedek
III	B	8:1–9:28	Come to fulfilment
	C	10:1–18	Cause of an eternal salvation
		10:19–39	Final exhortation
IV	A	11:1–40	The faith of the men of old
	B	12:1–13	The endurance required
V		12:14–13:18	The peaceful fruit of righteousness
		13:20–21	Conclusion

---

65. His work is in French and is entitled *La Structure Littéraire de l'Épître aux Hébreux* (Paris, 1963). He has also made a translation of Hebrews based on its structure. This has been translated into English by James Swetnam (*A Structured Translation of the Epistle to the Hebrews* [Rome, 1964]). Although the latter volume lacks Vanhoye's discussion and explanation of the principles of the structure of Hebrews, it gives the English reader Vanhoye's outline and indicates by the use of different type such things as inclusions, hook words, and announcements.

Outline of Epistle

HEBREWS ONE

Opening Statement
(1:1-4)

The Epistle begins with the most beautifully constructed and expressive sentence in the New Testament. Full of his subject, without the use of customary greetings or the mention of his name, the author plunges directly into his theme of the person and work of the divine Son. The opening words are a kind of foretaste of all that is to follow, in which the author will seek to demonstrate the absolute supremacy of the Christian religion. The construction of the sentence, which runs to the end of verse 4, is elaborate. The style is refined and literary. Of the first twelve words employed, five begin with the letter "p." The sweep of the thought can only be grasped by reading the sentence straight through, although for practical purposes it is necessary to break it down into separate parts. **In many and various ways God spoke of** 1 **old to our fathers by the prophets.** A God who speaks to men His will is the distinguishing mark of true religion.[1] This is the basic assumption of the author, and it furnishes the starting point of his work. God has, he says, spoken to men in the past. He has never left Himself without witness. He spoke to **our fathers,** meaning not simply the patriarchs but all the faithful of the Old Testament duration. He spoke by means of **the prophets;**[2] this refers to all those who had spoken for God, espe-

---

1. The verb *lalein* is used characteristically in the Epistle to denote a divine speaking or inspired oracle (cf. 2:2; 3:5; 5:5, etc.).

2. There is no manuscript evidence whatever for emending "prophets" *(prophētais)* to read "angels." Although the passage proceeds to speak of the angels, they are mentioned solely by way of contrast with the Son, and this contrast only begins with "having become as much superior" (v. 4). In verses 1-2 the antithesis is between God's former speaking and His recent, final speaking in Jesus. On the whole question, see Héring, p. 1f.

cially to Moses and those who succeeded him. The term is thus of wide application and, in effect, stands for the contents of the entire Old Testament revelation.[3] And God, in His speaking, spoke in a variety of ways. He spoke here through a prophet and there through a priest; in visions and in dreams; in symbols and in natural phenomena; in mighty deeds of history and in written oracle.

But the earlier speaking, presented in multifarious forms, cannot compare with the later. It was preliminary, destined to be superseded from the outset. It was preparatory, awaiting a final, definitive speaking. 2 God spoke before, **but in these last days** (literally, "at the end of these days") **he has spoken to us by a Son.** The **last days** are in contrast to the days of old. The Old Testament often speaks of "the last days" (Gen. 49:1; Num. 24:14; Isa. 2:2; Hos. 3:5), by which is meant the future in general or the Messianic age in particular, the time when prophecy would find its fulfilment. The New Testament writers speak of their own time as the time of this fulfilment (Acts 2:17; cf. Heb. 9:26; 1 Pet. 1:20; 1 Cor. 10:11). **These last days** denotes the final phase of history, brought on by the entry of the Son into the world and continuing until the consummation of all things. The author speaks not of "the Son" but of **a son.** This is his typical manner of expression (3:6; 5:8; 7:28). By speaking of **son,** he draws attention to His rank and dignity. The later revelation comes not through many voices but in one full gush through Him who has the dignity of a Son. In His Son God speaks His final, satisfying word to men.

But who is this Son? What are His privileges and powers? The author now lists a number of His distinguishing marks. **He is appointed the heir of all things.** "Ask of me, and I will make the nations your heritage, and the ends of the earth your possession" (Ps. 2:8). Perhaps these words were on the author's mind, for in verse 5 he quotes the previous lines of the psalm (2:7). The designation to be **heir** is a natural consequence of sonship, an appointment that partakes of the eternal sphere even as (as implied) His nature is eternal. He is Sovereign Lord of creation (Acts 10:36). All that the Father has belongs to Him (Jn. 16:15). As the "beloved son" He is the only rightful heir (Mk. 12:6-7; Lk. 20:13-14; Mt. 21:37-38). He is also the one **through whom** God

3. This is evident, as G. B. Caird has pointed out, from the author's use of the Old Testament. Of the twenty-nine quotations in the Epistle, twelve are from the Pentateuch, five from the prophets, eleven from Psalms, and one from Proverbs. Of the fifty-three allusions in the Epistle, thirty-nine are to the Pentateuch, eleven to the prophets, two to Psalms and one to Proverbs. This is sufficient to show that God's having spoken "by the prophets" is not to be taken in any narrow sense. See G. B. Caird, "The Exegetical Method of the Epistle to the Hebrews," CJT 5 (1959), 47.

created the world.[4] The two descriptive clauses are closely connected.
Since the Son is Heir, He is also Creator; or rather being Creator, He
is the undisputed Heir. The thoughts are similar to those found in John
and Paul (cf. Jn. 1:3; 1 Cor. 8:6; Col. 1:16). Through the Son's agency
the universe came into being. It has, therefore, always been His. He
is the sole, rightful owner of all things.

The dignity of the Son, however, depends not just on world-making.
It is involved in the eternal order of things and is best seen in the Son's
relation to the Father. **He,** like no other, **reflects the glory of God.** The 3
language points again to the pre-existent state of the Son, to His eternal
essence. There was a time when God was without a world, but there
never was a time when He was without glory.[5] The word translated
"reflects" may also be rendered "radiates,"[6] the idea being that the Son
radiates the ineffable light of the divine glory. In either case, the two
meanings are interrelated since Jesus Christ is the perfect shining forth
and reflection of God among men.

The Son, further, **bears the very stamp of** God's **nature.** He is the
counterpart of the Father. The two retain their individual identities, but
their essential nature is one. The Greek word *charactēr,* appearing only
here in the New Testament, refers to an exact reproduction, as a statue
of a person or as an impression made by a seal. Originally the term
denoted a die or stamp or branding iron; then it came to apply to the
mark engraved or the image of a person or thing. The Son is the impress
or image of the Father. He does not exhibit the Father in certain respects
but He is exactly like the Father (cf. Jn. 14:9; Col. 1:15). He possesses
the very likeness of the divine nature. In Him there reside all the
qualities that make God be God. The author clearly wishes to emphasize
that the nature of God and not only His message was revealed in Jesus.

These are some of the Son's wonderful attributes, and the author
adds one more as preliminary to his main thought. He says that the
Son is ever **upholding the universe by his word of power.** The Son is
Creator and Sustainer of the cosmos. He bears or guides along *(pherōn)*
the universe in the way that He wants it to go. This he accomplishes
by His omnipotent word, even as the worlds were called into existence
by the mighty word of God (11:3). The idea is not that the Son like a
weight lifter holds the universe up, but rather that He is responsible for
its providential government. The thought is similarly expressed in Colossians 1:17, although there Christ is seen as the basic element that holds

---

4. The Greek word *aiōnas* can mean "ages," referring to the ages of the world's
history. It is preferable here, however, to understand it spatially and translate it
(as in 11:3) "worlds" or "world."
5. A. B. Bruce, "Epistle to Hebrews," HDB, II, 329.
6. Greek *apaugasma,* meaning either "radiance" or "reflection."

everything together, here as the power that consciously directs its destiny.

Now the author reaches the climax of his long sentence. He is interested in all the Son is and does, but he is especially interested in what the Son has done for sin and in His consequent exaltation. It was He who made **purification for sins** and **sat down at the right hand of the Majesty on high.** Here the Son incarnate becomes visible, for He could have done all the things previously ascribed to Him and remained in heaven. But in order to deal with sin He had to come to earth and become man. That is precisely what He did, achieving for humanity a thorough **purification for sins.** These words stem from priestly symbolism and supply an early hint to the major theme of the Epistle that will be treated later on. Christ's death and sacrifice secured what could never be attained through Levitical procedures—a satisfactory and enduring cleansing from sin. Thus the Son is also Redeemer.

The exaltation following the earthly humiliation is described in the terms of Psalm 110:1: "Sit at my right hand. . . ." The **right hand** indicates the place of power and highest honor (1 Kings 2:19; cf. Ps. 45:9) and **sat down** implies dignity and dominion. **Majesty on high** is a periphrasis for God. Jews and early Christians so reverenced God that often they would not pronounce His name. Instead they would use such expressions for God as "throne of the Majesty" (8:1), Heaven (Lk. 15:18), and Power (Mk. 14:62). The whole clause vividly depicts the entrance of the Son on His reign. He shares rulership from the heavenly throne. To Him, therefore, is assigned a unique position in the world-order. Being distinct from the Father, He is nonetheless *near* Him, at His right-hand side; and yet being one with the Father, He is enthroned *with* Him.

The closing words of the long introductory sentence enlarge on the
4 Son's right to a throne: **having become as much superior to angels as the name he has obtained is more excellent than theirs.** The participle **having become** points back to a certain point in time. The Son became superior to the angels when He took His seat at God's right hand. Prior to this, while in human form, His position was a little lower than the angels. The Son's eternal existence and nature are not here in view (as in vv. 2b-3a); rather His work of redemption and His consequent exaltation.

Angels, though they are lofty beings, have never been enthroned like the Son. This is what the author wishes to stress. They do not have a **name** like His. Here **name** is possibly used in the sense of dignity or rank or reputation. But in light of verse 5, the **name** seems to be that of "Son" or "my Son." The word "Son" suggests a sweeping range of prerogatives. This means that the Son is radically different from the angels. He is **superior** to them—as the name "Son" is higher than the name "angels" or "messengers"—and this superiority is not only of degree but of essence.[7]

Son Superior to Angels
(1:5-14)

To a modern mind it would seem wholly unnecessary to prove that Jesus the Son of God is greater than the angels. But the ancient world at that time made much over the angels. Angels were prominent in various religions of the Near East. Among the Greeks there were considerable expectations of a coming divine messenger, of a messenger from heaven, of a messenger of light.[8] In the Old Testament angels often appeared: to Abraham (Gen. 18); to Lot (Gen. 19); at the sacrifice of Isaac (Gen. 22:11); to Moses at the burning bush (Ex. 3:2); in the desert wanderings to guard the Israelites (Ex. 23:20-23); and so forth. From the literature between the testaments, from the Pseudepigrapha and Dead Sea Scrolls, it is evident that more and more speculation about angels had developed.[9] With some, by the time of the first century, these speculations had been transformed into an elaborate system of angelology.

In the midst of this it is difficult to know how new Christians fitted Christ in with their conceptions. The temptation for the ancients was to overemphasize either His humanity or His divinity. Perhaps the readers of the Epistle, or at least some of them, avoided both extremes by associating Jesus with the angelic creation. He was neither man nor God but an angel. On the other hand, there is evidence that at Colossae a spirit of heresy was at work which had as one of its central doctrines the worship of angels (Col. 2:18). This kind of problem may lie in the background of the Epistle; and, if so, might account for the author's attention to the subject.[10] It is certain that he was concerned about "diverse and strange teachings" (13:9); but what they were, and whether they were in any way related to false notions about angels, is purely conjectural. On this the Epistle gives no hint. It is safe to conclude, however, that the contrast of the Son with the angels is made in order to show the superiority of the Son to all beings, and especially the angels, because they were the ones who mediated the Mosaic law

---

7. The word "superior" (*kreittōn*) appears thirteen times in the Epistle and carries in itself a special message. See Introduction, p. 37.

8. TDNT, I, 57.

9. IDB, I, 132.

10. This is the view of T. W. Manson; see his *Studies in the Gospels and Epistles,* p. 252ff. Because of this and other affinities with the Epistle to the Colossians, Manson argues that Hebrews was directed to churches in the Lycus Valley.

(Gal. 3:19; Acts 7:53). This becomes later an important aspect in the author's argument.

That the Son holds an unchallenged supremacy is, for the author, a matter capable of full demonstration. For in his mind nothing is more solid than divine Scripture, nothing more incontrovertibly true. Thus he always resorts to the authority of Scripture, and practically always to the Septuagint (LXX) text. His proof that the Son is superior to the angels comes from seven quotations of the Old Testament, five of which are derived from the Psalms. (For New Testament use of the Old Testament, see Additional Note.) The first quotation is from Psalm 2:7, a great Messianic passage (cf. Acts 13:33), and is set in the form of a
5 question. The author asks: **For to what angel did God ever say, "Thou art my Son, today I have begotten thee"?** Psalm 2 is a passage that probably reflects the enthronement of a Davidic king. On ascending the throne, the king became God's son by adoption. In Psalm 2:7-9 God puts His anointed on the throne and gives him unrivaled power. He will break the nations with a rod of iron, he will dash them in pieces like a potter's vessel. God says, "You are my son, today I have begotten you."[11] It is clearly the author's view, and the view of the early church (Acts 4:25-27; 13:33), that such words do not take on their full meaning except in the Messiah. In Scripture God speaks to the Messiah and designates Him as Son. Though the angels as a class are referred to as "sons of God" (Jb. 1:6; 2:1, etc.), to no individual angel has it ever been said, **Thou art my Son.** The words, **today I have begotten thee,** probably are best understood as a poetic metaphor for the act of enthronement.[12] The words should not be pressed, although the early church undoubtedly saw Jesus' resurrection and heavenly session as their fulfilment. The author uses the quotation simply to bring out that Jesus so very appropriately is called Son.

The next quotation is also in question form. This is evident from the author's connective **Or again.** When did God ever say to an angel, the author asks, **"I will be to him a father, and he will be to me a son"?**

---

11. The adoption formula in Ps. 2 is typical of the custom among the ancient kings of Babylon, Assyria, and Egypt (cf. A. Bentzen, *King and Messiah* [London, 1955], pp. 16-19). Eric Voegelin (*Order and History*, vol. I, *Israel and Revelation* [Baton Rouge, 1956], p. 305) cites parallels from the Pyramid texts 1 a-b and 42-b: "This is my Son, my first born. . . . This is my beloved with whom I have been satisfied" and "This is my beloved, my son; I have given the horizons to him. . . ." R. de Vaux (p. 112) also sees Ps. 2 as adoption language. "According to the Code of Hammurabi, when someone adopted a person, he said to him, 'You are my son,' and if the latter wanted to break the bond thus created, he would say, 'You are not my Father' or 'You are not my mother.'" But compare Schweizer (TDNT, VIII, 350f.), who views Ps. 2 as using the language of legitimation, the legal process by which the father acknowledges his son as his legitimate son and heir.
12. See Lindars, p. 141ff.

The quotation is taken from 2 Samuel 7:14 (cf. 1 Chron. 17:13). The Old Testament background for the passage is that Nathan the prophet has told David that God's house would be built not by David but by his son. In so saying, God gives assurance through Nathan that He will graciously provide for David's son: "I will be his father, and he shall be my son." Though spoken directly to Solomon, the promise indirectly applies to all of David's ruling descendants, and in particular, as the author sees it, to Jesus the Son, apart from whom the Davidic throne could never be "established for ever" (2 Sam. 7:16). To the Son God vowed in the supreme sense that He would be His Father. But at what time and in what place did God so speak to any of His angels? The point is confirmed from Scripture, then, that the Son has received a better name than the angels.

The argument advances another step. Jesus is lifted above the angels because He is Son and, further, He is superior to them because they owe Him worship. This is shown by a third quotation from the Old Testament, a quotation whose precise wording occasions difficulty. There is no Hebrew equivalent for **Let all God's angels worship him.** **6** The words, however, are found in the Septuagint translation of Deuteronomy 32:43 and in substance in Psalm 97:7.[13] In Deuteronomy the words relate to the worship of the God of Israel; and since the author maintains that the Son is divine, "the stamp of God's very being" (1:3, NEB), he feels no hesitancy in adapting the quotation to the Son. The command in the quotation is universal, for *all* the angels are to pay homage to the Son.

Prefacing the command are the words, **And again, when he brings the first-born into the world.** The translation should stand as is, the **again** being understood as introducing a new quotation. The thought is not "when he brings again the first-born," as though a reference to the Second Coming of Christ. (See Additional Note.) Nor does **when** point precisely to some event in the human career of Jesus, such as His incarnation or resurrection. "It is not so much a question of His being brought into the world as of His being introduced to it as the Son of God. . . ."[14] If a particular occasion is in view, it would seem

---

13. The Hebrew (MT) of Ps. 97:7 reads, "Worship him, all you gods." The LXX translates this as "Worship him, all you angels." Supporting the longer reading of the LXX of Deut. 32:43 is now a Hebrew fragment from Qumran Cave 4 which reads, "And prostrate yourselves before him, all you gods." See P. W. Skehan, "A Fragment of the 'Song of Moses' (Deut 32) from Qumran," BASOR 136 (1954), 12-15; cf. F. M. Cross, Jr., *The Ancient Library of Qumran and Modern Biblical Studies* (Garden City, 1958), pp. 135-37; P. Katz, "The Quotations from Deuteronomy in Hebrews," ZNW 49 (1958), 217ff.

14. F. F. Bruce, *Hebrews*, p. 17. Cf. Moffatt, *Hebrews*, p. 11. This idea is brought out in the NEB translation: "Again, when he presents the first-born to the world, he says. . . ."

that reference is being made to the Son's enthronement in heaven, when all the angelic hosts are summoned to worship their Lord.[15] Such an introduction, then, must be understood as poetic, not historic. The author is drawing on the quotation for dramatic effect, laying stress on the angelic acknowledgement of the Son's pre-eminence.

The Son here, as elsewhere (Rom. 8:29; Col. 1:15, 18; Rev. 1:5), is called **the first-born** (*prōtotokos;* cf. Ps. 89:27). The term may denote either "priority" or "superiority"; in this instance the concept of priority phases into superiority. (See Additional Note.) It cannot be taken in the sense that Jesus was the first to be created, for all along the author has been contending that He is eternal. As the first-born the Son sustains a special nearness to God and holds an unrivaled position among the heavenly host.

The remainder of the chapter is a remarkable combination of Old Testament citations from the Psalms. Angels are inferior beings, for

7 **Of the angels he** (God) **says, "Who makes his angels winds, and his servants flames of fire."** The quotation is from Psalm 104:4. According to the usual translation of the Hebrew text, the **winds** are God's messengers and **flames of fire** are His servants. But another rendering of the Hebrew is possible which, instead of making winds His messengers, makes His messengers (or angels) winds. This is the translation of the Septuagint, which is followed by the author, showing that God is able to do with the angels whatever He desires. He can change them into winds or into flames of fire. Angels, at their highest, are mere servants. They have no will or rule of their own. They do not give orders, they follow them.

The evanescent nature of angels is in contrast to the eternal exist-

8 ence and reign of the Son. **But of the Son he says, "Thy throne, O God, is for ever and ever."** Verses 7 and 8 are closely tied together; indeed, in the Greek language they are parts of the same sentence, the construction being "with respect to the angels, he says" and "with respect to the Son, he says." The speaker in both verses is, of course, God. God speaks to the angels as messengers, He addresses the Son as "God," who has an everlasting sovereignty. The angels stand before the throne; the Son sits on the throne. A full quotation from the psalm (Ps. 45:6-7) is now

9 made. God the Father continues to speak to the Son: **"The righteous scepter is the scepter of thy kingdom. Thou hast loved righteousness and hated lawlessness; therefore God, thy God, has anointed thee with the oil of gladness beyond thy comrades.** Psalm 45 is a festal marriage

---

15. The word translated "world" (*oikoumenē*) ordinarily refers to "the inhabited world." But it is also used in the sense of the *kosmos* (1 Clement 60:1), probably including the world of angelic powers. In 2:5 *oikoumenē* refers to all that is subject to Christ and is equivalent to "everything" in verse 8.

song that celebrates a royal wedding. The psalm is divided into two parts, the first part being addressed to the royal bridegroom and the second part to the bride. In its original setting it referred to the throne of a Davidic king, established and strengthened by divine power. (In the Old Testament God is always King and no king rules apart from His will.) The psalm is an ideal representation of the king and his kingdom, not a description of things as they actually were at any one time in history. The author of Hebrews regards the passage as intensely messianic and sees the reign of the Messiah as the perfect fulfilment of the ideal depicted in the Old Testament. "No earthly king of Israel ever fully answered to this description till Jesus came."[16] The Son's reign is eternal, for His throne endures **for ever and ever** (cf. Dan. 7:14; Lk. 1:33). The Son's reign is universal, for the **scepter** is a symbol of His absolute authority. The Son's reign is just, for He sways an upright scepter. His rule is not one of arbitrary power but of justice (cf. Ps. 89:14). The Son's reign is good. He has loved right and hated wrong, and the strong implication is that it has always been so.

The last line of the quotation supplies the author with additional proof of the Son's superiority to the angels. In the psalm the king's **comrades** might be either his fellow princes or his companions at court. **Oil of gladness** is a Semitic expression, referring to the occasion as an occasion of joy. The anointing probably is not that of a king's coronation but of a feast. It was customary in ancient times to anoint guests at a feast with perfumed oil (cf. Ps. 23:5). Here the anointing is metaphorical and expresses a high feeling of exultation, for Christ has been set above His **comrades.** If it is asked who are His comrades, the response must be the angels. The argument thus far irresistibly suggests this. They are His celestial comrades who constitute His heavenly court. The word "comrade" is not to be pressed, as if to say that the Son is like the angels. Everything in the context is against this, and indeed here in this verse the Son is made superior to the angels. Besides, it should be remembered that the author's choice of terms is compressed by the quotation. Still he feels that the word "comrade" is not inappropriate— and it is not if understood along the lines suggested above.

A further quotation attests to the uniqueness of the Son, the author's citation now coming from Psalm 102:25-27. The beautiful language is quoted at some length, revealing the Son as Creator and by nature imperishable. **"Thou, Lord, didst found the earth in the beginning** 10 (a figurative expression denoting the creation of the earth), **and the** 11 **heavens are the work of thy hands; they will perish, but thou remainest; they will all grow old like a garment, like a mantle thou wilt roll them** 12

---

16. Tasker, *Old Testament,* p. 121.

up, and they will be changed. But thou art the same, and thy years will never end." The words are similar to Isaiah 51:6; see also Matthew 24:35 and 2 Peter 3:10-12. The psalm quotation was first spoken with reference to God and to His eternal purposes. The anonymous writer of the psalm takes his grief to the Lord. He is overwhelmed by personal sufferings and prays that God may not take his life in the mid-course of his years—the God "whose years endure throughout all generations" because He is Creator. But the author of the Epistle, as he reads the psalm, quite naturally applies the passage to the Son because (1) He also is "Lord,"[17] and (2) He also is Creator (v. 2). The Son is over the universe because it came into being through His agency. (The angels, to the contrary, are not creators.) He is before the world, for He laid its foundations. He is after the world, for He will roll up the heavens and the heavenly bodies like a cloak. "The world wears out, even the sky (12:26) is cast aside, and with it the heavenly lights, but the Son remains . . . nature is at His mercy, not He at nature's."[18]

13 For his final Biblical proof on the Son the author cites Psalm 110:1, to which he has already made allusion in verse 3. The psalm is important in the scope of the Epistle (5:6, 10; 6:20; 8:1; 12:2) and especially in connection with Christ and Melchizedek (ch. 7). The argument is as incisive as it possibly can be, the tone quite emphatic. **But to what angel has he ever said, "Sit at my right hand, till I make thy enemies a stool for thy feet"?** The introductory formula is like that of verse 5; verse 5 and verse 13 are the opening and closing parts of the inclusion.[19] The figure arose from the Oriental custom of the victor's putting his foot on the neck of the defeated enemy (cf. Josh. 10:24). Jesus in His public teaching, as the apostles did later, interpreted this psalm messianically and applied it to Himself (Mt. 22:41-46; Acts 2:34). In the words of the psalm the Father says to the Son, **Sit at my right hand.** This position of royalty was never offered to an angel. The imperative **Sit** (*kathou*) is in the present tense, implying that the Son not only is to take a seat but is to continue to sit in the divine presence. There He will remain, awaiting final victory over His foes.

14 By contrast the angels are mere servants. **Are they not all ministering spirits sent forth to serve, for the sake of those who are to obtain salvation?** They are all servants. Their function is not to rule but to serve, and they do this not of their own initiative but they are **sent.** Here and there they go. As their name implies, they are messengers. Like Gabriel, they stand in the presence of God (Lk. 1:19). They stand

---

17. The LXX, from which the author is quoting, reads "Lord"; this facilitates the application of the quotation to Jesus Christ.

18. Moffatt, *Hebrews*, p. 15.

19. See Introduction, p. 47.

there always to execute with promptness the divine will. And for whom do they serve? Not simply for Him who is on the throne but for believers as well. It is not said that they serve Christians, but that they serve for their sake. Christians "inherit" (KJV, ASV, NEB)[20] or **obtain** salvation in the sense that they experience the joys of salvation while on earth and look forward to its full reward in heaven. The clause, **those who are to obtain salvation,** is transitional, leading the reader on to the main theme of the ensuing paragraph.

Thus a radical and indisputable difference exists between Christ and the angels. He is God's Son; they are God's servants. As Son Christ is also King, asserting His power from the throne for righteousness. But angels have no thrones. Christ the King is also Christ the Creator. He is eternal. They, like all creatures, are changeable and perishable. To worship them or give them undue honor would be to establish a form of paganism. This is why the author insists so much on the complete subservience of the angels. In heaven there are, to be sure, myriads of angels (12:22), but they are of a different order and rank than the Son. Through Him alone do men gain a right relationship with God. This the author proceeds to demonstrate.

Additional Notes

Hendiadys

V. 1. It is probably better to understand "in many and various ways" *(polumerōs kai polutropōs)* as hendiadys. The term "hendiadys" literally means "one through two" and denotes the expression of one idea by the use of two words joined together by the conjunction "and." Here there is scarcely any difference of meaning between *polumerōs* and *polutropōs,* the thought being simply that "in various ways" God formerly spoke to the fathers. In Hebrews cf. "transgression and disobedience" (2:2), "faith and patience" (6:12), "the table and the bread of the Presence" (9:2), "chains and imprisonment" (11:36), etc.

In Scripture the literary form of hendiadys is more common than is often realized. Some clear examples in the New Testament are: "power and coming" for "powerful coming" (2 Pet. 1:16), "suffering and patience" for "patience in suffering" (Js. 5:10), "hope and the resurrection" for "hope of the resurrection" (Acts 23:6).[21]

The author's use of the Old Testament

V. 5. Beginning here and going to the end of the chapter, the author

---

20. The word "inherit" *(klēronomeō)* and its cognates, used three times in ch. 1, occur nine times in the Epistle (1:2, 4, 14; 6:12, 17; 9:15; 11:7, 8; 12:17).
21. For further reference, see Blass-Debrunner-Funk, Section 442.

strings together seven quotations from the Old Testament on the relationship of the Son and the angels. Since at first glance he seems to select his passages arbitrarily and even capriciously, legitimate questions are raised as to how the author understood or undertook to explain his Old Testament. This, in turn, opens up the whole area of the connections between the testaments and of how diverse New Testament writers make citations from the Old Testament.

The subject is not new, but in the last decade or so it has been discussed with new vigor and flare. This is evident from the recent essays and books that have been published on the subject.[22] Aside from questions on variant forms of texts and manner of quotation, much of the discussion has centered on the Old Testament contexts of the quotations and whether the New Testament author respected, modified, or violated the original contexts. And on this score the general view has been that the tendency of the New Testament author was to look high and low for "proof texts" without regard for the original meaning of a passage.

The work of Dodd and Tasker, among others, runs counter to this view. Dodd attempts to show that practically all of the New Testament citations from the Old Testament, instead of being detached like bits and pieces, are more like parts of a whole—that the writers did not draw from isolated contexts but from whole contexts which they recognized as appropriate sources for their quotations.[23] In other words, Dodd finds more method and understanding of redemptive history in the New Testament writers than has often been allowed. Tasker expresses a similar view, but with a different emphasis. He laments that Biblical scholars, searching for the precise historical situation which prompted a prophet's utterance, have forgotten the truth "that the divine revelation is not conditioned entirely by the circumstances in which it was first given, nor is its significance limited to the historical

22. The literature is extensive, but certain works stand out. Books—C. H. Dodd, *According to the Scriptures* (London, 1952); R. V. G. Tasker, *The Old Testament in the New Testament* (London, 1954); E. Earle Ellis, *Paul's Use of the Old Testament* (Edinburgh, 1957); B. Lindars, *New Testament Apologetic* (London, 1961); James Barr, *Old and New in Interpretation: A Study of the Two Testaments* (New York, 1966); F. F. Bruce, *The New Testament Development of Old Testament Themes.* Essays—B. S. Childs, "Prophecy and Fulfillment," *Interpretation* 12 (1958), 250-71; J. A. Fitzmyer, "The Use of Explicit Old Testament Quotations in Qumran Literature and in the New Testament," NTS 7 (1960-61), 298-333; R. E. Murphy, "The Relationship Between the Testaments," CBQ 26 (1964), 349-59; C. K. Barrett, "The Interpretation of the Old Testament in the New," *The Cambridge History of the Bible*, vol. I, *From the Beginning to Jerome* (Cambridge, 1970), pp. 377-411; Moody Smith, Jr., "The Use of the Old Testament in the New," *The Use of the Old Testament in the New and Other Essays*, ed. J. M. Efird (Durham, N. C., 1972), pp. 3-65.
23. Dodd, *According to the Scriptures*, p. 60ff.

situation in which man first gave utterance to it, but that it has a far wider reference."[24]

G. B. Caird speaks similarly as he addresses himself to the interpretative method of the author of Hebrews.[25] Caird reacts strongly against any viewpoint that would represent the author as employing farfetched exegesis. "I should like to suggest that, so far from being an example of fantastic exegesis which can be totally disregarded by modern Christians, Hebrews is one of the earliest and most successful attempts to define the relation between the Old and New Testaments, and that a large part of the value of the book is to be found in the method of exegesis which was formerly dismissed with contempt."[26] Hebrews, by means of the author's approach to the Old Testament, ties the testaments together as perhaps no other book of the New Testament does. The God who spoke in the former covenant speaks much more in the latter. Indeed, He is still speaking—through the Son, to be sure, but in the "living," written word as well (4:12). For this reason the formulas that introduce the quotations are, for example, "God says" (1:5, 6ff.), "Christ says" (10:5), and the "Holy Spirit says" (3:7; 10:15)—with emphasis on the present tense. The author's consistent view of Scripture is that it is indisputably authoritative and normative.

The word *fulfil* does not occur in the Epistle. Yet it is true that everything in the Epistle has the stamp of fulfilment on it. Events of Israel's past and its holy institutions are alike seen as shadows and types of a greater, fuller reality in Christ. It is no wonder that Scripture, too, partakes of this character of fulfilment.

This is why the New Testament elsewhere does not hesitate to speak of itself in terms of fulfilment—"to fulfil what the Lord had spoken through the prophet," "in order that the Scripture might be fulfilled," etc. The term itself needs explanation, for without it there can be no true conception of fulfilment. The word *fulfil* (the Greek *plēroō*) means "to fill up," "to make completely full," "to complete," "to bring into full effect," etc. As the word is applied to Scripture, the thing to remember is that it is God who fills or fulfils His word. It is not possible that His word be empty or unfilled. From the moment His word is spoken it

---

24. Tasker, *Old Testament*, p. 15.
25. Caird, "The Exegetical Method of the Epistle to the Hebrews," CJT 5 (1959), 44-51. On Hebrews and Old Testament quotations, see P. Katz, "The Quotations from Deuteronomy in Hebrews," ZNW 49 (1958), 213-23; S. Kistemaker, *The Psalm Citations in the Epistle to the Hebrews* (Amsterdam, 1961); K. J. Thomas, "The Old Testament Citations in Hebrews," NTS 11 (1964-65), 303-25; M. Barth, "The Old Testament in Hebrews," *Current Issues in New Testament Interpretation*, ed. W. Klassen and G. F. Snyder (New York, 1962), pp. 53-78; G. Howard, "Hebrews and the Old Testament Quotations," NovTest 10 (1968), 208-16; and Westcott's special notes (pp. 68ff., 90ff., 471ff.), which are still of great value.
26. Caird, "The Exegetical Method," p. 45.

has meaning. The appropriate terms, then, are not "empty" and "full," but "full" and "fuller," with "fulfilment" suggesting that God has filled up the full measure of His word.

This suggests antecedents that become basic presuppositions for a Christian understanding of fulfilled Scripture. God moved in Israel's history. He worked His world-plan by means of this history, which reached its climax in Christ. Therefore, Old Testament events and institutions point beyond themselves. A prophet's statement might refer back to past history, or relate to a contemporary scene, or speak predictively with reference to the future. Jeremiah's "Rachel weeping for her children" (Jer. 31:15) is a poetic picture relating to a contemporary scene of lamentation over the impending bondage of the nation of Israel. But the words are relevant—have their full meaning—in connection with the slaughter of infants at Bethlehem when Messiah was born (Mt. 2:18). Hosea is speaking of God's love for Israel and of His deliverance of Israel from Egypt when he says, "Out of Egypt I called my son" (Hos. 11:1). Matthew's use of this statement, with application to Jesus' return from Egypt (Mt. 2:15), is indiscriminate only if in his eyes it has no fuller meaning in Jesus. If redemptive history is not piecemeal, if it forms a line of continuity from testament to testament, such prophetic words do have fulfilment—call it illustrative or analogical or typological or verbal or whatever—and real meaning.

The author of Hebrews possessed just this perspective of history. Writing in the "today" of God's saving act in Christ, with the light of the gospel and the gift of the Spirit, he is sure that the Spirit spoke and still speaks in Scripture. For the specific applications he makes of Old Testament texts, see the discussions on the pertinent passages.

Palin, "again"

V. 6. The word "again" (palin) has been the subject of much discussion. Is it to be understood as a connecting particle, simply introducing another quotation from the Old Testament? Or is it to be taken with the verb that follows—"And when again he brings the first-born into the world..."? Westcott, Hewitt, and Héring argue for the latter and thus interpret the clause as referring to the Second Coming of Christ. On the other hand, Moffatt, Michel, Spicq, Bruce, and others, along with the KJV, RSV, and NEB, see "again" as having no more than a connective function. For further discussion, see F. F. Bruce, *Hebrews*, p. 15; W. Michaelis, TDNT, VI, 880.

Prōtotokos, "first-born"

V. 6. In the early church an important title applied to Christ was "first-born" (Greek, prōtotokos; Rom. 8:29; Col. 1:15, 18; Heb. 1:6; Rev. 1:5). Paul, for example, describes Christ as "the first-born of all creation" (Col. 1:15). Does this mean that Christ is the first of all creatures, the first to be created, or does it mean that He has inherent priority over all creation?

The term is derived from Old Testament usage. Moses was told to say to Pharaoh: "Thus says the Lord, Israel is my first-born son" (Ex. 4:22). God speaks through Jeremiah, saying: "I am a father to Israel, and Ephraim is my first-born" (Jer. 31:9). Of the messianic King God says: "I will make him the first-born, the highest of the kings of the earth" (Ps. 89:27).

J. B. Lightfoot wrote an excellent note on *prōtotokos*, in which he showed that the term has two main ideas: (1) priority to all creation, and (2) sovereignty over all creation.[27] On the idea of priority to creation, Lightfoot showed that the patristic writers distinguished between *prōtoktistos* ("first-created") and *prōtotokos* ("first-born"); that Clement of Alexandria, for example, used *prōtoktistos* ("first-created") to refer to the angels, while he used *prōtotokos* ("first-born") with reference to the Son. Lightfoot continued: "... the description *prōtotokos pasēs ktiseōs* [first-born of all creation] must be interpreted in such a way that it is not inconsistent with His other title of *monogenēs, unicus*, alone of His kind and therefore distinct from created things. The two words express the same eternal fact; but while *monogenēs* states it in itself, *prōtotokos* places it in relation to the Universe."

On the conception of sovereignty over creation, Psalm 89:27 was sufficient for Lightfoot to show that rulership and pre-eminence are necessarily involved in *prōtotokos*, for the adjoining line explains "first-born" in the sense of "the highest of the kings of the earth."

As the term is applied to Christ in Hebrews 1:6, the immediate context suggests both sovereignty and priority. As first-born, He is Sovereign Lord and "the heir of all things" (1:2). As first-born, He is before all things (cf. Col. 1:16-17), the Pre-existent One whose throne is "for ever and ever" (1:8), the One who in the beginning "didst found the earth" (1:10).

The term *prōtotokos*, therefore, is the very opposite of what it is sometimes mistaken to be. It does not mean the first of created beings. It signifies pre-existence and rank of the highest order.

Ho theos, "O God"

V. 8. Various opinions exist as to how *ho theos* (translated "O God") is to be understood. Some commentators maintain that *ho theos* must be taken in the nominative case as the subject of the sentence: "God is thy

---

27. J. B. Lightfoot, *Saint Paul's Epistles to the Colossians and to Philemon* (London, 1900 reprint), p. 144f. In addition to Lightfoot's valuable note, see Vincent Taylor, *The Names of Jesus* (New York, 1953), pp. 147-49; K. L. Schmidt, TDNT, VI, 871ff.

throne for ever and ever." Others say that *ho theos* is a predicate nominative, the translation being "Thy throne is God. . . ." Westcott, going back
to the original quotation in Psalm 45:6, argues that it is hardly possible
that *ho theos* in the Septuagint can refer to the Davidic king; that,
therefore, "God is thy throne" is the preferred translation.[28] Interpreted
in this way, the idea is similar to "thou art my rock and my fortress"
(Ps. 71:3), "the Lord God is an everlasting rock" (Isa. 26:4), etc. Others,
however, including the KJV, ASV, RSV and NEB, regard *ho theos* as
vocative: "Thy throne, O God, is for ever and ever." When viewed from
the author's standpoint, the latter rendering seems to be the better one.
In either case, however, the author's main argument is not essentially
affected, for his point is not to establish that the Messiah is divine but
that He possesses a throne and everlasting dominion.

Sōtēria, "salvation"

V. 14. In the Greek classics "salvation" *(sōtēria)* predominantly
stands for "preservation" or "deliverance," deliverance from such as the
calamities of war or from dangers of the sea. In the Old Testament
again and again the thought is likewise deliverance from some mortal
danger. In the non-literary papyri the term ordinarily denotes "bodily
health." A letter written in the second century reads: "Write me a letter
first about your *sōtēria,* second about that of my brothers."[29] This means,
"Let me know how you are doing. . . ."

In the New Testament, in addition to these meanings (Lk. 1:69, 71;
Acts 27:20, 34), *sōtēria* takes on the significance of "salvation from sin"
or "salvation from impending wrath" (Mt. 1:21; Rom. 5:9; etc.). The
New Testament writers speak of salvation as a past act (Rom. 8:24), a
present state (1 Cor. 1:18), and a future expectation (Rom. 13:11).
Romans 5:1-2 takes in all three senses: "Therefore, since we are justified
by faith, we have peace with God through our Lord Jesus Christ.
Through him we have obtained access to this grace in which we stand,
and we rejoice in our hope of sharing the glory of God."[30]

Here in 1:14, as in other instances in the Epistle (5:9; 9:28), salvation
has a future reference. It is something that Christians will inherit at the
close of the age. At other points, it is something already present, co-
extensive with the salvation which began to be spoken by the Lord
(2:3) and the intercession He continues to make for those "who draw
near to God through him" (7:25).

---

28. Westcott, p. 25f.
29. Moulton-Milligan, p. 622.
30. See A. M. Hunter, *Interpreting Paul's Gospel* (London, 1954), p. 21ff. Hunter
has three chapters on salvation as "a past event," "a present experience," and "a
future hope." See also William Barclay, *A New Testament Wordbook* (London,
1955) and TDNT, VII, 965ff.

HEBREWS TWO

An Exhortation and a Warning
(2:1-4)

The theme of chapter 1 is that Christ is superior to the angels. His power is great, His name is unrivaled, His office and function are eternal. **Therefore,** the author says, **we must pay the closer attention to what** 1 **we have heard.** Here is what is usually termed the author's first digression from the main argument. Yet, strictly speaking, this is not a digression but the climax and necessary conclusion to the foregoing. Since God has spoken through the Son (1:2), men **must pay ... attention** to that message (2:1). Exhortations to faithfulness that break the logical thread are characteristic of the Epistle. The author is not concerned with mere theological abstractions, nor is his purpose to delve into impenetrable mysteries and reveal new truths. He wishes only to remind his readers (and himself) of what they have already heard. He is anxious about the spiritual progress of his friends and fears that they may be allowing their unique Christian opportunities to pass them by. What they have heard are words of great consequence. They are matters of life and death. The gospel message deserves, then, the most earnest heed possible, for the danger is ever present that men will **drift away from it.** The Greek word *pararreō,* translated **drift away,** has an interesting background.[1] It is often used to refer to something that slips away (see the KJV), as an arrow that slips from its quiver, or a ring that slips from the finger, or an idea that slips from the mind. It literally means "to flow by" or "flow past" and seems to be used here in the

---

1. Cf. Prov. 3:21, where the LXX employs the same verb *pararreō*—"Son, do not wander away [or, let escape from the mind], but keep my counsel and intention." The author wants his readers to heed his admonitions.

sense of a boat that is adrift. The warning is that as a boat might glide past its landing place, so Christians might be swept downstream from the truths of the gospel. The author feels that the readers' situation demands effort and diligence, for to drift away is to die.

The gravity of the situation is further explained, the necessity for attentive obedience being grounded on the fact of certain retribution.

2 **For if the message declared by angels was valid and every transgression**
3 **or disobedience received a just retribution, how shall we escape if we neglect such a great salvation?** The argument is in the form of "the lesser to the greater," what the Jews called "light and heavy" (Hebrew, *qal waḥomer*). (See Additional Note.) If in the Old Testament era every violation of law inevitably received its due punishment (the lighter instance), how can Christians expect to escape (the heavy case) if they drift away from the faith? **The message declared by angels** is the author's way of referring to the old Mosaic code, for the law was believed by Jews to be a revelation "delivered by angels" (Acts 7:53). Paul says that the law "was ordained by angels through an intermediary" (Gal. 3:19); and Josephus represents Herod as saying to his soldiers, "We have learned the noblest of our doctrines and the holiest of our laws from God through the angels."[2]

Although given through angels, the old law held good. It was steadfast and rigid, never a thing to be lightly regarded by God's people. It inflicted pains and imposed penalties on all who violated its requirements. No "transgression or disobedience" went by unaccounted for. (There seems little difference of meaning between the two terms, unless "transgression" indicates a positive offense and "disobedience" a negative offense. See Additional Note on 1:1.) That being the case, if the word of angels stood firm—and the message of a Son deserves more respect than the message of angels—what hope is there for those who would **neglect such a great salvation?** The author's pointed question strongly implies that no escape from retribution is possible if one is careless with the **great salvation.** He does not say "if we reject" but simply **if we neglect.** The Greek word translated "neglect" *(amelēsantes)* also appears in Matthew 22:5, where the guests "made light of" their invitation to come to the marriage feast of the king's son. What an outrage that the invited guests should disdain the king's grace. And likewise, here, how unthinkable that men should ignore their sole means of deliverance. For men who do so, the author is sure that God's judgment rests upon them; for, as he later says, "It is a fearful thing to fall into the hands of the living God" (10:31).

---

2. *Antiquities* 15.5.3. It is possible, however, to translate "messengers" instead of "angels."

The greatness of this salvation, its essential nature, its methods and results, become the theme of the remainder of the chapter. But first the author deals with the certainty of the salvation he has mentioned. The old covenant had proved its validity by condemnation of transgressors. The author assures his readers that the new covenant has no less confirmation. It is guaranteed as trustworthy by a threefold attestation. (1) **It was declared at first by the Lord.** The contrast between the law and the gospel is marked: one was spoken by angels, the other was spoken by the Lord Himself. It had, therefore, the authority of heaven and earth behind it. The title **Lord** adds emphasis to this authority. (2) **It was attested to us by those who heard him.** Was attested to *(ebebaiōthē)* refers back to **valid** *(bebaios)* in verse 2 and shows that the second revelation was just as inviolable as the first. The author makes no claim for firsthand knowledge. In fact, his language implies that he was not of the original apostolic circle. Author and readers alike were earwitnesses of the truth. They received the gospel from others. The statement "stands in strong contrast to the attitude of St. Paul, who, though not one of the original Twelve, yet always claimed that his authority was as direct and as valid as theirs. He would never have suggested that he relied on the reports brought to him by his predecessors in the Apostleship, still less would he have used their testimony as an argument for the validity of his message."[3] Yet the important thing is that the message was confirmed, for the author firmly believes that a report from the apostolic band is next to hearing Jesus Himself.

To the first and second aspects of the gospel's authentication, still another feature is added. (3) **God also bore witness by signs and wonders** 4 **and various miracles and by gifts of the Holy Spirit distributed according to his own will.** The witness borne by God was all-convincing. The combination **signs and wonders** is found frequently in the New Testament, **signs** indicating the inner significance of the miraculous deed, **wonders** the astonishment evoked by the unusual nature of the deed. The **miracles,** literally "powers," point to their superhuman source. They were not all of one class but were **various,** negating the possibility of fraud or deception. The **gifts of the Holy Spirit** refer to the spiritual gifts that attended the apostolic proclamation, showing that God was present with it. These gifts are of the sort listed in 1 Corinthians 12. They were not mere ecstatic manifestations, but the solemn witness borne by God to the truth of the gospel. This was all in keeping with God's express intention, it was **according to his own will.**

---

3. Robinson, pp. 13-14.

The Humiliation and Glory of Christ
(2:5-9)

The author now picks up the main lines of his presentation. Christ is indeed exalted above the angels, having seated Himself at God's right hand. Yet for a while He was made lower than the angels. This fact must be accounted for, and the author feels that he can. The starting point of his argument is once again a contrast of the Son and the angels, but soon this phases out and there remains only an incidental mention of the angels in verse 16. This is the last time the angels figure in the argument of the Epistle.

5   The author begins by insisting, **For it was not to angels that God subjected the world to come.**[4] The expression **world to come** has often been mistakenly thought to refer to heaven, but this is not its meaning. Throughout the Epistle "this world" and "the world to come" stand as opposites. One world, of which the old covenant is a part, is material and temporary, a world of shadows. The other world is spiritual and eternal, to which the new covenant rightly belongs. The Jews often spoke of "the world to come," meaning "the days of the Messiah."[5] The author clarifies his use of the expression by adding **of which we are speaking.** He means by **the world to come** the Christian world-order, the glorious era of salvation inaugurated by the Messiah and pressing on toward consummation at His second coming—the new order which by its very existence renders obsolete the prior dispensation.[6] The point which the author wishes to underscore is that the angels, though they had acted as revealers of the old law, have no rule in the Christian order.

The new order is subjected to men and, in particular, to the ideal man, Jesus Christ. The proof of this may be seen in a citation from the Psalms. The author regards the Old Testament as a God-given oracle, the express embodiment of the voice of the Holy Spirit. Only here in the Epistle (cf. 4:7, which is not an exception) is a quotation in any sense associated with a human author, and even so it is introduced by

---

4. Cf. "age to come" in 6:5, which is an equivalent expression. Here the term for "world" is *oikoumenē*, as in 1:6.

5. Michel thinks that 2:5 "clearly represents" the Jewish phrase, "the coming age" (TDNT, V, 159). Cf. G. Johnston, "*Oikoumenē* and Kosmos in the NT," NTS 10 (1963-64), 353-54; A. Vanhoye, "L'Oikoumenē dans l'épître aux Hébreux," *Biblica* 45 (1964), 248-53.

6. On the meaning of "the world to come," Westcott (p. 42) says: "The phrase is not to be understood simply of 'the future life' or, more generally, of 'heaven.' It describes, in relation to that which we may call its constitution, the state of things which, in relation to its development in time, is called 'the age to come' (*ho mellōn aiōn*) and, in relation to its supreme Ruler and characteristics, 'the Kingdom of God,' or 'the Kingdom of heaven,' even the order which corresponds with the completed work of Christ."

the indefinite formula, **It has been testified somewhere.** Leading into **6**
the quotation in this manner does not indicate any lack of information
on the author's part. It was a passage well known to both author and
readers. To cite a familiar passage with a vague formula was a mark
of good rhetoric. Also, the oblique reference to the human author lays
stress on the divine origin of the message. The readers would immediately recognize it as Holy Scripture.

The passage quoted is Psalm 8:4-6. **"What is man that thou art**
mindful of him, or the son of man, that thou carest for him?" The
subject of the psalm is man, and the point of the author is that all
things at the time of creation were placed under his control and juris-
diction. **Son of man** is a Semitic way of saying "man."[7] The first two
lines in the quotation are examples of synonymous parallelism characteristic of Hebrew poetry.

The remainder of the quotation (vv. 7-8a) should be read together.
The modern verse division is unfortunate, for the ending of verse 7
and the close of the quotation should coincide. **"Thou didst make him** **7**
for a little while lower than the angels, thou hast crowned him with
glory and honor, putting everything in subjection under his feet." By **8**
reading **angels** the author again follows the Septuagint, for the Hebrew
says "thou hast made him little less than God" (Ps. 8:5).[8] **Little,** in
Hebrew and Greek, can denote either position or time, and the exact
sense here is difficult to discern. Man, as the crown of creation, was
made a little lower than the angels; but perhaps the reference is temporal as in the RSV and in the NEB: "Thou didst make him for a short
while lower than the angels." In verse 9, when the line is directly
applied to Christ, the temporal significance better suits the sense of
the argument.

The author now presses the **everything** mentioned in the quotation
and argues from it. **Now in putting everything in subjection to him, he**
left nothing outside his control. In the psalm **everything** refers to the
sheep and oxen, the beasts of the field, and the birds of the air (Ps. 8:7-8).
The same general sense is found here, although the author's use of
everything is obviously more inclusive. Nevertheless, he is still thinking
of the dominion of mankind. Jesus is not mentioned until the following
verse, and then by way of contrast. Besides, when Jesus is mentioned,

7. Probably the author sees in "son of man" a heightened meaning, which may
have affected his choice of quotation at this point. But, if so, he does not strain the
expression. As he quotes, he leaves it to the reader to make the almost unconscious
identification with Jesus.
8. It may be, however, that the LXX has preserved the correct sense of the passage,
interpreting the Hebrew *elōhim* to stand for "divine beings" or "angels." The
thought of the Hebrew thus would be that man is made just a step under the
angels, not that he was created slightly inferior to God.

the specific reference is to the earlier part of the citation. But **As it is,** the author says, **we do not yet see everything in subjection to him.** The author continues to speak of man, as is made clear by the NEB, "But in fact we do not yet see all things in subjection to man." The "not yet" implies an unfulfilled promise. At present things may be in a frustrating condition; in the future things will be reversed.

The drift of the quotation and the author's meaning may be summarized as follows: God, mindful of man from the beginning, gave him a high place. He bestowed on him glory and honor and made him lord of creation (Gen. 1:26-28). All things were put under his feet. But man rebelled and lost his universal dominion. Man originally was given dominion. He is still destined to achieve it. But this dominion can only be realized, as the author goes on to say, through the ideal or representative man, Jesus Christ. Not everything is under man's control; **But,** the author says, **we do see Jesus ... crowned with glory and honor.** That is to say, in Christ the complete fulfilment of the psalm is realized and true dominion conferred. Man is not crowned as yet; but Jesus is crowned, even though **for a little while He was made lower than the angels.** This Christians see through faith.

That Jesus became flesh is a fact of history. Yet that was not the extent of His humiliation. It was necessary, also, that He suffer; indeed His enthronement in glory is precisely **because of the suffering of death.** These words must not be connected with **made lower than the angels,** with the meaning that Jesus became incarnate in order that He might die. The construction of the Greek sentence perhaps allows this, but the immediate context does not. (See Additional Note.) He was not crowned with a view to suffering but because He died in suffering. (For his first reference to the death of Jesus the author uses tautology— the **suffering** equals **death. Suffering** is underscored, not simply His act of dying. The concept of suffering is prominent in the whole Epistle; see especially 12:2ff.) And why, according to the author, did Jesus die? Not because of any claim man had but **that by the grace of God he might taste death for every one.** The reading **by the grace of God** is much to be preferred to the rendering "apart from God" and goes well with **it was fitting** in the next verse. (See Additional Note.) "Taste of death" is a Semitism found elsewhere (Mk. 9:1; Jn. 8:52), comparing the bitterness of death to something unpleasant to the taste. The expression **for every one,** if taken as a neuter instead of a masculine, would be translated "for everything." But the context of the passage argues against it. The meaning is that Jesus died for the whole human race. He did not die instead of men, for all men still must die. He died in their behalf, He died as their representative. So rather than dishonor and shame being attached to the death of Jesus, as any Jew might reason, the author shows that Jesus' death was a glorious death. He put down His life for others, and thus was "crowned with glory and honor."

The Savior of Men
(2:10-18)

To people of Jewish mind, a suffering Messiah was an obstacle to faith, a barrier so high and difficult that it could neither be scaled nor penetrated. The author now meets this problem head-on. He maintains that no matter what objections might be raised against it (1 Cor. 1:23), the cross was an event appropriate to heaven's supreme will. James Moffatt introduces and explains the thinking of the author so well here that at least part of his paragraph deserves quotation:

> To die for everyone meant that Jesus had to enter human life and identify himself with men; suffering is the badge and lot of the race, and a Saviour must be a sufferer.... For the first time, the conception of suffering occurs, and the situation which gave rise to the author's handling of the subject arose out of what he felt to be his reader's attitude. "We are suffering hardships on account of our religion." But so did Jesus, the writer replies. "Well, but was it necessary for him any more than for us? And if so, how does that consideration help us in our plight?" To this there is a twofold answer. (a) Suffering made Jesus a real Saviour; it enabled him to offer his perfect sacrifice, on which fellowship with God depends. (b) He suffered not only for you but like you, undergoing the same temptations to faith and loyalty as you have to meet. The threefold inference is: (i) do not give way, but realize all you have in his sacrifice, and what a perfect help and sympathy you can enjoy. (ii) Remember, this is a warning as well as an encouragement; it will be a fearful thing to disparage a religious tie of such privilege. (iii) Also, let his example nerve you.[9]

In this new section the author starts out by basing the death of Jesus on necessary moral grounds. Behind the cross there lay the action of God proportionate to the need of man. Verse 10 is closely linked with the words in verse 9, **by the grace of God.** In view of God's incomparable grace, **it was** entirely **fitting that he** perfectly qualify Jesus **10** to be Leader of His people by means of suffering. This is the main thought of the verse. The **he,** of course, is God. God, **for whom and by whom all things exist** (cf. Rom. 11:36; 1 Cor. 8:6), always does what is right and appropriate. He is the basis and cause of all existence. In Him, therefore, everything must find its reason; and the passion of Jesus corresponds with this eternal reason. God's purpose is, **in bringing many sons to glory,** to **make the pioneer of their salvation perfect through suffering.** Here for the first time the author speaks of Christians as God's **sons**—sons, as is made clear elsewhere in the New Testament,

9. Moffatt, *Hebrews,* p. 28.

by the process of adoption (Rom. 8:15; Gal. 4:5). **Many** is not used to indicate how many people will be in heaven, but rather to indicate that it was God's purpose to have not one Son but many sons to share His glory. This glory has been destined for men, as verse 7 shows. That they are truly sons will be brought out in the next verses.

Many are called **sons;** only one can be described as **the pioneer of their salvation.** The word here translated is *archēgos*. Applied in other New Testament passages to Jesus (Acts 3:15; 5:31; Heb. 12:2), it is a term of unusual interest. In secular Greek writings it was used of a "hero" who founded a city, gave it its name and became its guardian. Similarly, it denoted one who was "head" of a family or the "founder" of a philosophic school. The term also had a distinct military connotation (thus the KJV's "captain"), referring to a commander of an army who went ahead of his men and blazed the trail for them. All these terms fit Jesus; but the idea of a leader who opens up a new way seems here to be uppermost in the author's mind. As a pioneer the Son goes ahead of the saved, opening up a path.

Their salvation implies what is later (4:15) made more explicit: Jesus did not save Himself from sin because He had no sin. He had no moral faults or imperfections (cf. 2 Cor. 5:21; 1 Pet. 2:22). This being so, then in what sense was Jesus made **perfect through suffering?** Some understand the author to be saying simply that through death Jesus completed His earthly work and overcame all His earthly limitations. But the word **perfect,** which with its cognates is characteristic of the Epistle, demands more than this. Ordinarily it means to bring to completeness or wholeness; to do a thing fully; to put into effect; to finish, for example, a tower or a work of art. But here its meaning is determined by the Septuagint, which regularly uses the term in the Pentateuch to refer to the consecration of priests (Ex. 29:9, 29, 33, 35, etc.). As in the Old Testament the priests were perfected or consecrated by various rites, so Christ in the New was perfected or consecrated or qualified.[10] The thought is that, apart from suffering, Christ could not have been made a thoroughly effective, perfect Leader of His people.

11 The author now speaks of the relationship between the **Sons** of God and the Son of God. **For he who sanctifies,** he says, referring to Christ, **and those who are sanctified,** meaning Christians, **have all one origin.** Here the work of sanctification, as later (13:12), is assigned to Jesus, for it is "the offering of the body of Jesus Christ once for all"

---

10. The Greek verb is *teleioō*, which, with its related forms, occurs fourteen times in the Epistle (2:10; 5:9, 14; 6:1; 7:11, 19, 28; 9:9, 11; 10:1, 14; 11:40; 12:2, 23). It is significant that *teleioō* occurs in Hebrews more often than in any other New Testament book.

(10:10) that makes it possible for men to be sanctified. This is consistent with the Biblical view that holiness belongs essentially to God alone. To sanctify is to make holy, for "sanctify" and "holy" come from the same root. If there were such a word as "holify," the connection between the two terms would be obvious to the English reader. Sanctification is thus the action of setting aside something or some one as peculiarly belonging to God. It is the state or condition essential for access into God's presence, for only those who are sanctified can draw near to God. In this Epistle it is the practical equivalent of justification, and is based on the atoning blood of Christ. **Of one origin** probably refers not to Adam or to Abraham but to God the Father.

The Leader and the followers form one unit, they are brothers in one family. **That is why he is not ashamed to call them brethren. Not ashamed** implies the superior order of the Son: He does not blush to look on them as His brothers. Three Old Testament proofs are now submitted to point up the common tie of Christ and the redeemed. In all three quotations Christ is the speaker, evincing the author's full persuasion that they must be understood messianically. The first of these is from Psalm 22:22, a psalm the first verse of which Jesus applied to Himself while agonizing on the cross (Mk. 15:34). **"I will proclaim** 12 **thy name to my brethren, in the midst of the congregation I will praise thee."** In the first line the significant words are **my brethren;** in the second line the special thought is that the Son joins His brothers in praising God in the community. The parallelism of **brethren** and **congregation** incidentally shows that Christ counts as His brothers those who are members of His church.

The second and third quotations are taken from Isaiah 8:17b-18a. Jesus is represented as saying, **"I will put my trust in him [God]." And** 13 **again, "Here am I, and the children God has given me."** Originally these statements were made by the prophet Isaiah concerning himself and his two sons, Shearjashub and Mahershalalhashbaz. Distressed and rejected by a disobedient people, the prophet affirmed his faith in God and looked to his children as witnesses to the salvation that God would bring. The author regards Isaiah's words as illustrative of higher truths. First, the Messiah expresses His complete trust in God. He, too, is wholly dependent on God, which demonstrates His sonship and brotherhood with all men. Second, the Messiah willingly associates Himself with God's children. He says, "Here I am among men, on equal footing with those God has given me." The three Old Testament quotations throw emphasis on the spiritual links of the Sanctifier and the sanctified.

Jesus, then, is closely connected with God's children. **Since there-** 14 **fore the children share in flesh and blood, he himself likewise partook** of the same nature.[11] Since they are men, He had to become man. He had to likewise share in flesh and blood, an expression synonymous with the weaker and perishable aspect of man's nature (cf. 1 Cor. 15:50). His intention was that through death he might destroy him who has the power of death, that is, the devil. "To destroy" (katargeō) means "to make ineffective," "to render powerless," "to put out of use." Jesus became incarnate that He might subdue Satan's power; as another writer says, "The reason the Son of God appeared was to destroy the works of the devil" (1 Jn. 3:8). Satan had the power of death. He introduced it into the world and exercised his dominion in his own realm, the realm of death. ("Death as death is no part of the divine order.")[12] He was lord of death because sin, which produces death, was under his control. To overthrow this control, to destroy this dominion, to save man that he might never die again, this is what Jesus came to do—and this is what He did when He offered Himself as the perfect atonement for sin (9:28). Thus in one sense death is no more; in and through Him death is already destroyed (2 Tim. 1:10). In another sense complete victory over death awaits the final consummation, for "the last enemy to be destroyed is death" (1 Cor. 15:26; cf. Rev. 20:14).

15   By death Jesus also was able to deliver all those who through fear of death were subject to lifelong bondage. The figures in verses 14-15 are figures of conquest and liberation, expressing the two sides of Christ's triumph over death: He destroyed him who had the power of death and set at liberty those who were the bondservants of death. Death held sway. Men, all through their earthly years, were bent low in the fear of death. Men feared death and its consequences.[13] But as a victorious Captain or Leader, Christ has beaten back the enemy and has opened the way of escape. He has released them from captivity, for it is not fitting that sons should be in bondage (cf. Rom. 6:17-18). In these verses the resurrection of Jesus is strongly implied,[14] for otherwise it would not have been possible through death to break the iron grip of the ruler of death.

16   One final reference is now made to the angels. For surely it is not with angels that he is concerned but with the descendants of Abraham. Since men are His brothers, it is they that Christ came to save, not

---

11. The tenses of the Greek verbs are instructive. The children "share" (kekoinōnē-ken, perfect tense) in flesh and blood; He "partook" (meteschen, aorist tense) of their human nature. He partook, but does not now partake.

12. Westcott, p. 54.

13. On the extent of the fear of death in the ancient world, see Moffatt, Hebrews, p. 35f.

14. In fact, the Epistle everywhere assumes the resurrection of Jesus as an accomplished fact, though it makes only one pointed reference to the event (13:20).

angels. The translation here is a rather weak rendering of the author's idea.[15] The Greek verb translated "is concerned with" would be better translated "helps." The word used here is *epilambanō*, which literally means "to take hold of"; in a given context it can be extended to mean "help." It appears again in 8:9, where it is said that God "took hold" of His people and led them out of the land of Egypt. The author is not simply saying that Jesus is concerned with men but that He helps them and delivers them. The entire thought is that He laid hold of men in order to help them out of their distressed condition. **The descendants of Abraham** might well refer to fleshly Israel; that is, that the author writes as "a Hebrew to Hebrews" and asserts that Christ came especially to save them. This would have the advantage of taking **the descendants of Abraham** quite literally, in line with other literal references to His sharing in flesh and blood, to His death and the deliverance gained by it, and so forth. But in the next verse the author concludes that it was necessary for Christ **to be made like his brethren.** This must mean, in light of his previous statements, that Christ had to be made like men, not that He had to be made like the Hebrew race. It seems better to understand, therefore, that **the descendants of Abraham** has a broader reference, and that the author is using one of those archaic phrases of which he is fond,[16] by which he includes all God's children of faith (cf. Gal. 3:7, 9, 29).

It was necessary, then, the author repeats, that Jesus become a real man. **Therefore he had to be made like his brethren in every respect.** Christ became **in every respect** a human being—except that He did not sin, as is stated directly in 4:15 and implied in 2:11, since He is the Sanctifier. He had to partake of the human predicament and be one with His brothers of flesh. Their trials and burdens, their pains and sighs, became His. He learned to see things from the human plane. This was essential if He was to act as a representative of men, if He was to **become a merciful and faithful high priest in the service of God** (literally, "in the things pertaining to God").[17] These words provide the first glimpse of what surely has been in the author's mind from the outset, *the high priesthood of Christ.* But this grand subject, which

15. The KJV reads, "For verily he took not on *him the nature of* angels." This rendering of the clause is unfortunate, being influenced by the patristic writers who understood the verse to refer to Christ's human nature. The KJV margin, a literal rendering of the verse, is more to the point: "He taketh not hold of angels, but of the seed of Abraham he taketh hold."

16. See Moffatt, *Hebrews*, p. 37.

17. *Ta pros ton theon*, "the things pertaining to God," is the same idiom that is found in Rom. 15:17 in reference to the Gentile gifts that Paul brought to Jerusalem. In the OT (LXX) Moses was to be for Aaron (Ex. 4:16) and for the people (Ex. 18:19) "the things pertaining to God" (cf. Deut. 31:27).

stands as one of the originalities of the Epistle, is not developed at this time; it is merely introduced here and will be taken up again in 4:14. The author says nothing about "gifts and sacrifices" (5:1), nothing yet of Jesus' offering of Himself. This master thought he will hold in reserve. He speaks now only in a general way of those qualities that enabled Jesus to be high priest. He was **merciful and faithful.** In respect to God He proved Himself faithful, as indeed all good servants do (3:2, 6; 1 Cor. 4:2). He suffered, but He was never shaken in His purpose. But the author's perspective at this point is somewhat different. He is speaking of Jesus as a merciful and faithful high priest *in regard to men.* (Here the words "high priest" and "faithful" are hook words,[18] connecting the verse with 3:1-2.) Jesus is a faithful priest in the sense that He is reliable and dependable: believers can trust in Him with absolute confidence.

In regard to men He also showed Himself merciful and compassionate. If it is "want of sympathy that makes officials perfunctory,"[19] it is the broad course of human experiences as a background that guarantees Jesus as a compassionate priest. He knows and understands. He thus represents men to God. As priest it is His function **to make expiation for the sins of the people.** Men's sins separate them from God, blur their vision of Him, and prevent fellowship with Him. But Christ procures forgiveness and removes every tinge of guilt from the sinner's heart. He expiates or atones for sin.[20] This is His primary function as high priest, a function which in itself inspires trust.

The concluding statement of the chapter further draws out the meaning of Jesus as a merciful and faithful priest. **For because he himself has suffered and been tempted, he is able to help those who are tempted.** As high priest He deals not only with sinners, expiating their sins, but He deals also with the saints. He aids them daily as they are exposed to various trials. He feels for them. He understands their lot. He was severely tempted; and in this connection one thinks of all the earthly temptations which in full force were unleashed upon Him. But the author is not thinking of His temptations generally, but of the one great temptation He experienced in His death. **He himself has suffered and been tempted** goes back to 2:9, "the suffering of death." In death, and all associated with it, He was tempted in particular

18

18. See Introduction, p. 48.

19. A. B. Bruce, *Hebrews,* p. 127.

20. In recent years the meaning of the verb *hilaskomai,* whether "to propitiate" or "to expiate," has been abundantly discussed. F. F. Bruce's excellent note (*Hebrews,* p. 41f.), along with the bibliographical sources indicated, should be consulted. In addition, see John R. W. Stott's note in his *The Epistles of John* (London, 1964), pp. 84-88.

(cf. 5:7ff.). This temptation, and His triumph over it, can always serve to inspire His weaker brothers.[21] "Courage, the writer cries, Jesus understands; he has been through it all, he knows how hard it is to bear suffering without being deflected from the will of God."[22]

Additional Notes

The qal waḥomer argument

V. 2. In this verse the author's reasoning follows the well-known form of "the lesser to the greater," the "how-much-more" principle. The argument is also known as *a minori ad maius* and as *qal waḥomer* ("light and heavy"). Rabbi Hillel (first cent. A.D.) listed this as one of his seven rules of interpretation of the law. According to this principle one proceeds from the fuller conditions in the law to the lesser ones, or from the lesser to the fuller. The presupposition is that the law is especially inviolable in weightier matters, and less so in lighter matters. It follows, then, that if a stipulation is made in the case of the lighter, how much more will it apply in a similar case of the heavier, even though there may be no specific statement in the law governing it.

The New Testament gives expression to reasoning in this form on a number of occasions. It is perhaps significant that most of these instances go back to the teachings of Jesus. A good illustration is Matthew 12:11-12, when Jesus asks, "What man of you, if he has one sheep and it falls into a pit on the sabbath, will not lay hold of it and lift it out? Of how much more value is a man than a sheep! So it is lawful to do good on the sabbath." (See also Mt. 6:30; 7:11; Lk. 13:15-16; 14:3-5; Jn. 7:22-23; Rom. 11:12, 24; 2 Cor. 3:7-11).

Philo, too, employs this type of argument. Two examples are especially noteworthy. "But if he who swears a wrongful oath is guilty, how great a punishment does he deserve who denies the truly existing God and honors created beings before their Maker..." *(The Special Laws* 2.255). "For if those who reviled mortal parents are led away for execution, what penalty must we consider those have merited who take upon them to blaspheme the Father and Maker of the universe?" *(On Flight and Finding* 84).

Because Hebrews deals so much with contrasts of the old and new covenants, the author is able to take special advantage of the "how-much-more" principle in his argumentation. "For if," he says, "the sprinkling of defiled persons with the blood of goats and bulls and with the ashes of a heifer sanctifies for the purification of the flesh, how much more shall the blood of Christ... purify your conscience from dead

---

21. See W. Michaelis, TDNT, V, 917f.
22. Moffatt, *Hebrews,* p. 39.

works to serve the living God" (9:13-14). The argument here expresses very well much of the message of the Epistle.

Again, "A man who has violated the law of Moses dies without mercy at the testimony of two or three witnesses. How much worse punishment do you think will be deserved by the man who has spurned the Son of God ... ?" (10:28-29). Very similar to 2:2-3 is 12:25: "See that you do not refuse him who is speaking. For if they did not escape when they refused him who warned them on earth, much less shall we escape if we reject him who warns from heaven." The argument for paying attention to the divine oracle in Christ could scarcely be stated in a more convincing form.

For further reference, see Sowers, p. 127ff.; Kistemaker, p. 62ff., p. 71ff.

"Gifts of the Holy Spirit"

V. 4. "Gifts of the Holy Spirit" may be understood in one of two ways: either in the sense of the Holy Spirit as the Giver, or the Holy Spirit as a gift. The New Testament speaks in both senses. (In the case of the former, see 1 Corinthians 12:11; Acts 2:3-4; for the latter, see Galatians 3:5; Acts 2:38; 5:32.) Here the correct interpretation turns on the use of the genitive case in Greek, whether "gifts of the Holy Spirit" is a subjective or objective genitive. Since in this passage it is God who bears witness with the gifts, it is probably better to construe the genitive objectively—"distributions consisting of the Holy Spirit." In this way the Holy Spirit is regarded as given in various functions. The idea is that God has certified the gospel with signs, wonders, miracles, and distributions of the Spirit, and all of this is according to His will.

"Because of the suffering of death"

V. 9. Some commentators hold that the sentence here means that Jesus was crowned prior to His suffering, that He was crowned for death, or that He was crowned with a view to the suffering of death. Marcus Dods identified the crowning with the recognition, on such occasions as His baptism and His transfiguration, that Jesus was the Messiah. But the passage makes perfectly good sense by rendering *dia to pathēma tou thanatou* as "because of the suffering of death" (ASV, RSV). Thus translated, the exaltation is understood as the consequence of Jesus' suffering (cf. Phil. 2:8-9). Westcott has correctly stated that "for the purpose of suffering death" is contrary to the New Testament usage of *dia* with the accusative, that this construction "always expresses the *ground* and not the *object: because* something is, and not *in order that* something may be realised."[23]

---

23. Westcott, p. 45.

The reading of 2:9

Instead of "by the grace of God" *(chariti theou)* some textual critics have preferred the reading "apart from God" *(chōris theou)*. Both forms of the text were current in the second century. Origen and Jerome were acquainted with both readings; and Origen, finding significance in both, refused to choose between the two. Important patristic evidence for *chōris theou* comes from Theodore of Mopsuestia, Theodoret, Ambrose, and others. This reading has received various interpretations. It has been said that Jesus died "apart from God" in the sense that (1) He was forsaken on the cross by God—"My God, my God, why hast thou forsaken me?" (Mk. 15:34); (2) He died apart from His divinity—the human Jesus died but His divine nature survived; or (3) He died for everyone or everything *(pantos)* except for God.

But the reading *chōris theou* ("apart from God") is highly questionable. Aside from certain patristic writers who know of it (and there are many others who apparently do not know of it), the evidence of the Greek manuscripts and versions is practically nil. Witnesses in its favor are M, 424 (margin), 1739 (margin), one manuscript of the Vulgate, and several manuscripts of the Syriac Peshitta. All other textual authorities, including a host of Greek manuscripts and versions, stand against *chōris theou*. Although it can be defended as the more difficult reading, it seems more plausible to regard *chōris theou* as an unexplained primitive corruption.[24]

The conception of Jesus as high priest

V. 17. "The suddenness with which the notion of Jesus as 'a merciful and faithful high priest' is first introduced in ii. 17 suggests that it is no invention of the writer, but was a belief already familiar to Christians" (A. J. B. Higgins, "The Priestly Messiah," NTS 13 [1966-67], 235). The question has often been raised as to the source of the author's conception of Jesus as high priest. Higgins is correct in saying that the author did not originate the idea. Although there are no specific references to Jesus as Priest outside Hebrews, there are a number of statements in various sections of the New Testament that imply His priesthood (Rom. 5:2; 8:34; Eph. 2:18; 5:2; 1 Tim. 2:5; 1 Jn. 2:1). And there are the

---

24. G. Zuntz (p. 34f.) in recent years has argued that *chōris theou* is the original reading of the text. R. V. G. Tasker has taken exception to Zuntz on this point; he agrees with Tischendorf "that *chōris theou* is a later correction made in the light of 1 Cor. xv.27 to exclude God from the inclusiveness implied in *huper pantos.*" See Tasker, "The Text of the 'Corpus Paulinum,'" NTS 1 (1954-55), 84. J. K. Elliott ("When Jesus Was Apart from God: An Examination of Hebrews 2:9," ExpTimes 83 [1971-72], 339-41) more recently has argued for *chōris theou*. He maintains that "apart from God" is consistent with the author's style and usage, and further that the Epistle elsewhere (4:15; 5:7ff.; 12:2; 13:12f.) depicts Jesus in death as separated from God.

words of Jesus Himself that point to Him as Intercessor (Jn. 17:9ff.; Lk. 22:32; 12:8). As to the possibility of Hebrews deriving its conception from Qumran and on the whole question of a Jewish expectation of a priestly Messiah, see Higgins' article, p. 221ff. and his essay, "The Old Testament and Some Aspects of New Testament Christology," *Promise and Fulfillment*, pp. 128-41; cf. G. R. Beasley-Murray, "The Two Messiahs in the Testaments of the Twelve Patriarchs," JTS 48 (1947), 1-12; F. F. Bruce, *Biblical Exegesis in the Qumran Texts*, p. 37ff.; James R. Schaefer, "The Relationship Between Priestly and Servant Messianism in the Epistle to the Hebrews," CBQ 30 (1968), 362ff.

HEBREWS THREE

Jesus Superior to Moses
(3:1-6)

In the preceding section it has been shown that Jesus Christ is the Author of the Great Salvation. Salvation began with Him and was perfected by Him. His words, therefore, deserve greater respect than the words of angels. This is true even though for a little while Christ was made lower than the angels. Not ceasing to be God, He became man; and the dominion and glory that were destined to be man's have become His. As man He shared with men the frustrations of the human condition. As man He, too, put His trust in God. As man He faced temptations, especially that of suffering and death. This is why He can serve, in behalf of men, as a compassionate and trustworthy high priest. He, as no one else, can be heart and soul concerned about those whom He is not ashamed to call His brothers.

In what follows the author develops the theme of Christ's supremacy over Moses and Aaron, and over the old covenant of worship and sacrifice they represent.

He begins with a contrast of Moses and Christ. The Moses-Christ parallelism was especially meaningful to the primitive church. In the New Testament Moses is mentioned more often (some eighty times) than any other Old Testament figure. Christ came as a second Moses, and J. Jeremias has shown that the messianic hope of a later Moses probably is to be dated before the Christian era.[1] The parallels of Moses and Christ are numerous. Moses' lifting up the serpent is a type of

---

1. See Jeremias' article on Moses in TDNT, IV, 848-73. See also T. F. Glasson, *Moses in the Fourth Gospel* (Naperville, Ill., 1963), p. 20ff.

Christ's being lifted up on the cross (Jn. 3:14). Moses gave the manna in the desert, but Christ gives the true bread from heaven (Jn. 6:31ff.). The prophetic word of Moses in Deuteronomy 18:15ff. is applied in Acts (3:22; 7:37) to Christ. Both Moses and Christ as deliverers were misunderstood and rejected by the people (Acts 7:20-44). Thus many examples of Moses-Christ typology found in the New Testament could be cited. The author of the Epistle himself will draw a number of parallels and contrasts.

At the end of the previous chapter the conclusion was reached that Jesus is a merciful and faithful high priest. The author now moves on to lay stress on those words, showing, first of all, the extent of Jesus' faithfulness to God and then, later, the depth of His feelings for men

1   as their priestly representative. He begins by saying: **Therefore, holy brethren, who share in a heavenly call, consider Jesus, the apostle and high priest of our confession.** Every word of this direct appeal to the readers is meaningful. **Therefore** calls to mind the convincing argument on the Son's unique rank and the efficacy of His redemptive work. The recipients of the Epistle are termed **holy brethren**—**holy** because of the action of the Sanctifier and **brethren** because they constitute one family with whom Christ was willing to be identified. These share not in an earthly call, such as the Israelite call to the land of Canaan, but in a **heavenly call** (cf. Phil. 3:14). The word **heavenly** suggests the contrast that appears again and again in the Epistle, a contrast between the present, visible, material world and that of the truly real world—immaterial, eternal and heavenly. Christians have been summoned to the celestial country, to the land of real and abiding things. They prospectively share with Christ His inheritance in heaven as He shared with them their human nature on earth.

The titles **apostle** and **high priest,** applied to Jesus, are chosen for a special purpose. They serve to introduce to the readers the great contrasts that are to follow between Moses and Christ, and between Aaron and Christ. The first of these titles the author immediately begins to deal with, postponing for a while his consideration of the second. When he terms Jesus an **apostle,** he is not thinking of one who simply was sent. Although this is the common definition, **apostle** is a term that means much more in the New Testament. It is the equivalent of the Hebrew term *shāliāh* which, at least by the time of the first century A.D., had come to stand for a person "sent with authority."[2] An apostle, therefore, is one who is sent with full authority to represent the sender. He is an "authoritative representative." **Apostle** is here appropriately applied to Jesus; for, as seen in 1:2-3, God speaks and acts through His Son.

---

2. See K. H. Rengstorf's instructive article on *apostolos,* TDNT, I, 398-447.

Moses, too, was an apostle, but God has sent out Jesus as the **apostle** of the great salvation. As such, He is the center of **our confession.** The **our** is emphatic: Christ, not Moses, is at the head of the Christian religion. The point is that the readers are to consider this remarkable Jesus, fasten their attention on Him, and hold on to Him whom they have confessed. (See Additional Note.)

It is necessary that God's stewards be faithful (1 Cor. 4:2). Christ proved to be no exception to the rule. **He was faithful to him who 2 appointed him, just as Moses also was faithful in God's house.** The last clause is taken from Numbers 12:7, where Moses is said to have been faithful in his appointment with reference to God's house (the people of Israel). The occasion of the statement was Miriam's and Aaron's opposition to Moses and their claim that God had also spoken through them (Num. 12:1ff.). In response God says: "Hear my words: If there is a prophet among you, I the Lord make myself known to him in a vision, I speak with him in a dream. Not so with my servant Moses; he is entrusted with all my house. With him I speak mouth to mouth...." It is important to notice that the author, as he speaks of Moses, in no way reflects on him. He could have pointed to some instance of disobedience in the desert wanderings, such as that at Meribah (Num. 20:7-13), to show that Moses' faith was not always satisfactory; but he does not choose to follow this line. He will lift up Christ but he will not disparage Moses. He acknowledges the value of the old dispensation, and proves that the new is better. Moses was faithful. Jesus was faithful—faithful in the tasks assigned to Him as apostle and high priest.

Yet there is a wide gap between Christ and Moses. **Jesus has been 3 counted worthy of as much more glory than Moses as the builder of a house has more honor than the house.** The word **house** is used in the sense of "household." The author is not speaking of a material house, constructed of wood or stone, but rather of the personnel or people who inhabit the house. God's people of both old and new covenants comprise the house. This becomes clear in verses 5-6. Christ is the builder of the house. Moses is the house, that is, he is part of the house, is a servant in it (v. 5). Christ's glory outshines the glory of Moses, as cause takes precedence over effect, as the builder is over the house. This is the same type of comparison as is employed earlier when it is declared that Jesus is better than the angels because to Him belongs the better name of Son.

Christ is indeed the Builder, the author goes on to say, **For every 4 house is built by some one.** No household springs into existence by itself. No nation spontaneously appears on the stage of history. Everything has its cause, and the author believes even a First Cause. Christ as Founder was under God, for **the builder of all things is God.** The author's choice of words is significant, indicating that the closest possible relationship exists between God and Christ. According to verse 3, Christ is the Builder; in verse 4 God is the Builder of all things. In 1:2 God is described as the Creator and the Son is spoken of as the agent of creation; in 1:10, however, the Son is represented as laying the foundation of the earth. Such language as appears here, in which the work of one divine person is ascribed to another, is typical of the various New Testament writers and stands as proof of their persuasion of the complete divinity of Christ the Son.

5
6   Christ is seen as superior to Moses in another respect. **Now Moses was faithful in all God's house as a servant, to testify to the things that were to be spoken later, but Christ was faithful over God's house as a son.** Moses simply did what He was told. He did not originate the laws of the old covenant, nor did he tamper with them. His loyal service is chronicled in the words, "According to all that the Lord commanded him so he did" (Ex. 40:16).

The word for **servant** is not *doulos*, the ordinary word for slave. It is *therapōn*, a word that suggests a free, personal service. It is often used of those who wait on the gods. The term indicates both a position of honor and a role of subservience, appropriate for Moses. Yet though it was an honor for Moses to be God's servant, Christ is exalted as God's Son; and while Moses served **in** God's house, Christ showed Himself faithful **over** God's house. Again, the contrast is like that of chapter 1: Christ as Son over the angels as ministers, so Christ as Son over Moses as servant. Moses' position was preliminary and preparatory, looking to those things that were to be later revealed. It was a position, as Moffatt has said, "which pointed beyond itself to a future and higher revelation,"[3] or one which, in the subsequent words of the author, was associated with "a shadow of the good things to come" (10:1).

A further statement of encouragement and warning is added, which serves as a transition to the solemn passage that is to follow (3:7—4:13). **And we are his house if we hold fast our confidence and pride in our hope.** Throughout the Epistle, everything depends on perseverance. This is one of the grand marks of faith, indeed, the practical equivalent of it (ch. 11). The words **we are** God's **house** are a definite assurance to Christian readers that they—not Moses and the Israelites—are now God's people. But the privilege is not irrevocable; its continuance depends on holding on to a joyful confidence and an enthusiastic hope. **Confidence** here means the bold, open profession of the Christian religion. (See comments on 4:16.) This was the very thing needed by the Epistle's first readers. Their trying circumstances demanded that they not lose

---

3. Moffatt, *Hebrews*, p. 43.

their grip. **Pride in our hope** is not boasting in one's own strength. It is rather a self-assertive, forward thrust. Christians instead of being ashamed should exult in their heavenly calling and in its anticipations of the future.

A Warning from the Wilderness
(3:7-19)

The Epistle now moves from argument to exhortation. The author has established the absolute supremacy of Jesus over Moses. Yet Moses was a great leader, and this very fact causes the author to ponder the possibility of failure under outstanding leadership. His inference is that Christians too, like the Israelites in the wilderness, can fall short of their promised inheritance.

The author's appeals for faithfulness here are in three parts, which include most of chapters three and four (3:7-19; 4:1-10; 4:11-13). The first two appeals are based on Psalm 95:7-11. **Therefore, as the Holy** **7** **Spirit says, "Today, when you hear his voice, do not harden your hearts** **8** **as in the rebellion, on the day of testing in the wilderness, where your** **9** **fathers put me to the test and saw my works for forty years."**[4] The connection suggested by **Therefore** is that Christians are God's house, if only they hold fast, if they do not prove faithless as Israel did in the past. The introductory formula of the quotation clearly shows that the psalm was regarded as divinely inspired and authoritative (cf. 10:15). The Holy Spirit, the author says, is still speaking these words, and these words must be heeded. **Today** is emphatic. Today God is speaking through a greater Someone than Moses, and today God expects men to be responsive. The implication is that it is within the power of man not to harden his heart.

One instance of disobedience alluded to took place shortly after the nation of Israel fled from Egypt. At Rephidim the people threatened revolt against Moses because they had no water to drink. Because of their faultfinding and testing of the Lord, the place was called "Massah and Meribah" (Ex. 17:1-7). (In the LXX, these two place names are translated by the more general words "testing" and "rebellion"; and thus they appear in the author's citation of the psalm.) There were numerous other occasions, such as the events at Kadesh (Num. 14:1-38; 20:1-13), on which God's patience was tried. In fact, the author seems not to be thinking so much of separate incidents of rebellion but of a

---

4. The author connects the forty years with God's works instead of with His grief (as in the Hebrew and LXX). This shift of emphasis focuses attention on the goodness of God displayed over the forty year period and thus makes Israel's rejection all the more unaccountable.

prolonged obstinancy: all through the desert wanderings of forty years
the people persisted in their stubborn ways. +

10   "Therefore," God says, "I was provoked with that generation, and
said, 'They always go astray in their hearts; they have not known my
ways.'" The word provoked suggests extreme displeasure; in the psalm
the verb means "to feel a loathing." God was greatly displeased with
the rebellious Israelites, which accounts for His solemn vow against

11 them: "As I swore in my wrath, 'They shall never enter my rest.'" God
is often represented in Scripture as swearing, generally by Himself or
by His own existence. It is a figurative expression, indicating a strong
affirmation of His set purpose. The rest referred to is the land of Canaan;
it is called my rest because it was provided by God (cf. Deut. 12:9).
That wonderful rest in Canaan, the author wishes to remind his readers,
the people as a whole were never allowed to enter. Because of their
habitual waywardness, they shut themselves out of their promised
homeland.

12   The author's exhortation now becomes direct. Take care, brethren,
lest there be in any of you an evil, unbelieving heart, leading you to
fall away from the living God. The living God is a favorite Old Testament designation for God—"the Lord is the true God; he is the living
God and the everlasting King" (Jer. 10:10; cf. Deut. 5:26; Ps. 42:1-2;
84:1-2; etc.).[5] Living God is used several times in the Epistle (9:14;
10:31; 12:22) and often in other parts of the New Testament (Mt. 16:16;
Acts 14:15; 1 Tim. 3:15; etc.). It marks off the true God from lifeless
idols and shows His constant concern and vigilance over His people.
The danger of apostasy is always present, and for the readers of the
Epistle the danger was doubly great. Apostasy is the ultimate consequence of unbelief; and unbelief, as the next verse indicates, is brought
on by the heart that is hardened through sin. Thus the logical order of
the downward process is sin, a hardened heart, unbelief, apostasy. The
objection that this language would not be appropriate in describing a
possible departure of Jewish Christians is not valid. The very point of
the author is that to lapse back into Judaism is to fall away from the
living God (cf. Gal. 5:4). In other words, the author is contending that
one cannot reject Christ without rejecting God as well.

13   To keep from falling away, individual action is required. But exhort
one another every day, as long as it is called "today," that none of you
may be hardened by the deceitfulness of sin. The word for deceitfulness
(apatē) may also be translated "pleasure" or "delight," as in Matthew
13:22 (RSV), but the context suggests a guarding against the tricks of
sin instead of a temptation to gross wantonness. The author attaches

---

5. See W. Sanday, "The Living God," ExpTimes 16 (1904-05), 153-56.

much importance to the spiritual strength that Christians can lend to each other, both in the worship of the public assembly (10:25) and in private meetings. Every day is a day for mutual encouragement. **Today** is the best time—when God is still speaking to men, while yet there is opportunity, as long as the day of grace lasts. Much exhortation is needed to gain the upper hand on sin. It is deceptive by nature. Attractive externally, it is corrupt within; appearing to be wise, it blinds men to truth; offering promises of gain, it leads inexorably to ruin. The form of the author's sentence makes the warning especially personal. "Take care . . . lest there be in *any* of you. . . .Exhort one another . . . that *none* of you may be hardened." The demand is for an exacting self-evaluation.

In verse 6 the author has already stated the reason why Christians should maintain their confident expectations of the future. He now returns to the same thought and sounds a similar warning. **For we 14 share in Christ, if only we hold our first confidence[6] firm to the end.** The idea here is not so much that Christians share in Christ as that they share with Him (cf. Rev. 3:21). They "have become Christ's partners" (NEB), even as they "share in a heavenly call" (v. 1) and as they "have become partakers of the Holy Spirit" (6:4). The perfect tense is employed *(gegonamen),* showing that this partnership with Christ began in the past and continues into the present. This wonderful participation, however, is qualified. Christians must hold on to the confident assurance they had when they started out on their heavenly journey. The author wishes to stress that it is not enough to have made a beginning, not enough to have once known the unutterable joy of the Christian hope. Everything depends on their persevering to the end.

The author turns again to the passage on which he has based his appeal. **While it is said, "Today, when you hear his voice, do not harden 15 your hearts as in the rebellion."** He wants his readers to consider the whole passage, of course, but he quotes only the first verse; and as they recall the events represented in the passage, he bears down on them with a series of rhetorical questions.[7] **Who were they that heard 16 and yet were rebellious? Was it not all those who left Egypt under the leadership of Moses?** (Moses, indeed, was a great leader, yet apostasy under him was practically universal. The point of the questions is that no one should feel himself overly secure.) **And with whom was he pro- 17 voked forty years? Was it not with those who sinned, whose bodies fell**

---

6. The word here for "confidence" is *hupostasis* and means, as in 11:1, the ground or basis of hope, conviction, assurance. It is a different word from "confidence" *(parrēsia)* in verse 6.

7. Rhetorical questions are characteristic of diatribes (Hellenistic popular sermons), a literary form with which the Epistle has certain similarities. See Introduction, p. 42; see also Ropes, p. 13.

in the wilderness? ("'As I live,' says the Lord, 'what you have said in my hearing I will do to you: your dead bodies shall fall in this wilderness; and of all your number, numbered from twenty years old and upward, who have murmured against me, not one shall come into the land where I swore that I would make you dwell, except Caleb the son of Jephunneh and Joshua the son of Nun. But your little ones . . . I will bring in, and they shall know the land which you have despised. But as for you, your dead bodies shall fall in this wilderness'"—Num. 14:28-32.)

18   **And to whom did he swear that they should never enter his rest, but to those who were disobedient?** The questions are penetrating, leading
19   to the inevitable conclusion: **So we see that they were unable to enter because of unbelief.** The people of Israel did not put their trust in God (cf. Deut. 32:20). They set out from Egypt with abounding confidence, yet they left their bones in forgotten graves of sand. Why? Because God was unable to overcome their opposition and bring them to their hoped-for destination? No; but because of their sin.

The concluding verse of the chapter contains several key terms. One is the word "enter," a hook word that leads into 4:1ff. Another key term is "unbelief," which with "unbelieving" in verse 12, forms an inclusion. Unbelief—how fatal it was to the Israelites. (The chapter begins with the faithfulness of Christ and ends with the unfaithfulness of Israel.) Still another key expression is "we see." This, too, forms an inclusion with "see" (translated "take care") in verse 12. Above all, the readers are to see to it that they do not fall like Israel did.

Additional Notes

Homologia, "confession"

V. 1. The word *homologia* may be taken in one of two senses: either actively, to refer to the act of confessing, or passively, to denote what is confessed. The two senses are well illustrated by the NEB text and margin. The passive is read in the text ("Apostle and High Priest of the religion we profess"), the active is read in the margin ("him whom we confess as God's Envoy and High Priest"). The passive sense is probably correct; this is the view of Arndt-Gingrich, Westcott, Moffatt, Montefiore, F. F. Bruce (though William Manson dissents). Thus "confession" here means about the same as "our religion" (cf. 4:14). It has, moreover, a strong connotation. The first readers of the Epistle, who were wavering, need to hold firmly to the faith they have confessed. Their confession ties them and obligates them to Christ. They are not to go back on their word of allegiance.

"Appointed"

V. 2. "Appointed" is the translation generally adopted and is undoubtedly correct (cf. 1 Sam. 12:6; Mk. 3:14). The verb *poieō*, however, also means "to make" or "to create." That it in no way can mean that Jesus was a created being is made clear in 1:2-3. Early Christian writers took it as a reference to Jesus' incarnation, that is, that His human nature was "made" by God. This interpretation is not impossible, although it scarcely fits the context. It is Jesus' office, not origin, that is in view.

The reading of 3:6

Some of the earliest manuscripts (P^{13}, P^{46}, B; also the Sahidic and Ethiopic versions) omit the words "firm to the end" at the close of the verse. The words are found in the majority of the later manuscripts (thus also in the KJV) and also in Aleph, A, C, D, etc. The phrase appears at the end of v. 14, and there seems no question but that its presence there accounts for the reading here, the repetition of the phrase being made by an early scribe.

Tines as an interrogative

V. 16. The KJV translates this verse as a declarative statement: "For some, when they had heard, did provoke...." The KJV translators read *tines* as the indefinite pronoun, meaning "some." On the other hand, the ASV, RSV, and other recent translations, take *tines* as an interrogative. This is much to be preferred because of the position of *tines* at the beginning of the sentence and because this fits in better with the following interrogatives.

HEBREWS FOUR

The Rest that Remains
(4:1-10)

No break in thought comes between chapters 3 and 4. Drawing on the unfavorable example of the Israelites who failed to enter God's rest, the author shows that the divine rest is still left open. This new section goes back to the words, "Today, when you hear his voice," words which to the author imply that God is still making His rest available in the Christian era. The author's exhortation continues: **Therefore, while the promise of entering his rest remains, let us fear lest any of you be judged to have failed to reach it.** Though Israel was shut out of the land of Canaan, this in no way has affected God's rest. God's promise of rest has neither been fulfilled nor withdrawn; it is still open and prepared for men. The proof of this is found in verses 2-10. **1**

A further parallel (and thus warning) exists between God's ancient people and God's people in the new age. **For good news came to us just as to them.** The Israelites in former days were evangelized; their good news consisted of the divine offer of a land of rest and plenty. **But the message which they heard did not benefit them, because it did not meet with faith in the hearers.** Having heard the good news, the Israelites did not trust God enough to believe that He would go with them and conquer a land for them (Num. 13:1-33). As in the Parable of the Sower, the trouble was not in the message but in the hearers. Likewise, the readers of the Epistle had heard good news (2:1-3). Would they, too, just hear the word and do nothing about it? **2**

Assurance is now given that true believers can enter the divine rest. **For we who have believed enter that rest, as he has said, "As I swore in my wrath, 'they shall never enter my rest,'"** although his works were **3**

finished from the foundation of the world.[1] It is possible that what is meant here is that Christians, when they believe, begin to enter rest. The word for **enter** (*eiserchometha*) is in the present tense and might well indicate a process of entering—"we are entering into rest." In this case the idea would be that the believer now has spiritual rest in Jesus Christ (Mt. 11:28), that this rest continues throughout life and meets its full fruition in the heavenly rest. But this interpretation is by no means certain. In the context of the chapter, rather, it seems that **rest** refers to a future state, to something that the readers might fail to reach (v. 1), and something, therefore, that they must make every effort to enter (v. 11). So understood, the present tense would then be rendered "do enter" (emphatic) or "will enter" (futuristic present). But no matter which alternative is taken, the important fact is that only through faith can the Christian enter rest.

The King James Version reads here "if they shall enter into my rest." This is a literal translation of a Semitic idiom for a strong negative; it is more correctly translated in 3:11 as "they shall not enter my rest." The final clause, **although his works were finished,** further explains the nature of the rest under discussion. The rest is God's rest. It is His not only because it comes from Him but because He Himself entered into it when He finished the works of creation. The failure of a past generation to enter in was not because it was not ready; to the contrary, since it goes back to the foundation of the world, it is a rest that is eternally valid.

The author as usual confirms his point by appeal to the Old Testament, introducing his quotations in the vague manner typical of his
4 literary style (cf. 2:6). **For he has somewhere spoken of the seventh day in this way, "And God rested on the seventh day from all his works."**
5 **And again in this place he said, "They shall never enter my rest."** These passages prove, says the author, that God's rest has long been in existence. He began His rest on the seventh day of the creation week and continues in that rest. That rest has been available ever since the world began; and though the Israelites excluded themselves from it, God still desires to share it with men. The disobedience of some does not void His generous intentions.

Verse 6 presents a restatement of what is said in verses 3-5, and verse 7 adds another Scriptural argument to show that the promised
6 divine rest is still open. **Since therefore it remains for some to enter it, and those who formerly received the good news failed to enter because**

---

1. The expression, "from the foundation of the world," does not suggest that the earth has some kind of foundation. It rather refers to a "laying down" or "casting down" of the kosmos—to the creation, to the beginning of history. Cf. 9:16; Mt. 13:35; 25:34; Lk. 11:50; Jn. 17:24; Eph. 1:4; 1 Pet. 1:20; Rev. 13:8; 17:8.

of disobedience, again he sets a certain day, "today," saying through 7
David so long afterward, in the words already quoted, "Today, when
you hear his voice, do not harden your hearts." The quotation is, of
course, the one previously employed from Psalm 95; but this time the
author seizes upon the significance of **today.** In David's time, he says,
long after the desert experiences, the Holy Spirit spoke of **today.** That
must mean, then, that the divine rest had not been cancelled; and if it
had not been cancelled in David's time, the author reasons that the
promised rest remains for Christians. **For if Joshua had given them** 8
rest, God would not speak later of another day. The names Joshua and
Jesus have the same form in the Greek text, which explains why the
King James Version here reads "Jesus." Joshua was the commander
under whose leadership the Israelites entered Canaan. Jesus is the
Leader and Pioneer of faith for His people. But the rest that Joshua
gave to his followers was only physical; it was only temporary and it
did not really satisfy. If it had been adequate, the psalm would not
speak about another day. Jesus, however, it is implied, is able to lead
His own to their eternal destination. The contrast of Joshua and Jesus
is a rather incidental contrast, one that the author does not seek to
extend; but there is little doubt that it entered into his thinking.

The conclusion of it all is finally reached. **So then, there remains a** 9
sabbath rest for the people of God; for whoever enters God's rest also 10
ceases from his labors as God did from his. The author in speaking of
a **sabbath rest** uses a thought-provoking word found nowhere else in
Biblical Greek. The term is *sabbatismos* and can also be translated as
"sabbath keeping." It is not, however, as is clear from the context, a
literal "sabbath keeping."[2] The author who has so much to say about
the better hope and the better way of life in the new covenant cannot
be understood as enforcing the observance of the Mosaic sabbath. The
rest that he speaks of is not a thing they are *keeping* but something that
can be entered (vv. 1, 3, 6, 10, 11). And that rest is specifically said to
be **for the people of God.** This rest—"God's own rest for God's own true
people, an ideal rest for an ideal community"[3]—will be like the keeping
of a sabbath. As God in the beginning entered His sabbath, they too
will enter theirs—"that they may rest from their labors, for their deeds
follow them" (Rev. 14:13).

The Word of God
(4:11-13)

God has a perfect rest, and that rest is destined for the people of

2. The author's choice of terms might well be determined by his belief that the
Jewish law, with its sabbath keeping, utterly failed to give the people rest.
3. A. B. Bruce, *Hebrews,* p. 161.

God. Of these truths the author is positively certain. But as he contemplates the conditions of his readers, he flinches momentarily; and then,
11 as he had done in verse 1, he sounds a solemn warning. **Let us therefore strive to enter that rest, that no one fall by the same sort of disobedience.** The author speaks urgently. When he says **strive,** he uses a forceful Greek verb, *spoudazō,* which means "to haste," "to be zealous," "to exert oneself," "to make every effort." In the New Testament it is often used "to characterize the total conduct of the Christian in the sense of an actualising of his saved position, a fulfilling of what grace has opened up for him."[4] This demands that the Christian "make every effort" to present himself acceptable to God (2 Tim. 2:15), that he "pursue intensely" the unity of the Spirit (Eph. 4:3), that he "give diligence" to confirm his calling (2 Pet. 1:10). Here the author says that his Christian readers are to "strive zealously" for the rest that is worth everything.

Verses 12-13 center on one grand thought, the power of the Judge. This is not apparent at first, but gradually through these verses the author builds to a climactic point—"all are open and laid bare to the eyes of him with whom we have to do." Initially the author speaks of God's word, then of the God of creation before whom all must stand.

12 **For the word of God is living and active, sharper than any two-edged sword.** The **For** is quite significant, linking the statement directly with the foregoing. **The word of God** does not refer to the person of the Son. (See Additional Note.) Although in other places Jesus is described as the Word (Jn. 1:1, 14; Rev. 19:13), He is not so designated in this Epistle. Rather **the word of God** is here poetically personified. It is endowed with the attributes of God, with whom it is identified in the next verse. The thrust of the passage is that God's written word, which tells of Israel's fall, must be heeded. It is no dead letter. It cannot be trifled with (cf. Deut. 32:46-47). To the contrary, it is **living.** It partakes of God's life; as He is "the living God" (3:12), so it is "the living and abiding word of God" (1 Pet. 1:23). It is, therefore, inherently **active,**[5] constantly working His will, never returning to Him empty, always accomplishing His purpose (cf. Isa. 55:11). The promises and warnings of Scripture, then, are ever new. Scripture does not speak only in the past but in the present. "Today," it says. The word of God, in such passages as Genesis 2 and Psalm 95, offers man rest; and the word of God, by cataloguing the consequences of disobedience, warns him against hardening his heart.

4. G. Harder, TDNT, VII, 565.

5. The Greek term is *energēs* (cf. the English "energy," "energetic," etc.), which means "active," "effective," "powerful." In the Epistle of Barnabas (1.7) a related form of the word *(energoumena)* is applied to prophetic things in the sense that they "come to pass." The author's use of the term in 4:12 is similar. He means that God's word is fully effective and applicable to his readers.

The word of God is also sharp like a **sword.**[6] The comparison is frequently made in Scripture (Eph. 6:17; Rev. 1:16; 2:12; 19:15; Isa. 49:2), perhaps because of the similarity in the shape of a tongue and a dagger. God's word is no dull blade but, being two-edged, cuts in every direction; it penetrates to the inner parts of human nature, **piercing** even **to the division of soul and spirit,** and **of joints and marrow.** This does not mean that the word literally divides the soul from the spirit, the joints from the marrow. The author is merely heaping up terms to show that the divine word cuts sharp through everything that is in man. No segment of the human personality can escape its keen edge. It commands and threatens. It lays open the secret places of men's lives, **discerning the thoughts and intentions of the heart.** It thoroughly sifts the stored-up matters of the **heart.**[7] It has, like God, the capacity to examine all that is laid up in the hidden chambers of man, "for the Lord searches all hearts, and understands every plan and thought" (1 Chron. 28:9; cf. 1 Sam. 16:7; Ps. 139:1-2).

The author now passes easily from the word to God, who is its source and who is present in it. **And before him no creature is hidden,** 13 **but all are open and laid bare to the eyes of him with whom we have to do.** The picture of God as Judge now emerges. This is clearer if **him with whom we have to do** is translated, as in the New English Bible, "the One with whom we have to reckon."[8] The range of God's scrutinizing eye covers all creation. He reduces all things to their basic elements. His judgment is infallible. Before Him everything is **open and laid bare.** The verb translated **laid bare** *(tetrachēlismena)* is found only here in the New Testament. It probably refers to an exposure of the throat, as when a person's head is thrown back and his throat is laid bare. (See Additional Note.) That is how men are before God—to whom they must render account—naked and exposed, stripped of every possible concealment.

The Compassionate Christ (4:14-16)

The verses in this short section are transitional: they serve both as

---

6. *Machaira* may refer to a knife as well as a sword; it would be a knife used in sacrifice or surgery to sever "joints and marrow." Sacrificial imagery may provide the appropriate background for "laid bare" in v. 13. Yet ordinarily knives, except the surgeon's knife, were not two-edged.

7. "Heart" calls to mind the "evil, unbelieving heart" of 3:12. The word "heart" is central in the Epistle (3:8, 10, 12, 15; 4:7; 8:10; 10:16, 22; 13:9).

8. The clause, if rendered literally, would read, "to whom is our word." This makes it possible to see the literary beauty of this small unit. V. 12 begins with "For the word of God," and v. 13 ends with "to whom is our word." "Word" thus forms another impressive inclusion.

a conclusion and as an introduction. Verse 14 touches again the key terms of 3:1—"heavenly," "Jesus," "high priest," and "confession." Therefore, 4:14 supplies the concluding part of the larger inclusion begun in chapter 3. These verses also conclude the author's direct admonitions begun in 3:7. The exhortations here are the last in a series of exhortations: "let us fear" (4:1), "let us ... strive to enter that rest" (4:11), "let us hold fast our confession" (4:14), and "let us ... draw near" (4:16).

But these verses introduce the subject of the high priesthood of Christ. This is the main theme of Hebrews. It occupies much of what remains (4:14—10:18). It is the topic toward which the author has been moving from the beginning, as evidenced by his previous allusions to the priestly office of the Son (1:3; 2:9, 17, 18; 3:1).

The significance of Christ's priesthood is the essence of the Epistle's argument. On the priesthood and its adequacy depend, in the author's mind, the whole question of whether a man can really gain access to God. The priesthood of Christ, and His sacrificial death that went with it, opened heaven (cf. 10:19ff.). For the author, therefore, the nature of the priesthood defined the nature of the religion.

In 2:17 Jesus is described as a merciful and faithful high priest. In 3:1-6 Jesus' faithfulness to God is established. The author now turns his attention to Christ as One who is merciful. **Since then we have a great high priest who has passed through the heavens, Jesus, the Son of God, let us hold fast our confession** (cf. 3:1; 10:23). Every word descriptive of Christ is important. Christians *do* have a **high priest,** the implication being perhaps that some were in doubt on this point. Not only so, but Christians have a **great** high priest, One who is great in His own right— greater than Aaron and greater than all the priests. His greatness is seen in the fact that He has **passed through the heavens** (cf. 7:26; 9:24). Some Jewish writings speak of seven heavens;[9] but Paul's mention of "the third heaven" (2 Cor. 12:2), apparently in reference to a specially privileged state, would seem to exclude the idea of there being four other higher heavens. In Ephesians 4:10 Christ is described as "he who ascended far above all heavens" (NEB); so here the author means that Christ has passed through the heavens in the sense that He has entered into heaven itself. Other high priests like Aaron passed through a material veil into the Holy of Holies, but He as Son of God has gone directly into the presence of God.

Another mark of the great high priest is suggested in the designation **Jesus, the Son of God.** The phrase is significant, joining together the human and the divine natures of the Christian high priest. As Son of God He is strong and dependable and on intimate terms with the Father; as son of man He has behind Him a distinct human history

14

---

9. Cf. *The Testaments of the Twelve Patriarchs,* "Testament of Levi," ch. iii.

which enables Him to understand men. **For we have not a high priest** **15**
who is unable to sympathize[10] **with our weaknesses, but one who in**
every respect has been tempted as we are, yet without sinning. The
author puts down any supposed objection that one who is so exalted
can not be concerned about the human predicament. By **weaknesses**
he means both physical and moral limitations, the frailties that are
characteristic of men. With these Jesus is able to sympathize. He has
gone over the broad course of temptations just as others have. In fact,
He has felt the full force of temptation that men do not experience; for
having never given in to sin, He knows its incalculable intensity and
power. He was tempted **in every respect**—from all sides the darts of the
tempter were cast at His soul. Like men physically, He was unlike them
in always resisting sin. The sinlessness of Jesus is stated here for the
first time in Hebrews, but it is stated elsewhere as well (2 Cor. 5:21;
1 Pet. 2:22; 1 Jn. 3:5; cf. Jn. 8:29, 46; 10:32).

Since Jesus knows the power of sin and understands sinners, the
appeal is: **Let us then with confidence draw near to the throne of** **16**
grace, that we may receive mercy and find grace to help in time of need.
The exhortation to **draw near** strikes one of the doctrinal keynotes of
the Epistle, for the religion of Christ is the religion of access to God.
Under the old covenant, only the priests could draw near—and they
only on stipulated conditions—and the people could not draw near at
all. But Christ's sympathy and suffering for mankind make access
possible. The way to God, so long closed, is now open. It is therefore
possible to speak of **the throne of grace** on which God sits, with Christ
at His hand, and deals benevolently with all who approach Him.

Precisely because it is a throne of grace and not a judgment seat,
this is why it can be approached with **confidence** *(parrēsia). Parrēsia*
(from *pan* + *rēsia* = full story) in ancient Greece denoted the right of
a full citizen to speak his mind on any subject in the town assembly—a
right that the slave did not have. In the Epistle it stands for freedom
to approach God on the basis of the blood of Jesus (10:19). Before
God's throne Christians need not have fears and inhibitions. They can
come just as they are. At God's throne there is "timely help" (NEB),
help that is needed in the hour of temptation. Men cannot save themselves or remedy their ills by their own strength; and because their
times of need are many, the implication of the author is that they should
come regularly and often to the divine throne.

---

10. The Greek term is *sumpathēsai*, literally, "to suffer with." The verb form is
found only here and in 10:34; the adjective form is found in 1 Pet. 3:8. The Greek
word suggests an intensity that is lost in the English word "sympathy." It sees the
suffering of another not from the outside, but rather it is, as Westcott says (p. 108),
"the feeling of one who enters into the suffering and makes it his own."

Chapters 3 and 4, although to some extent doctrinal, are given mostly to practical exhortations and encouragement. The small doctrinal portion (3:1-6) contributes to the apologetic purpose of the Epistle by contrasting Moses and Christ. This contrast, as distinct from that of Joshua and Jesus later on, is an essential one; for while it has been proved that Christ is better than the angels, it must also be shown that He is superior to the founder of the Jewish system. And Christ does, beyond question, have this necessary superiority. Moses was a part of the house, Christ is the builder of the house. Moses was a servant in the house, Christ is a Son over the house. Both were faithful to God, but beyond this they cannot be compared.

The thought of Moses causes the author to digress from his main theme and prompts him to clarify the critical position that his readers are in. He goes to the book of Psalms and takes a text. From this he deduces that his readers are faced with exactly the same danger that the Israelites were faced with in the wilderness. What was wrong with those ancient people? How did they meet such disaster? They failed because sin was in their hearts, the sin of unbelief. "They despised the pleasant land, having no faith in his promise. They murmured in their tents, and did not obey the voice of the Lord" (Ps. 106:24-25).

In 4:1-13 the author has two main objectives, which he skillfully blends into one. First, he proves that a rest does in fact remain for believers. To them, as well as to a past generation of Israelites, the gospel of rest has been preached and for them that rest is preserved. It is God's rest, the rest that He Himself enjoyed and prepared when He created the world. It is a rest that human disobedience cannot void, for David in his time was still speaking of it as being in the present. It is a rest the like of which Joshua could never give.

Second, the author continues his line of thinking from the previous chapter and warns his readers of the possibility of losing that rest. Again he reminds them that in the Old Testament God's own people failed, that those who started out from the land of slavery died short of the land of promise. The thought—so tragic and horrible when he realizes that the same fate might befall any Christian—never leaves him. So he pleads with his readers that they pay attention to the all-powerful message of God's word and that they remember that they always remain within the scope of the divine gaze. And for their aid he points them to Jesus, their great high priest, and to the throne in heaven that is distinguished by grace.

Additional Notes

The reading of 4:2

The last clause of this verse is read variously in the manuscripts and presents a difficult problem for textual critics. The RSV, preceded by the KJV and ASV, reads "it did not meet with faith in the hearers." The alternative reading is found in the RSV margin: "they were not united in faith with the hearers." The difference turns on an -os (nominative singular) or -ous (accusative plural) ending for the participle of the Greek verb sunkerannumi, "to mix with," "to unite." Much of the evidence (P[13], P[46], A, B, D, etc.) supports the RSV marginal reading instead of the text (based on Aleph, Peshitta, Sahidic). But how does the marginal reading fit the context? Presumably the meaning is "they [the Israelites] were not united with those who heard it [such as Moses, Joshua, and Caleb] in faith." But there is nothing in the passage about anyone hearing the message in faith. Accordingly, the reading of the RSV text is to be preferred to that of the margin.

Ho logos tou theou, "the word of God"

V. 12. Early Christian writers, and others since, have mistakenly identified "the word of God" (ho logos tou theou) in this verse with Jesus the Son. This doubtless was occasioned by the passages in the prologue to the Gospel of John that speak of the logos who "was in the beginning with God" and "became flesh" like men (1:1, 14). These references clearly point to Christ (cf. Rev. 19:13). There are several reasons, however, why logos is not to be interpreted as having the same meaning here as in John: (1) the context is not speaking of Jesus; (2) the language is inappropriate to Jesus: He would not be described as "sharper than any two-edged sword"; (3) the idea of Jesus as Logos appears nowhere else in the Epistle; (4) the connective "for" (gar) goes back to the preceding promise of rest and threat of failure to obtain the promise; and (5) the argument throughout refers either to the word preached (4:2, literally, "the word of hearing") or to the word written (3:7, 15; 4:4, 7, 8). The passage, therefore, must be seen as a warning to the readers that God's word—by implication, every word of God— demands undistracted attention.

Tetrachēlismena, "laid bare"

V. 13. The word tetrachēlismena, translated "laid bare" (RSV) and "exposed" (NEB), presents difficulties; for, although its general sense is plain, its precise meaning is uncertain. The related noun form, trachēlos, means "throat" or "neck." In the active voice the verb occurs in the sense of bending or twisting the neck of a victim: in wrestling, for example, to the twisting of the neck of an opponent. The word is also used for the skinning of animals; for the exposure of the throat of an animal about to be sacrificed; for the subjection of an enemy to public shame; and for forcing a captive, with his neck at sword point, to show his face and bear the full brunt of dishonor. Thus here the word has been thought to mean: (1) to prostrate or render helpless in the presence of Almighty God (Montefiore); (2) to be compelled to raise the head and to meet God's eyes in judgment (William Barclay); (3) to bend back and lay bare the neck, to expose the throat like a victim's ready for sacrifice (Arndt-Gingrich, Moulton-Milligan, Liddell-Scott-Jones, Moffatt, RSV, NEB). The translation "laid bare" or "exposed" seems to fit best with the word *gumna,* "naked" or "bare."

Proserchōmetha, "let us draw near"

V. 16. "Let us draw near" *(proserchōmetha)* is a priestly expression that denotes approach to God for worship and prayer. This usage is well illustrated in 1 Clement: "Let us then approach him in holiness of soul, raising pure and undefiled hands to him..." (29:1). Among the Greeks it occurs as a typical expression for approaching deity. The term is used seven times in the Epistle (see especially 7:25; 10:1, 22; 11:6). Since in the Old Testament it is used of priests in their approach to God (Lev. 21:17-21, etc.), the author's use and application of the term suggest that the priestly privilege of access to God is now extended to all Christians.

HEBREWS FIVE

Qualifications of the High Priest
(5:1-4)

Now begins in earnest a discussion of Christ's priesthood. It was necessary in the earlier chapters to demonstrate Christ as Son because Sonship is the essential predicate of eternal priesthood. This explains the combination of texts in 5:5-6, "Thou art my Son . . . Thou art a priest for ever."

The author believed, as he will show, that the new covenant had displaced the old; and so he believed that the priestly ministry of Christ far excelled that of Aaron and his Levitical successors. The chapters that follow, therefore, form an extended discussion of the old Aaronic type of priesthood, on one hand, and the new Christ-type of priesthood (like Melchizedek's) on the other. The author's presentation on priesthood may be divided into four parts:

1. Christ supremely qualified as high priest—compassionate, chosen from among men, and called by God (5:1-10).

2. The need for progress by the readers—rebuked for their immaturity, threatened by the possibility of apostasy, yet encouraged to hold on to their hope to the end (5:11—6:20).

3. Christ, a high priest like Melchizedek, with attendant consequences and blessings (7:1-28).

4. The two covenants and the superior ministry of Christ's priesthood (8:1—10:18).

The immediate section begins not with the grandeur of Christ's priestly office but with its lowliness. Throughout the discussion there remains the distinction of two statements that are juxtaposed: "like his

105

brethren in every respect" (2:17; cf. 4:15) and "separated from sinners" (7:26).[1]

The author first lists some of the basic qualifications of the high priest under the Levitical arrangement, and then he shows how Christ
1 meets these qualifications. **For every high priest chosen from among men is appointed to act on behalf of men in relation to God, to offer gifts and sacrifices for men.** The first qualification mentioned is that the high priest must be selected from among men. The statement is not a truism: it is necessary that a *man* be chosen to represent *men* in dealing with *their* sins against God. **Gifts and sacrifices,** mentioned several times in the Epistle (8:3, 4; 9:9; 11:4), are general terms that refer to all kinds of offerings. The reference is probably to the Day of Atonement, when the high priest was the central functionary and when both vegetable and animal sacrifices were offered.

A second qualification of the high priest, closely related to the
2 first, is next stated. **He can deal gently with the ignorant and wayward, since he himself is beset with weakness.** The high priest, being a man and having the weaknesses of men, is better able to minister in behalf of men. He, too, is liable to error and, like all men, is answerable to God. He is therefore able to **deal gently** *(metriopathein)* with his fellows. *Metriopatheia* (the noun form) was used by the Greeks as the mid-point between the extremes of deep grief and lazy indifference.[2] Here the thought is that of gentleness and forbearance toward offenders whose misdeeds otherwise would incite harsh judgment. Under the old dispensation such gentleness was ideally in the character of every high priest; in point of fact, however, it was found in the life of no Levitical high priest and never existed until the Perfect Priest appeared. How wonderful that Christ possesses this *metriopatheia!* As high priest He is concerned with men, but His concern for them never drives Him to the point of irritation or annoyance with them. He is always gentle and patient and ready to bear with them in their mistakes.

Those who were to receive the high priest's gentle treatment were **the ignorant and wayward,** those who erred through ignorance.[3] In reference to the man guilty of these sins, the law said: "And the priest

---

1. G. Schrenk, TDNT, III, 279.

2. A passage in Philo *(On Abraham,* 255-57) well illustrates *metriopatheia* as the golden mean. In commenting on Abraham's grief over the death of Sarah, he explains that Abraham acted in accordance with reason. He did not grieve "over-bitterly" nor did he assume "indifference" as though nothing painful had happened; but his decision was "to choose the mean rather than the extremes and aim at moderation of feeling [*metriopathein*]."

3. The words *tois agnoousin kai planōmenois*, with a single article, are probably to be understood as hendiadys: "those who go astray through ignorance." See p. 63.

shall make atonement before the Lord for the person who commits an error, when he sins unwittingly, to make atonement for him; and he shall be forgiven" (Num. 15:28). Sins committed "unwittingly" were both sins committed in ignorance and sins into which a man fell through passion. But the law also stated that anyone who committed sin "with a high hand" was to be cut off from the people and was to atone for his sin with his life (Num. 15:30). This kind of sin consisted of open rebellion against God, in such as blasphemy, sin for which no sacrifice was available. For the author sin like this, for which there was no remedy, was nothing other than the sin of apostasy (3:12; 10:26; cf. 6:4-6).

That the Jewish high priests were **beset with weakness** can be abundantly illustrated. In the Roman period, for example, some were notorious renegades. Even the first high priest, Aaron, succumbed to the pressure of the masses for a visible god and vainly tried to explain: "I said to them, 'Let any who have gold take it off'; so they gave it to me, and I threw it into the fire, and there came out this calf" (Ex. 32:24).

Under the old covenant the high priest was officially different from others. Officially he was a very holy man, arrayed in gorgeous robes and "required to be so devoted to his sacred calling and so dead to the world" that he was not to mourn over the death of his loved ones. "How oppressive the burden of this official sanctity must have been to a thoughtful, humble man . . . knowing himself to be of like passions and sinful tendencies with his fellow-worshippers. How the very sanctity of his office would force on the attention of one who was not a mere puppet priest the contrast between his official and his personal character, as a subject of solemn reflection."[4] **Because of this**, with a deep sense 3 of his own unworthiness, with a view of himself as one who is also tempted, the high priest is **bound** (Lev. 16:1-24) **to offer sacrifice for his own sins as well as for those of the people.**

The third qualification given by the author is that the high priest-hood must be a matter of divine appointment. **And one does not take** 4 **the honor upon himself** (not if he is really conscious of his sins) **but he is called by God, just as Aaron was.** The word **honor** here is used in the sense of "position" or "office." A responsible office like this is not filled by self-designation. All devout, deep-thinking men would shrink from such an office, and anyone who would magnify himself by seeking it would lack the quality of compassion so essential to the office.

The author's thinking is based on scenes of the Pentateuch. Aaron is the model of that priesthood just as the tabernacle is the type of ritual service the author later appeals to. He is not thinking of the succession to the high priesthood which in his own day had become

4. A. B. Bruce, *Hebrews*, p. 180.

arbitrary and contrary to the principle of Aaronic descent.⁵ But, as Westcott remarks, "the notoriousness of the High-priestly corruption at the time could not fail to give point to the language of the Epistle."⁶

Aaron received his call to priesthood from God (Ex. 28:1ff.; Ps. 105:26), and likewise Aaron's son, Eleazar, and his descendants (Num. 20:23-29; 25:10-13). They did not appoint themselves. In the lifetime of Aaron, Korah and his followers were destroyed precisely because without a divine call they sought to usurp the Aaronic privilege of burning incense to the Lord (Num. 16:1-35).

Jesus' Qualifications
(5:5-10)

Having stated that a divine appointment is essential for the priestly
5 office, the author now comes to consider the case of Jesus. **So also Christ did not exalt himself to be made a high priest, but was appointed by him who said to him, "Thou art my Son, today I have begotten**
6 **thee"; as he says also in another place, "Thou art a priest for ever, after the order of Melchizedek."** Jesus, even though Messiah, did not glorify Himself to be made a high priest (cf. Jn. 8:54). He did not come in His own name nor did He rely solely on His own testimony (Jn. 5:43, 31).

Again the author makes reference to the Old Testament, and again God is represented as speaking to His Son. His first quotation, which he had previously cited (1:5), is from Psalm 2:7. His second quotation, from Psalm 110:4, is given here for the first time. Earlier he has made use of this psalm (1:13) and later he will return to it as his chief Scriptural proof to show the nature of the Messiah's priesthood. Christ is a priest, he will argue in chapter 7, of the Melchizedek sort or order of priests.

The question here is why the author selects two quotations to prove his one point. The two quotations are not disparate, for together they show Christ's priesthood and His sonship: Christ is high priest *because* He is the divine Son. Does not the Christian high priest minister in the heavenly sanctuary (8:2)? Is He not seated eternally at God's hand, always able to save and always living to intercede (8:1; 7:25)? Sonship and priesthood, therefore, are inseparable.

7 The author now speaks of Jesus' human history. **In the days of his flesh, Jesus offered⁷ up prayers and supplications, with loud cries and**

---

5. On the whimsical selections of high priests made by Herod and later by the Romans, see Josephus, *Antiquities* 15.3.1; 20.10.5.

6. Westcott, p. 123.

7. Jesus offered (*prosenenkas*) petitions in Gethsemane, and it is the duty of the high priest to offer (*prosphere*) gifts and sacrifices (v. 1). Such a subtle comparison is not intended. Later (8:3ff.), the author will take up the thought of Jesus' perfect offering.

tears. Why is reference now made to Jesus' earthly days, and what connection is there between this and the previous quotations concerning Jesus' priesthood? The passage doubtless refers to Jesus' agony in Gethsemane, where, according to Mark, "horror and dismay came over him." There He said, "My heart is ready to break with grief," and there He prayed, "Abba, Father . . . all things are possible to thee; take this cup away from me. Yet not what I will, but what thou wilt" (Mk. 14:33-36, NEB). Here, as in Mark, the grim reality of Jesus' struggles is exposed. How intensely He entered the human drama! How real and deep His experiences of suffering! If ever there was a time when Jesus was beset with weakness (v. 2), it was in Gethsemane. This seems to be the connection and the explanation as to why the author casts a backward look at Jesus **in the days of his flesh.**

The drift of the passage is as follows: "Look at Jesus on earth. See Him in Gethsemane—how intense were His sufferings, how urgent He was in His petitions, how dependent He was on His Father. He prayed **with loud cries and tears** [a statement not found in the Gospels]. It is absurd to think that such a Person, so obedient and humble, so molested with weakness and grief, would be unable to sympathize with human weaknesses." In Gethsemane Jesus wholly identified Himself with men, not in flesh only but in distressing weakness. There, like all men, *Jesus needed to pray:* He needed to submit absolutely to God's will and feel firsthand the frustration of not giving in to His own human desires.

The prayer of Gethsemane was addressed **to him who was able to save him from death.** The language implies that Jesus prayed for His physical deliverance ("take this cup away from me") and also that His prayer for physical deliverance was not heard. If not, why would the author emphasize that God was **able** to grant His request? Jesus knew that God was able to unleash the power of angel-legions (Mt. 26:53), and this very knowledge intensified His trials.

Jesus' prayer, offered with loud cries and tears, **was heard,** the author now says, because of **his godly fear.** On another occasion, according to John, Jesus had prayed: "Father, I thank thee that thou hast heard me. I knew that thou hearest me always . . ." (Jn. 11:41-42). So, too, in Gethsemane He was heard. But how, or in what way, since the cup of suffering was not withdrawn? Several suggestions have been made in an attempt to alleviate the difficulty. (See Additional Note.) In the New Testament the term *eulabeia* seems always to denote "fear of God," "awe," "reverence" (cf. 12:28); thus the translation here **godly fear.** The term even suggests cautious reverence. The thought is that Jesus prayed out of great reverence and submission to God—He did not wish to oppose God's will or prevail upon Him. He prayed out of a godly fear "which leaves everything to the will of God."[8] And in this sense Jesus' prayer was heard. Yet throughout the passage the main point to remember, as A. B. Bruce has said, is "not so much that the prayer of Jesus was heard, as that it *needed* to be heard: that He needed heavenly aid to drink the appointed cup."[9]

8   The thought of 2:10 is now reintroduced, showing that sonship does not exempt one from suffering. **Although he was a Son, he learned obedience through what he suffered.** Ordinarily the word **Son** implies obedience, but when applied to Jesus it suggests something special. Although Son, he still had to suffer. This was a consequence of His incarnation and an essential qualification of leadership. All of God's sons, the author will note later on (12:5-11), must be subject to discipline.

Learning and suffering are linked together by many Greek writers from Herodotus onward, the combination being facilitated by verbal wordplay (here, *emathen . . . epathen*). Often it was used of a person who was a hardhead, of one who could only learn the hard way. It is interesting to note that the author does not refrain from applying this expression to the sinless Jesus. His boldness is purposeful. He wishes to underscore in the strongest terms that in suffering Jesus **learned obedience.** When a child is told to do something that he does not want to do—something that might be even painful for him—and he does it, then he learns the lesson of obedience. So Jesus did not do His own will but the will of God (cf. 10:5-10); He obeyed to the point of death, "even death on a cross" (Phil. 2:8). It is not as though He had not known obedience before. But being Son, it was still necessary for Him, through the bitterest of all trials, to learn perfect obedience and so be perfectly qualified as God's chosen high priest.

It was in this sense, in view of equipping Him for His priestly 9 function, that Jesus was "perfected": **And being made perfect he became the source of eternal salvation to all who obey him.** By going through the school of suffering, Jesus was perfectly qualified to be Priest. Because of His suffering, He became the **source** (*aitios*, literally, "cause") of men's salvation.[10] Through Him salvation was made possible. He tasted death for everyone (2:9). Men are consecrated to God because He offered up His body (10:10).

The salvation He makes available is characterized in two ways: it is an **eternal** (*aiōnios*) salvation and it is a salvation accessible to all

---

8. Moffatt, *Hebrews,* p. 66.

9. A. B. Bruce, *Hebrews,* p. 186.

10. Other writers, Philo and Josephus in particular, use the expression "cause of salvation." Philo (*Special Laws* 1.252), for example, contrasts physicians, who are unable to secure man's health, with God, who has lordship over man's physical faculties and who is "the Author of his preservation" (*tēs sōtērias aition*).

who **obey** Him. The term *aiōnios* is fundamental to the author's main thesis. Appearing here for the first time, it is a carefully chosen word showing the absoluteness of the Christian religion as compared with Judaism (cf. 6:2; 9:12, 14, 15; 13:20). The salvation Christ bestows is eternal. It, in contrast with the annual atonement of the Jewish ritual, completely satisfies; and, like the Melchizedek order of priests, it endures forever. But that salvation is restricted to those who obey Him. Christ as Son had to obey the Father, and all who expect salvation must first learn obedience as He did.

Having begun his paragraph by saying that Christ did not exalt Himself to be made a high priest, the author now concludes by emphasizing that Christ was **designated by God a high priest after the order** 10 **of Melchizedek.** The author puts the words of the ancient oracle (Ps. 110:4) in the mouth of God. By so doing he makes it clear that not by men but by God has Christ been designated as high priest. And if Christ is a high priest like Melchizedek, that can only mean, as the author will later show, that the Aaronic order of priests has passed away.

Spiritual Childhood *(5:11-14)*

This section is a hortatory digression from the main thought that the author wishes to pursue. He has assured his readers that they do have a great high priest, Jesus Christ. In broad outline He meets the requirements for priesthood. Yet His priesthood possesses a distinctive character, for it is like the order of Melchizedek. And it is precisely at this point, on the transcendent doctrine of the priesthood of Melchizedek, that the author pauses to ponder (and regret) the mental outreach of his readers.[11] **About this we have much to say which is hard to explain.** 11 The author had in mind to treat the Christ-Melchizedek subject rather extensively. To him it was not a question of small significance. He believed that if the nature of Christ's priesthood was grasped, it had to be viewed from the standpoint of the Melchizedek type. And the author was aware that it was a matter difficult to express in the right words (literally, "hard to be interpreted to say"). It was especially difficult **since** his readers had **become dull of hearing.** It was a condition into which they had gradually lapsed. They had not always been like this.

---

11. "This he does with very great plainness of speech, for which all Christian teachers have reason to thank him; for what he has written may be regarded as an assertion of the right of the Church to be something more than an infant school, and as a defence of the liberty of prophesying on all themes pertaining to Christ as their centre against the intolerance always manifested by ignorance, stupidity, indolence, and prejudice towards everything that is not old, familiar, and perfectly elementary" (A. B. Bruce, *Hebrews,* p. 197).

Formerly they had had eager minds, but over the years they had **become dull.** Dullness of hearing is a metaphor for mental sluggishness and spiritual apathy.[12] As it is difficult to communicate with a deaf person, so the author finds it difficult to get his thoughts into the ear of their intelligence.

12   The complaint of the author continues. **For though by this time you ought to be teachers, you need some one to teach you again the first principles of God's word.** The language perhaps suggests that the Epistle was addressed to a small group. But regardless, it is the task of all Christians to give reasons why they are what they are, and this they must always be prepared to do (1 Pet. 3:15). Yet this is not quite the author's thought. In saying **you ought to be teachers,** the author, rather than harassing them because they were not all teachers, is shaming them because they had not grown up in Christ. To be a teacher meant to the ancient mind that one was able to think and to act maturely—the very thing that these Christians could not do.[13] They had had enough time, indeed more than enough. But they had gone backward rather than forward. They still needed a teacher. They still needed to be taught, as literally rendered, "the rudiments of the beginning of the oracles of God." The meaning here must be seen in light of the similar expression in 6:1, which is literally translated as "the word of the beginning of Christ." Both expressions point back to the initial stages of salvation, when they were first taught the elementary truths of the gospel. The term *stoicheia* adds a deeper tone of reproach. Sometimes in the New Testament it denotes the physical elements of the universe (2 Pet. 3:10, 12), and sometimes it refers to "the elemental spirits of the universe" (Gal. 4:3, 9; Col. 2:8, 20 [RSV]). (See Additional Note.) Here it is used with reference to the first letters of the alphabet. Joined to the word "beginning,"[14] it is as though the author is saying that his readers need another lesson on "the rudiments of the rudiments," the very "ABC of God's oracles" (NEB). These oracles include not only the Old Testament but any portion of God's communication to man, especially the word given by Him through the Son (1:2; 2:3).

---

12. The terms, and the drift of the whole passage, do not fit in with the theory that the Epistle was written to a select group of gnostic intellectuals.

13. The point may be illustrated from Seneca's "On the Futility of Learning Maxims." Seneca decries men who do not think for themselves but hang on the opinions of others written down in notebooks. "Let there be a difference," he says, "between yourself and your book! How long shall you be a learner? From now on be a teacher as well!" (*Epistle* 33.9).

14. The Greek term is *archē*, the whole phrase being *ta stoicheia tēs archēs*. As such, *tēs archēs* must be understood as a genitive of apposition: the "rudiments of the beginning" does not mean "the beginning of the rudiments" but "the rudiments, the beginning," or "the rudiments of the rudiments."

By saying **You need milk, not solid food,** the author continues to use figurative language in depicting their state. The parallels of the child and milk and of the mature Christian and solid food were generally known (1 Cor. 2:6; 3:2; 14:20; Eph. 4:13-14; 1 Pet. 2:1-2).[15] The readers, as shown here and throughout the Epistle, were tending toward the wrong direction. They were in spiritual infancy once again; and some, in fact, were on the way to apostasy (3:12; 6:4-6; 10:26-31). They needed food for full-grown men, the very food that the author was seeking to give them.

The author elaborates his illustration. **For every one who lives on 13 milk is unskilled in the word of righteousness, for he is a child. Unskilled** means "without experience." **Word of righteousness** might mean "right teaching," "teaching concerning righteousness," or "teaching which leads to righteousness." The word for **child** is *nēpios*, a term that seemingly is derived from a verb that means "to be without power—weak, impotent." It is a term that is especially used of small children. But the term predominates in Greek literature in the sense of inexperience with things of the world. A person might even be physically mature; but if he knows nothing of the world, he would be called a babe. The general sense seems to be that the readers were amateurs in **the word of righteousness** (probably, God's word that makes men upright) because they had been feeding on milk. They had turned to their second childhood. On the other hand, **solid food is for the mature, for those who 14 have their faculties trained by practice to distinguish good from evil.** The expressions in this verse are in contrast to those of the previous verse—"solid food" to "milk," "mature" to "child," and "faculties trained by practice" to "unskilled in the word." Babies do not have the ability to discriminate. They cannot choose for themselves but must take what is put before them. But grownups are able to make proper distinctions. Such ability is not inborn but is gained through long use and habit. The senses are sharpened by experience. As an adult does not need someone to stand over him, always reminding him what foods are good and bad to eat, so the adult Christian is able to **distinguish good from evil.** The latter expression does not refer to good and bad in morals but to good and bad in teaching. It is a mark of maturity to be able to discern truth

---

15. The metaphor is an obvious one and is frequently found in contemporary Greek authors. The rabbis commonly spoke of their pupils as "sucklings." Pythagoras divided his pupils into two groups, the infants (*nēpioi*) and the mature (*teleioi*). Among the Hellenistic writers, the example of Philo may be cited. "And since milk is food for babes and wheat-pastries for the mature, there must also be nourishment for the soul, as is milk-like suited for childhood, in the form of the preliminary stages of school-learning, and such as is fitted for the mature in the form of instructions leading the way through wisdom and temperance and all virtue" (*On Husbandry* 9). For a detailed list of similar statements, see Michel, *ad loc.*; Spicq, *ad loc.* and I, 54; TDNT, I, 645ff.

from error, just as it is a mark of maturity to be able to teach. The two are linked inseparably.

Additional Notes

The interpretation of 5:7-10

Several passages in the Epistle are especially difficult for the interpreter, among them 5:7-10. Verse 7 alone raises many questions. What is the connection of "in the days of his flesh" with the larger context? What is the meaning of "prayers and supplications" and of "loud cries and tears," and out of what background do these expressions come? How was Jesus saved "from death" (*ek thanatou*)? Or was He? How was His prayer heard? And how is "godly fear" (*eulabeias*) to be understood?

The answers to many of these questions center on the meaning of the difficult clause "he was heard for his godly fear" (*eisakoustheis apo tēs eulabeias*). Perhaps it will be helpful to sketch some of the main lines of interpretation that have been followed and then to mention some of the points that should be kept in mind as one seeks a clearer understanding of the passage.[16]

1. Jesus' prayer was heard on the basis of His godly fear. So rendered, *apo* is taken as causal ("because of," "on acount of," "for") and *eulabeias* is understood as "piety," "awe," "godly fear." This view is supported by the Vulgate, similarly by the Greek commentators (Chrysostom, Photius, Oecumenius, Theophylact), almost all of the medieval writers, and a majority of the modern interpreters (Delitzsch, Westcott, Peake, Dods, Nairne, Riggenbach, Moffatt, etc.). Jesus prayed in Gethsemane that the Father would remove the cup of death, yet He prayed also that the Father's will might be done. He prayed this prayer in "godly fear." His prayer was heard, for God's will was done.

2. Jesus' prayer was heard and He was delivered from the fear of death. *Eulabeias*, taken with the "loud cries and tears" preceding, is understood to refer to "fear" or "apprehension." This is the translation of the Old Latin and the Peshitta Syriac. It is the view held by Calvin, Beza, Grotius, Bengel, M. Stuart, Robert Milligan, O. Michel, and

16. This note reproduces much of my article, "The Saving of the Savior: Hebrews 5:7ff.," *Restoration Quarterly* 16 (1973), 166-73. The title was suggested by Reuben E. Omark, "The Saving of the Savior," *Interpretation* 12 (1958), 39-51. Other than these articles I know of no recent summaries of various viewpoints on the passage available in English. For good summaries in foreign publications, see Michel, p. 222ff. and Spicq, II, p. 114ff. Other articles summarize in part: E. Brandenburger, "Text and Vorlagen von Hebr. V 7-10," NovTest 11 (1969), 190-95; P. Andriessen and A. Lenglet, "Quelques Passages Difficiles de l'Épître aux Hébreux (5,7.11; 10,20; 12,2)," *Biblica* 51 (1970), 208-12. For further bibliography and views, see my article.

Montefiore.[17] But the difficulties with this solution are not minor. *Eulabeia* and its related forms, *eulabeomai* and *eulabēs,* are not used in the New Testament to denote fear in general. As A. B. Davidson notes, "The term does not seem applicable to a terror such as death inspires, and such renderings as *heard* (and saved) from his mental *terror,* or from that which was his terror (death), seem inadmissable."[18] There is the difficulty also of fitting this in with the Gethsemane prayer, if indeed that is the background against which 5:7 is to be understood. Jesus' prayer in Gethsemane was a prayer for deliverance from death, not deliverance from fear of death. And more importantly, is this really what Hebrews is saying? Is the author's meaning that Jesus was delivered from the fear of death and so is able to identify Himself sympathetically with humanity?

3. Jesus' prayer was heard and He was delivered from death by means of resurrection. W. F. Moulton has succinctly stated this view: "The prayer, we are persuaded, was not that death might be averted, but that there might be granted deliverance out of death."[19] Or, in the words of G. H. Lang, it was a "prayer for resurrection."[20] Peake believes that the answer to Jesus' prayer was probably in the resurrection.[21] But was this what Jesus prayed for in Gethsemane? Did He agonize "with loud cries and tears" concerning the possibility of resurrection? And how would this be a test of His obedience (cf. v. 8), for Him to be raised from the dead?

4. Other solutions. A. F. Schauffler has suggested that Jesus prayed that He might not die "then and there" in the garden and thus frustrate His whole life's mission.[22] Blass-Debrunner-Funk[23] suggests a change in punctuation, *kai eisakoustheis, apo tēs eulabeias . . . emathen aph' hōn (t') epathen tēn hupakoēn,* with the result that "from fear He learned obedience." But, as Spicq says, this is very artificial and does not take into account the important intervening expression *kaiper ōn huios* ("al-

---

17. This is likewise the view of Bultmann, that is, if the present text is not to be corrected, TDNT, II, 753.

18. Davidson, p. 113. Arndt-Gingrich says of *eulabeia:* "in our lit. prob. only of reverent *awe* in the presence of God, fear of God" (p. 322); e.g., Heb. 12:28, *meta eulabeias kai deous* ("with awe and reverence"). So concerning *eulabēs* Arndt-Gingrich says, "in our lit. only of relig. attitudes *devout . . .*; e.g., Luke 2:25; Acts 2:5; 8:2; 22:12.

19. *A New Testament Commentary for English Readers,* ed. C. J. Ellicott (London, 1897), vol. III, p. 300.

20. *The Epistle to the Hebrews* (London, 1951), p. 92.

21. "Hebrews," *The Century Bible* (Edinburgh, 1914), p. 135.

22. ExpTimes 6 (1895), 433. More recently Hewitt (p. 100) apparently leans toward this view.

23. Blass-Debrunner-Funk, p. 114.

though He was Son."[24] Harnack's well-known conjecture, followed by Bultmann,[25] was that *ouk* ("not") originally belonged in the text before *eisakoustheis* ("he was heard") and was cut out on religious grounds. The text would read, according to Harnack, "He was not heard apart from His fear, although He was Son...."[26] The conjecture has not made much headway; for, void of any manuscript attestation, it depends on the fragile hypothesis of a very early corruption of the text. And what is more: any conjecture that results in a patent contradiction of passages such as John 11:41-42 ("Father...I knew that thou hearest me always....") does not really contribute to the solution of the problem.

With so many views on 5:7, some personal observations at this point will summarize and perhaps clarify some of the central issues at stake.

1. Meanings of terms.

(a) *Eulabeia*. The balance of weight seems to be on the side of "piety," "godliness," "godly fear." In the makeup of the word *eulabeia* (from *eu*, "well," and *labein*, "to take," thus denoting one who lays hold of a thing well or carefully) there is no special hint as to its precise meaning, as is usually the case with words; and a look at almost a full column of its usages annotated in Liddell-Scott-Jones confirms this.[27] The term suggests "discretion" and "caution," and this meaning might be expanded in the direction of either "fear" or "piety." But in the New Testament, and in Hebrews in particular, *eulabeia* consistently denotes reverence for God.

(b) *Apo*. The meaning of *eulabeia* determines the sense of *apo*. If *eulabeia* means "godly fear," *apo* must be causal. This accords with New Testament usage—"because of [*apo*] the crowd" (Lk. 19:3); "because of [*apo*] the persecution" (Acts 11:19); "because of [*apo*] the brightness of the light" (Acts 22:11); etc.

(c) *Sōzein ek thanatou*. It is much more natural to take the expression "to save from death," in the prayer of someone living, to refer to death impending, not to death already experienced. Compare the use of *ek thanatou* in such passages as James 5:20 and 2 Corinthians 1:10.

2. Intrinsic difficulties. There are many views that have been proposed on 5:7, but it should be kept in mind that not a few of these proposals involve greater difficulties than those they seek to explain. A number of these difficulties have already been noticed.

---

24. Spicq, II, p. 115.
25. TDNT, II, 753.
26. Harnack's view is discussed by J. Jeremias, "Hebräer 5, 7-10," ZNW 44 (1952-53), 108. For Jeremias' view, see my article, "The Saving of the Savior."
27. *Eulabeia* and cognates listed on p. 720.

3. Context. The setting of the passage is by far the most important consideration here. From 4:14ff. the author begins to sketch his portrait of Christ, the sympathizing High Priest. He refutes any potential objection that one who is as exalted as Christ can not be concerned about the human predicament. The high priest, who in the ancient order was surrounded with weakness, was a man who ideally could "deal gently" *(metriopathein)* with his fellows. Christ has this *metriopatheia.* He has gone over the broad course of temptations as other men have had to do.

The author's portrait of Jesus is no Docetic one. He purposely exposes the grim reality of Jesus' sufferings. He points to Gethsemane; for if ever there was a time when Jesus was surrounded with weakness, it was there. There He urgently prayed that death's cup might be withheld. But if this had been granted, He would not have been like His brothers in all respects. "The fact that the cup was not removed qualifies Him all the more to sympathize with His people.... At no point can the objection be voiced that because He was the Son of God it was different, or easier for Him."[28] But Jesus also prayed, "Not my will but Thy will be done!" This was His *eulabeia*—the godly fear that was willing to turn everything over to God. Because of this *eulabeia* His prayer was heard.

This seems to explain why the author casts a backward look at Jesus "in the days of his flesh." There is, therefore, a real sense in which it is possible to speak of "The Saving of the Savior." "The Epistle does not hesitate to use the word 'save' even of the Son, so complete is the parallel between His history and relation to God and that of men (ii. 9, 14)."[29] Through it all the Son learned in the hard school of suffering. Through it all He attained "perfection." Through it all He learned submission, the very trait that the high priest must have who does not honor himself.

It is remarkable that this verse, so filled with imponderables, marvelously explores and exposes much of the theme of the Epistle—a reverential Son, human like all other humans, who is submissive to God even to the point of severe suffering, and one thus qualified to be High Priest and Leader of His people.

Ta stoicheia tēs archēs, "first principles"

V. 12. When the author speaks of "first principles" *(ta stoicheia tēs archēs),* he uses a term, *stoicheia,* whose meaning has been discussed since the early Christian centuries. The term is also found in Galatians 4:3, 9; Colossians 2:8, 20; and 2 Peter 3:10, 12.

Stoicheia is the plural of *stoicheion.* It is related to *stoicheō,* which

28. F. F. Bruce, *Hebrews,* p. 102.
29. Davidson, p. 113.

often means "to march in line"; to *stichos*, often a "row" or "file" of soldiers; and to *stoichos*, a "row in an ascending series," often used of a "file" of persons marching, a "column" of ships, a "row" of verses, etc.

Stoicheion has many possible meanings. It was used of a "basic element" in speech, a "syllable" or "part" of speech. It often had the sense of "letters" in the alphabet (*ta stoicheia* = alphabet; *kata stoicheion* = alphabetically). In geometry and physics it meant "the basic elements," such as fire, air, earth, and water. (Euclid's work on the elements of geometry is entitled *Stoicheia*.) In astronomy *ta stoicheia* stood for "the heavenly bodies": the sun, planets, stars, constellations—and even the "gods" or "demons" or "spirits" behind them. In astrology *stoicheia* ultimately came to mean "the signs of the zodiac."

In the Pauline passages referred to, the RSV renders *ta stoicheia tou kosmou* as "the elemental spirits of the universe." The translators take Paul to be speaking of cosmic spiritual beings: with reference to Jews, "angels" (Gal. 4:3), with whom was associated the giving of the law (Gal. 3:19); with reference to Gentiles, the deities that they formerly had worshiped (Gal. 4:9). Thus in Colossians, too; for there "the elemental spirits" are connected with "principalities and powers" (2:15) and the worship of angels (2:18).[30]

Fortunately, the meaning of *stoicheia* in 5:12 is clear. It can mean nothing other than "rudiments," "beginnings," "the ABC." This meaning is intensified by *tēs archēs* ("the beginning"), and so the rendering "first principles."

---

30. It should be noticed, however, that this whole line of interpretation is disputed. Burton, in his extended note, questions whether *stoicheion* had the meaning of "angel" or "spirit" as early as the first century A.D. (Burton, *The Epistle to the Galatians*, p. 513). Delling (TDNT, VII, 682) likewise questions whether the evidence goes so far as to show "that the stars were regarded as beings in the NT age." Both Burton and Delling see the Pauline passages as relating to the weak and imperfect conceptions of the true religion in Christ. For the point of view that "the elemental spirits" were indeed cosmic spiritual beings, see A. Deissmann, EB, II, 1258ff.; P. L. Hammer, IDB, II, 82.

HEBREWS SIX

On to Maturity
(6:1-3)

The exhortation begun at the end of chapter 5 continues in the opening of chapter 6. Having severely rebuked his readers for their spiritual lethargy, the author now admonishes them to move beyond the rudiments of Christianity to that stage where they will be able to digest solid food. **Therefore, since growth is demanded of all Christians, 1 let us leave the elementary doctrines of Christ and go on to maturity.** The words express both purpose and encouragement. The **maturity** (translated "perfection" in the KJV) of which he speaks is not to be connected so much with the maturity of the readers (which was lacking) as with the maturity of the teaching which they needed. **Let us ... go on,** he says, to more advanced teaching, to such doctrines as the nature of Christ's priesthood, which they were scarcely able to grasp. They needed to push on to higher plains, to more advanced Christian truths than those to which they were accustomed.

As a child must leave behind the school books used in earlier years, so the author wants to carry his readers beyond the beginnings of Christianity. He has no intention of going back over the elementary truths of their faith: **not laying again,** he says, **a foundation of repentance from dead works and of faith toward God, with instruction about 2 ablutions, the laying on of hands, the resurrection of the dead, and eternal judgment.** The list of fundamentals is by no means exhaustive. Therefore, no conclusions can be reached from it as to what constituted the core of primitive instruction given to new converts.[1]

---

1. This is contrary to a recently developing view that the items listed here represent a basic outline of teaching for catechumens. See Robinson, pp. 69-70; Michel, p. 238; Spicq, II, p. 147; Buchanan, p. 103; etc.

What is striking about the list is how little that is specifically Christian it contains. There is in it no mention of Christ, even in connection with faith. This is in contrast to Paul's statement of his practice, that he testified "both to Jews and to Greeks of repentance to God and of faith in our Lord Jesus Christ" (Acts 20:21). Other items on the list, such as the laying on of hands, are characteristically Jewish; and when the author speaks of "ablutions" or "cleansing rites" (NEB), one thinks at once of the many ritual cleansings required in the Old Testament. For these reasons some have argued that the entire exhortation must be seen as an attempt on the part of the author to move his readers beyond matters that are basically Jewish to the distinctive truths of Christianity. A. Nairne, for example, sees essentials of Judaism in these points, of the kind that might well fit in the "creed of a Pharisaic Jew."[2] But this is probably carrying the matter too far. If the elementary principles are essentially Jewish, they are not exclusively so; for why should the author say (5:12) that his readers had need for someone to teach them these **first principles** again? Did he mean that they had need of these basic elements as taught in Judaism? And how would it be possible for these Jewish elements to be called **the elementary doctrines of Christ** (6:1)?

The list of basics includes six points. A slight variation in the readings of the manuscripts determines whether the six points are co-ordinate and together constitute the **foundation** that need not be laid again (v. 1), or whether the last four points are subordinate to the first two.[3] The texts of the King James and American Standard, on one hand, may be compared with the texts of the Revised Standard and New English Bible on the other. The difference is slight, the texts of the Revised Standard and New English Bible subordinating the teaching on **ablutions, laying on of hands, resurrection and eternal judgment** to the **foundation of repentance** and **faith.** In either case, the author's abbreviated list contains six items, given in three sets of pairs.

1. Repentance and faith. These are the first essentials to be preached to men in sin. This is what Jesus preached when He began His Galilean preaching ministry, saying, "The time is fulfilled, and the

---

2. Nairne, *Epistle of Priesthood*, p. 15.

3. The difference hinges on whether the reading is *didachēn* ("teaching" in the accusative case, supported by P[46], B, d, (e), syr[p]) or *didachēs* ("teaching" in the genitive case, supported by Aleph, A, C, and many other MSS). The RSV and NEB follow the earlier reading *(didachēn),* so that "the foundation of repentance . . . and of faith" is made up of (1) "ablutions," (2) "laying on of hands," (3) "resurrection," and (4) "judgment." Tasker *(Greek Testament,* p. 441), expressing the view of the NEB committee, says that the genitive is due to "early assimilation to the other genitives in the context"; Zuntz (p. 93) holds that the genitive is "inadmissible."

kingdom of God is at hand; repent, and believe in the gospel" (Mk. 1:15). **Repentance** and **faith** are interrelated because both have to do with a new attitude toward God. **Faith** is a subject the author will enlarge upon later, for "without faith it is impossible to please him" (11:6). It should be noticed here, however, that when the author speaks of **faith toward God,** this for him implicitly involves faith in the Son through whom God has spoken in the last days (1:2). In fact, from the standpoint of the Epistle, faith is always described as faith toward God, not faith in Christ. Christ is "the pioneer and perfecter of our faith" (12:2).

Repentance is a subject that the author will deal with momentarily (6:4ff.). Repentance is the basis of right, religious conduct. It is more than a change of mind. It is much more than sorrow for sin. It is a "turning" or "returning" to God. "It represents a reorientation of one's whole life and personality, which includes the adoption of a new ethical line of conduct, a forsaking of sin and a turning to righteousness."[4] It is here described as **repentance from dead works, from** being the appropriate preposition with the word "repentance." There is a slight possibility that **dead works** has reference to the ineffective sacrifices of the Jewish law which, with all its works, could never secure salvation (see 10:1-4; Gal. 2:16). It is probably better, however, to take **dead works,** as in 9:14, to refer to one's sinful practices, "the deadness of our former ways" (NEB). These works are dead because they lead to death (Rom. 6:23).

2. **Ablutions** and **laying on of hands.** The second pair of elementary principles concerns the individual's introduction into the Christian community. Here the term *baptismōn* is an unusual one. It is a plural form of *baptismos,* a term which in its other New Testament usages refers to ceremonial washings practiced by the Jews (see 9:10; Mk. 7:4). (The word *baptisma* is ordinarily used to denote Christian baptism.[5]) This explains the translations of the Revised Standard and the New English Bible, the former rendering the phrase "instruction about ablutions," the latter "instruction about cleansing rites." The plural form has been variously explained: a threefold baptism in the name of the Godhead (Didache 7, 1-3), the repetition of baptism practiced by heretics, the plurality of those baptized, outward and inner purification, and so forth. It is better, with Oepke, to say that the plural "denotes instruction on the difference between Jewish (and pagan?) 'washings' (including

---

4. Richardson, p. 191.
5. The one possible exception, unless here, is in Col. 2:12, where *baptismos* is strongly attested by P[46], B, D, G, etc. Blass-Debrunner-Funk (p. 59) distinguishes the terms: *baptismos* denotes the act of immersion, *baptisma* also includes the result of the act, although admittedly Josephus *(Antiquities* 18.5.2) uses *baptismos* in reference to the baptism of John.

John's baptism?) and Christian baptism."[6] Many ritual washings were, of course, practiced by the various sects of pagans and Jews. There were undoubtedly many disputes in ancient times about the efficacy of such rites (cf. Jn. 3:25). All of these practices would have to be carefully distinguished from Christian baptism, and this would naturally constitute part of the **instruction** directed to the penitent. Although the term *baptismos* does not usually denote Christian baptism, here it is the appropriate term since other washings as well as baptism are in view.

In the primitive church, baptism in water and in the name of Christ was done for the forgiveness of sins (Acts 10:47-48; 2:38; 22:16). Often following this came **the laying on of hands,** which generally indicated some endowment of the Holy Spirit or divine blessing (Acts 6:6; 8:17; 19:5-6). In the time of Christ and the early church the sick were healed by the laying on of hands (Mk. 7:32; Acts 9:12, 17). By this means in the Old Testament men were admitted to their calling (Num. 8:10; 27:18, 23); so also in the New Testament (Acts 6:6; 13:3; 1 Tim. 4:14; 2 Tim. 1:6). The laying on of hands was accompanied by prayer, the imposition of hands being the outward symbol of the prayer.[7]

3. **Resurrection** and **eternal judgment.** The final pair of truths deal primarily with the future. The apostolic proclamation centered on Jesus the Resurrected Lord (Acts 2:31-32; 10:40; 13:33). There was the promise, too, that all His followers would be raised like Him (Acts 4:2; 1 Cor. 15:12-23); indeed, that all men would be raised from their graves (Jn. 5:28-29). Nothing preached by the apostles was more fundamental than resurrection and judgment; and, according to the author, they form the sobering outlook with which the Christian is to live (10:36-37; 12:28-29).

So the author concludes his list of the ABC's of the Christian faith. It should be remembered that his list is not complete. He could have enumerated many fundamentals, but he hastens to bring his readers 3 from spiritual childhood to spiritual maturity. **And this we will do,** he says, adding reverently the qualifying clause, **if God permits** (cf. 1 Cor. 16:7).

A Warning Against Apostasy
(6:4-8)

The author now makes clear to his readers why they should press on beyond the elementary principles of their religion. To fail to advance would mean to fall back, and to fall back would be fatal. The author

---

6. TDNT, I, 545.
7. See Everett Ferguson, "Jewish and Christian Ordination," HTR 56 (1963), 15f.

ranges his thoughts in one long sentence. **For it is impossible** *(adunaton,* 4
"impossible," stands impressively at the beginning of the Greek sentence)
to restore again to repentance those who have once been enlightened,
who have tasted the heavenly gift, and have become partakers of the
Holy Spirit, and have tasted the goodness of the word of God and the 5
powers of the age to come, if they then commit apostasy, since they 6
crucify the Son of God on their own account and hold him up to
contempt.

The warning is one of the most severe in the New Testament. For
whom is it intended? Kenneth S. Wuest, among others, holds that the
author's concern is with the "unsaved Jew" and that the sin in question
is "the act of an unsaved Jew in the first century renouncing his pro-
fessed faith in Messiah as high priest, and returning to the abrogated
sacrifices of the First Testament...."[8] But against this view is the context of the whole passage; "for it is the very fact of these persons having
veritably entered the spiritual life, which makes it impossible to renew
them afresh if they fall away."[9] And why say impossible to renew
again to those who have not been renewed in the first place?

It seems correct, therefore, to say that the passage speaks of those
who have embraced the Christian religion. The author makes this even
clearer by describing, clause after clause, their condition.

1. They **have once been enlightened.** Their enlightenment took
place at the time of their conversion.[10] In 10:32 the author writes, "But
recall the former days when, after you were enlightened, you endured
a hard struggle with sufferings...." God who is light had given them
light (1 Jn. 1:5; Eph. 1:18; 5:14). The light of the gospel shined upon
them and they came to a "knowledge of the truth" (10:26; cf. 2 Cor.
4:4, 6). **Once** is in contrast with **again** in verse 6.[11] For them it was a
one time act of entrance into Christ that could never be duplicated.
"Once for all men enter into Christianity, it is an experience which,
like their own death (9:27) and the death of Jesus (9:28), can never
be repeated."[12]

---

8. K. S. Wuest, "Hebrews Six in the Greek New Testament," BibSac 119 (1962), 46.

9. Alford, IV, pt. 1, p. 113. Alford distinguishes between the "regenerate" and
the "elect" and applies this passage to the "regenerate."

10. In the second century, at least by the time of Justin, the word "enlightenment"
came to be used as a synonym for baptism (Justin, *Apology* 1.61.65). The Peshitta
Syriac translates here, "who have once descended to baptism." Such understanding
gave rise to heated discussions in the early centuries of the church concerning
post-baptismal sin and the possibility of forgiveness.

11. For clarity of translation the RSV places the phrase "to restore again to repentance" in v. 4.

12. Moffatt, *Hebrews,* p. 78.

2. They **have tasted the heavenly gift.** "Taste" suggests an element of deep personal experience. "Jesus ... was made lower than the angels ... that ... he might taste death for every one" (2:9). Peter speaks to Christians in terms of their having "tasted the kindness of the Lord" (1 Pet. 2:3; cf. Ps. 34:8), and this in connection with their need, like new babes, for "the pure spiritual milk." Their tasting **the heavenly gift** refers back to their past experience of salvation, including the forgiveness of sins and all the spiritual blessings in Christ which had become theirs to enjoy (8:12; 10:17; Eph. 1:3). As Behm says, the clause "describes vividly the reality of personal experiences of salvation enjoyed by Christians at conversion (baptism)."[13]

3. They **have become partakers of the Holy Spirit.** This, too, points back to the time of their conversion (Acts 2:38; 5:32). The word **partakers** *(metochous)* is significant. Christians "share [*metochoi*] in a heavenly call" (3:1); they "share [*metochoi*] in Christ" (3:14); so here they share in the Holy Spirit.[14]

4. They **have tasted the goodness of the word of God and the powers of the age to come.** Again, "taste" underscores the aspect of personal experience. The "good word of God" (KJV) may refer to God's promises (cf. Josh. 21:45), but more probably is to be taken to refer to the good news generally: they had heard the gospel, made trial of it, and had found in it blessings that truly were worthwhile. They had experienced also "the spiritual energies of the age to come" (NEB). They had felt in their own lives the extraordinary effects of spiritual powers, which perhaps included "signs and wonders and various miracles and ... gifts of the Holy Spirit" (2:4). **The age to come** does not refer to some age which for Christians lies in the future. It is, rather, equivalent to the Messianic Age, ushered in with the appearance of Christ, but still appropriately called **the age to come** because it awaits its consummation at the Second Advent of Christ. (See comments on 2:5).

By reminding his readers of the wonderful experiences of conversion, the author underscores the tragedy of falling from divine favor. He speaks here not of the possibility of sin (cf. 1 Jn. 1:8, 10) but of the possibility of apostasy. **If they then commit apostasy,** he says. The if has been much debated. Although it is found in the early English versions (including Tyndale's), as well as in the King James and the Revised Standard versions, the **if** has been charged as representing dogmatic bias. The whole question depends on the translation of the Greek

---

13. TDNT, I, 676.

14. "Think of the high privilege involved in such participation.... Once again we behold a Christianity that is deep and thrilling" (Herbert H. Hohenstein, "A Study of Hebrews 6:4-8," CTM 27 (1956), 440). Hohenstein's two excellent articles (433-44; 536-46) on this passage should be consulted.

participle *parapesontas* ("commit apostasy").[15] All along the author has expressed himself (in the Greek original) by the use of participles—**have been enlightened ... have tasted ... have become partakers ... have tasted.** Since all these are translated with past tenses, it is maintained that the next participle in the series *(parapesontas)* should also be translated in the past. And this is what the British and American revisions of 1881-1901 did, translating it "and *then* fell away." On the other hand, it is unquestionably permissible to translate *parapesontas* as a conditional participle, the **if** idea being included in the participle. There is a danger here, a danger of thinking that the author is presenting a mere vapid hypothesis, that he is dealing with a supposition that could never be a fact. Wuest, for example, says: "The participle is a conditional participle here presenting a hypothetical case, a straw man."[16] But F. F. Bruce counters by noting that the "biblical writers (the writer to Hebrews being no exception) are not given to the setting up of men of straw." Bruce continues: "The warning of this passage was a real warning against a real danger, a danger which is still present so long as 'an evil heart of unbelief' can result in 'falling away from the living God' (Ch 3:12)."[17] It seems more reasonable to think, therefore, that the author is describing a condition which he considers altogether possible, though he is persuaded of better things concerning his readers (v. 9).

Concerning those who became apostates, the author says that **it is impossible to restore** them **again to repentance.** Impossible how? What does this mean? Various efforts have been made to explain the stern words of the passage.

1. Some commentators in the past have thought that the passage means that there can be no restoration for Christians who slip into sin, that a believer who sins simply can never have forgiveness.[18]

2. Erasmus in the sixteenth century softened the word **impossible** with the word "difficult," and many since that time have urged that **impossible** must not be taken literally. Bengel in the eighteenth century tried to explain that the impossibility is with men and not with God,

---

15. The verb *parapiptō* indicates no more than a falling aside from the path, but the context here and the larger context of the Epistle requires the rendering "commit apostasy."

16. Wuest, "Hebrews Six," p. 52.

17. Bruce, *Hebrews*, p. 123.

18. Tertullian (third cent.), who believed that Barnabas wrote Hebrews, quotes 6:4-6 and then says: "He who learned this *from* apostles and taught it *with* apostles, never knew of any 'second repentance' promised by apostles to the adulterer and fornicator" *(On Modesty* 20). This was his response to the *Shepherd* of Hermas (second cent.), which he refers to as "that apocryphal Shepherd of adulteries," since it allowed *one* opportunity for repentance after baptism *(Shepherd,* Vision 2.2.4-5). Hermas believed, however, that there was no repentance for apostates *(Shepherd,* Similitude, 8.6.4).

that ministers of the gospel can do only so much in reclaiming the lost and that the rest must be left to God.

3. The margin of the American Standard Version suggests another possible explanation. Adopting the alternative reading, the text would read: "It is impossible to renew them again unto repentance, the while they crucify to themselves the Son of God afresh. . . ." This means that people can not be brought again to repentance as long as they continue to renounce Christ.

4. Some interpreters, noticing that the infinitive **to restore** is without a subject, are convinced that the sense of the passage requires additional wording. They add, then, from the context of the Epistle, an expression such as "the law of Moses," with the full sense of the passage being "it is impossible *for the law of Moses* to restore again to repentance. . . ."

5. Some think that a right understanding of these verses hinges on the infinitive *anakainizein* ("to restore"). The infinitive is a present infinitive and as such has the force of "to keep on doing a thing." Thus the meaning of the passage would be that "it is impossible to keep on renewing them again to repentance"—not that they can not be restored but that they can not be restored again and again without their going outside the bounds of hope.

Each of these briefly stated views offers a possible solution to the problem. It is especially helpful to keep in mind that the author, as he speaks of renewal, switches from a series of past tenses to the present tense. In so doing he says forcefully that for the enlightened man the process of falling away and of being restored again cannot continue interminably, that there is a line drawn beyond which, if the individual crosses over, he cannot be retrieved. Why can he not be? Because he has traveled the road of falling and renewal so much that for him the whole matter is a trifle. His heart has turned cold, his life listless, and his condition is such that he can no longer turn from sin. It is **impossible** for him to be saved because he is *incapable* of turning to God. He is void of conscience. He has lost his repenting-apparatus.

It remains to be emphasized that the author's main subject is *apostasy*. He is not speaking of mere backsliding, of the ordinary shortcomings and failures that go with human weakness. Falling short is not the same as falling away. It is one thing to yield to sin contrary to the new life in Christ, it is another thing to abandon that new life altogether. "What our author feared was that men should cease entirely to be Christians, and should wholly give up what they had known of

Christ."[19] So for him falling away is the equivalent of "departing from the living God" (3:12). It is the same as to "persist in sin after receiving the knowledge of the truth" (10:26, NEB).

Those who apostatize by their lives **crucify the Son of God** and **hold him up to contempt.** These words describe the enormity of the crime that hardened apostates commit, the title **Son of God** intensifying the sin. The Greek interpreters (Chrysostom, Theodoret, Oecumenius, etc.), along with the Vulgate, took *anastaurountas* in the sense of "crucify again"; and so the early English versions. But in ordinary Greek usage the verb *anastauroō* means simply "to crucify."[20] They crucify Jesus **on their own account** (literally, "to themselves"). This can mean that they do it to their own harm (the crucifiers hurt themselves rather than the Crucified) or it can mean that they themselves crucify Jesus (cf. NEB). And they **hold him up** in disgrace. Having torn Him from their hearts, they put Him on the cross for all the world to scoff at. No wonder, then, that for such people "there no longer remains a sacrifice for sins" (10:26).

Indeed, as the author goes on to conclude, their end is destruction. That certain doom is emphasized by an illustration from agriculture. **For land which has drunk the rain that often falls upon it, and brings** 7 **forth vegetation useful to those for whose sake it is cultivated, receives a blessing from God.** The language calls to mind some of the parables of Jesus, with the stress on the forces of nature that work in due course. The next lines retrace some of the words of Genesis 3:17-18. **But if it bears thorns and thistles, it is worthless and near to being** 8 **cursed; its end is to be burned.** The point of the comparison is not so much that there are two different types of soil, but that there are two widely different results that come from the soil. Some **land,** renewed by the frequent rains that come upon it, yields a **useful crop** and is blessed by God. This is typical of the Christian who, growing in grace and knowledge, bears fruit abundantly. Other land is not so rewarding. Bringing forth nothing but **thorns and thistles,** it is degenerate and a curse hangs upon it. So the apostate is like the thorn-bearing field destined for burning (cf. Mt. 13:30; Jn. 15:6; Heb. 12:29). The author's meaning stands clear: irrevocable destruction is the fate of those who cast themselves away from Christ.

---

19. Robinson, p. 77.
20. The *ana* prefix has the force of "up" rather than "again." Some believe, however, that a figurative meaning is required here and thus prefer "crucify again" (Arndt-Gingrich, p. 60). Kasch (TDNT, VII, 584) points to *palin anakainizein* ("to restore again"), and says that this "plainly supports the rendering 'to crucify a second time.' "

A Word of Encouragement
(6:9-12)

9   The words which follow mark a sudden transition in tone. **Though we speak thus, yet in your case, beloved, we feel sure of better things that belong to** (accompany, will lead to) **salvation.** After drawing a grave picture, the author pauses, reflects, and then hastens to assure his readers that he does not consider them apostates. To be sure, that terrible condition is a potential one for them; but for the present he overpowers his misgivings concerning them. His affection reaches out for them and he addresses them as **beloved,** a term that he uses nowhere

10   else. He "believes all things and hopes all things" for them: **For God is not so unjust as to overlook your work and the love which you showed for his sake in serving the saints, as you still do.** The saints are, of course, Christians. The essential meaning of the term is that of "consecration." Applied to God's holy people in the Old Testament, it was easily transferred to God's people in the New Testament.

The author's confidence in his readers has a twofold basis: (1) their acts of unselfishness, and (2) the character of God Himself. They had proved their love in an especially practical way, by rendering service to their fellow Christians. Their service, as the word in the original (*diakonēsantes*) indicates, was of a personal nature—they had "waited on" their companions, doing such things as sharing in their afflictions and showing compassion to the imprisoned (10:33-34). The author was persuaded that men who would show such kindness to Christ's followers were not the sort who would lift Him up to public contempt. Besides, the author was sure of God. He knew that, since God is just, He could not be unjust and forget to reward those who do good (cf. 11:6).

The personal tie that binds author and readers is noticeable once

11   again. **And we desire each of you to show the same earnestness in realizing the full assurance of hope until the end.** The author has a deep love for his readers. The word he employs for **desire** suggests an intense longing, as when Jesus spoke to His disciples on that fateful night and said, "How I have longed to eat this Passover with you before my death."[21] The author's love for them is not generic but individual. He is deeply concerned about **each** of them (3:12; 4:1, 11; 12:15, 16). One gets the impression that he could call all of them by name. He knows that some of them are in imminent danger. He feels that they must cling to their hope at all costs—a hope that is not counterfeit and superficial but real and full, a hope which must be sustained in fullness to the end. What was needed was for them to show as much diligence in regard to

---

21. Lk. 22:15 (NEB). The same verb *epithumeō* appears in both passages.

their hope as they had shown in their love, **so that,** he says, **you may** 12
**not be sluggish, but imitators of those who through faith and patience
inherit the promises.** Earnestness is in contrast with their sluggish
(nōthroi) condition, a condition which the author had previously la-
mented by noting that they were "dull" *(nōthroi)* of hearing (5:11).
The **promises** refer to the heavenly possession laid up for God's people,
though the failure of Israel (chs. 3 and 4) serves as a reminder that not
all anticipated goals are realized. **Faith** and **patience** stand in the closest
possible connection and probably are to be understood, with Moffatt,
in the sense of "steadfast faith."[22] That is, it was by means of "steadfast
faith" that the great heroes of the past launched out upon a shoreless
ocean; and the author is convinced that only through this faith will his
beloved reach the sure harbor. On this theme of **faith** he has much more
to say (ch. 11), but he will not take the subject in hand again until the
doctrinal section of his Epistle is completed.

The Certainty of God's Promises
(6:13-20)

The previous section ended with a reference to those who "are
inheriting the promises" (NEB).[23] The purpose of this section is to
demonstrate that the promises of God are sure and unbreakable and,
therefore, provide a solid foundation for hope. Hope, having been
introduced in verse 11, thus becomes an important concept in the paragraph, although the dominant thought is the certainty of the divine
promise. The author begins by appealing to a memorable occasion in
the life of Abraham. **For when God made a promise to Abraham, since** 13
he had no one greater by whom to swear, he swore by himself, saying, 14
"Surely I will bless you and multiply you." The specific promise cited
is found in Genesis 22:16-17. There, on the occasion of the offering of
Isaac, God promises Abraham: "By myself I have sworn, says the Lord,
because you have done this, and have not withheld your son, your only
son, I will indeed bless you, and I will multiply your descendants as
the stars of heaven and as the sand which is on the seashore." The
promise is a restatement of an earlier promise that God would make of
Abraham a great nation and would bless the world through him
(Gen. 12:2-3; cf. 12:7; 13:15; 15:5; 17:4-8). For a divine being, swearing
would seem to be wholly unnecessary; but since with men oaths are
important, God condescended and made Himself, so to speak, His own
witness. (See Additional Note.)

22. The two terms probably form a hendiadys. For similar constructions, see p. 63.
23. The word "promises" is a hook word, tying together vv. 12 and 13. The Greek
word *nōthroi* ("sluggish," "dull"), found in v. 12, frames an inclusion begun in 5:11.

Yet the promise given to Abraham, on the human side, was slow in fulfilment. When God called Abraham in Haran, and promised him that his posterity would be great, he was seventy-five years old (Gen. 12:4). Twenty-four years of sojourning in a strange land elapsed, and only then did Abraham learn how the promise would be kept through the birth of a son (Gen. 17:1-21). In the next year that son, Isaac, was born (Gen. 21:1-7). In Isaac's birth Abraham began to see the fulfilment of the promise; and later, with Abraham still believing the promise, this son was restored to him from death. These were pledges that all of the promises, which were not to be fully realized until Christ came

15 (Gal. 3:14, 16, 29), would someday be fulfilled. **And thus Abraham, having patiently endured, obtained the promise,** in the sense that before his death he began to see God working His purposes through Isaac. In a way it could be said that Abraham saw Messiah's day: through faith he saw it and was overjoyed (Jn. 8:56). Over the years "no distrust made him waver concerning the promise of God, but he grew strong in his faith as he gave glory to God, fully convinced that God was able to do what he had promised" (Rom. 4:20-21).

16 A general principle on oaths is now stated. **Men indeed swear by a greater than themselves, and in all their disputes an oath is final for confirmation.** The words **for confirmation** (eis bebaiōsin) have a legal connotation. In the secular papyri it was the expression used for more than 700 years to "legally guarantee" a sale.[24] Here the confirmation of a sale is not in view, but the phrase is more general, a "legal guarantee." When one man disputes with another, an oath puts an end to the

17 strife and guarantees the truthfulness of the claim that is made. **So,** similarly, **when God desired to show more convincingly to the heirs of the promise the unchangeable character of his purpose, he interposed with an oath.** The **heirs of the promise** are not confined to Abraham's physical offspring, but include all his spiritual descendants (Christians) as well (Gal. 3:7). The author is urging home the message that God's promise does not vacillate. It is solid, irrevocable. His mere word is enough; but God, wishing to make men feel doubly sure, stands Himself as the guarantee for His word. (The verb mesiteuō usually means "to act as a mediator," "to interpose" or "to intercede"; here, however, the meaning is "to guarantee."[25])

---

24. Deissmann, Bible Studies, pp. 104-09.

25. Greek expositors (Chrysostom, Oecumenius, Theophylact) misunderstood mesiteuō and took it as a reference to Christ's mediation of the oath. The NEB correctly translates, "so God ... guaranteed it by oath." This is the only occurrence of the verb in the New Testament. The noun form, mesitēs, appears in 8:6; 9:15; 12:24. Both the verb and noun forms are common in the papyri in legal transactions. Mesitēs generally means an "arbiter" or "intermediary," but it also refers to one who is the "surety" of a debt. Compare with 7:22, where "surety" (enguos) is equivalent to mesitēs. See TDNT, IV, 620.

God certified the promise with His oath, **so that through two un- 18 changeable things, in which it is impossible that God should prove false, we who have fled for refuge might have strong encouragement to seize the hope set before us.** The two immutable things are God's promise and His oath. It is impossible for Him to break His promise, it is impossible for Him to take an oath falsely. "God is not man, that he should lie" (Num. 23:19; cf. 1 Sam. 15:29; Tit. 1:2). If either His promise or His oath proved false, the very laws of His Being would be violated and He would cease to be God.

These gracious assurances are for the benefit of those **who have fled for refuge,** that is, for all Christian believers. How is it that they **have fled for refuge?** As involuntary lawbreakers who might rush to the cities of refuge (Num. 35), or, more probably, as seamen who might escape the fury of a storm in a protected harbor.[26] Like the sailor who struggles through the waves, intent on making the distant shore, the Christian is urged to grasp the **hope** that is **set before** him. This **hope** is objectively conceived (cf. Col. 1:5; Tit. 2:13). It has an object—that which is hoped for, the final realization of the Christian's anticipations. In all of this the author seeks to give **strong encouragement** to his readers whose vision of the future was growing dim.

Having mentioned **hope,** the author continues by saying that **We 19 have this as a sure and steadfast anchor of the soul.** This metaphor is often used in Greek and Roman writings.[27] On coins and medals **hope** is represented by an anchor. The figure is peculiarly appropriate for the expression of Christian truths.[28] **Hope** is to the believer what a secure **anchor** is to a ship. **Hope** sustains and braces the Christian in the midst of all of his trials; but when **hope** fails, he is left to drift aimlessly and falls victim to the merciless ocean.

The Christian **anchor** of **hope** is **sure and steadfast** because it is

---

26. Philo symbolically interprets the Old Testament place of refuge, for a person who unintentionally killed someone, as God Himself. He asks, "Is it not life eternal to take refuge with Him that IS, and death to flee away from Him?" (*On Flight and Finding* 78). The author's thought is similar, although here the refuge toward which men flee is hope itself (that is, the object of hope). Compare "the set-before-us hope" with "the set-before-us race" and "the set-before-Him joy" in 12:1-2. The verb "set before" (*prokeimai*) is often used of a prize offered at a contest, and that meaning fits in well here.

27. A statement attributed to Socrates is illustrative: "A ship cannot depend on one anchor, or a life on one hope." The adjectival combination "sure and steadfast" (*asphalē te kai bebaian*) is also common in the Greek ethical writings. Sextus Empiricus (*Against the Logicians* 2.374) speaks of an assumption that is "certain and sure" (*bebaian . . . kai asphales*); Philo (*Who Is the Heir* 314) of "the sure and steadfast apprehension of the wisdom of God." Cf. Wisdom 7.23, where these terms are listed together as two of the twenty-one qualities of Wisdom.

28. Thus Clement of Alexandria names the ship's anchor as one of the several devices permitted on rings worn by Christian men (*Christ the Educator* 3.59).

based on the **two unchangeable things** (v. 18) and because it is **a hope that enters into the inner shrine behind the curtain.** The picture of the **anchor** entering into the **shrine** beyond the veil seems at first awkward and difficult. What connection is there between a ship's anchor and the sacred enclosure in the tabernacle? Some seek to escape the difficulty by explaining that the figure is now dropped and that **enters** should be taken not with the **anchor** but with **hope.** Thus the Revised Standard Version, following the English and American revisions and in agreement with Westcott and Moffatt, has inserted the word **hope** in the clause. But even without the insertion the general sense is plain. The figures are not in violent contradiction with each other. Instead they are beautifully complementary. **Hope** is an **anchor** that enters the unseen realm and is grounded in the eternal order, as a ship's anchor enters the waters; but the region beyond, where **hope** is fixed, is like a place **behind the curtain.** This place, where God dwells, is typically described as **the inner shrine** and denotes the Holy of Holies, about which the author will speak in more detail later on (9:1-14, 23-28).

The language, of course, is the language of the old system of worship, of the tabernacle with its two central compartments. One compartment, the outer, could be entered by any qualified priest; the other, separated from the first by a veil or **curtain,** could be entered only by the high priest and then only on the annual Day of Atonement. Here, in the inmost enclosure, which contained the Ark of the Covenant, was the sacred spot where God was represented as dwelling with His

20 people. This is **where,** says the author, into the inner sanctuary, **Jesus has gone as a forerunner on our behalf.** Christ has gone into the very presence of God, "thus securing an eternal redemption" (9:12). And He has gone as **forerunner** *(prodromos),* a term that can also be translated "scout" or "advance guard" of an army. (See Additional Note.) Christ as Leader of His people has gone before them, as Pioneer He has cleared the way for others to follow in His steps. He goes nowhere His people cannot follow. His entrance **behind the curtain** is the pledge that His followers, too, will come into the holiest of all. He has entered **on our behalf.** But he has entered, not simply as Leader, but as High Priest. The Jewish high priest did not go into the most holy place as **forerunner,** but as the representative of the people. He went where none could follow.[29] But **behind the curtain** is "Christ Jesus our hope" (1 Tim. 1:1), **having become a high priest for ever** (the words are last

29. The author "means to point out a contrast between the two religions, saying in effect: That which was lacking in the old religion is at length come. Where the High Priest goeth we may also go, instead of, as of old, standing without, waiting anxiously for the exit of the high priest from that inaccessible, dark, awful, perilous, most holy place beyond the veil" (A. B. Bruce, *Hebrews,* p. 235).

in the Greek sentence for emphasis) **after the order of Melchizedek.** The author proceeds to explain what this means in the next chapter.

So concludes the finely wrought passage that is so characteristic of the Epistle. Chapter 5 presents Jesus as the magnificent high priest of the Christian religion. He meets and supersedes the qualifications of the Jewish high priest. He, like other high priests, was selected from men; and so He is able to deal understandingly with the ignorant and erring. And in being made a high priest, He did not take the honor upon Himself.

This Jesus, whom God called to be high priest, even when on earth was not self-exalting. Always He was submissive. Offering up prayers and petitions with tears, He like other men needed to lean on the Everlasting Arms; and leaning on that strength, He met the cross and qualified Himself as high priest in the school of suffering. He became a high priest like Melchizedek of old—a subject that the author returns to at the end of chapter 6.

Before this, however, there is grim language. The readers are intellectually and spiritually dull, and the author rebukes them for their lack of progress. Trying to impress upon them the serious consequences of this condition, he brings them to the edge of the precipice that they might look below and see the dismal end of apostates.

Having begun this section in despair, he moves toward eager expectancy. He is persuaded that his readers are still on the way of salvation. What is needed particularly, he believes, is for them to hold on to their hope at all costs. He points to the example of Abraham, and here once again the skill of the author comes to the fore. Why Abraham? Because from Abraham's life it can be shown that God has made His promises doubly sure, and because at the same time it can be seen that Abraham's life is exemplary of those who endure through steadfast faith. So underneath the surface of the paragraph on Abraham is an artful intertwining of the themes of faith and hope. The scene is no longer one of gloom and failure but of joy and anticipation. The Christian who resolutely maintains his hope of eternal life is like an anchored ship that calmly rides the waves. And in the end the author masterfully ties together this hope and the Melchizedek priesthood, the very subject that the readers would otherwise have scorned. Warned and stimulated by the author's attention to their needs, the readers are now prepared to consider once again the main theme of the Epistle.

Additional Notes

The doctrines of Christ

V. 1. The "doctrines of Christ" can be either subjective or objective genitive. If subjective genitive, this would be "Christ's doctrines," that is, what Christ Himself taught. If objective genitive, the meaning would be "doctrines about Christ" (Christology). The latter is more likely in view of the "higher Christology" the author goes on to discuss in chapter 7.

But J. Clifford Adams has argued that "doctrines of Christ" is to be taken subjectively, that the author is pointing to things that Jesus of Nazareth personally taught, such things as "ablutions," "laying on of hands," etc.[30] But much of the strength of Adams' case is drawn from his view that the verses only with difficulty fit the mold of a "primitive Christian catechism." If, however, the author really has no intention of giving a fully developed statement of fundamental Christian truths, then the argument for the subjective genitive is less persuasive.

Philo on divine oaths

V. 13. Philo, believing that the good man need not swear, wrestled with the problem of God's affirming His word with an oath. Explaining God's oath to Abraham, Philo says that God spoke to him as a friend. And then he says: "For He, with whom a word is an oath, yet says, 'By Myself I have sworn,' so that his mind might be established more securely and firmly even than it was before" (On Abraham 273). Elsewhere, he goes into the matter more fully. "But when he tells us that God swore an oath, we must consider whether he lays down that such a thing can with truth be ascribed to God, since to thousands it seems unworthy of Him.... Truly He [God] needs no witness, for there is no other god to be His peer.... Now men have recourse to oaths to win belief, when others deem them untrustworthy; but God is trustworthy in His speech as elsewhere, so that His words in certitude and assurance differ not a whit from oaths. And so it is that while with us the oath gives warrant for our sincerity, it is itself guaranteed by God. For the oath does not make God trustworthy; it is God that assures the oath."

If it be asked why God is represented as binding His word with an oath, Philo's answer is that this is an accommodation to humans—what would be called an anthropomorphism—"a mere crutch for our weakness" (The Sacrifices of Abel and Cain 94-96; cf. also Allegorical Interpretation 3.203-07).

Jesus as prodromos, "forerunner"

V. 20. The author describes Jesus as "forerunner" (prodromos). The Greek term is an old one, with a varied and interesting history. (1) It is used to refer to one who runs forward with headlong speed, one who rushes on. (2) It is used of one who runs before or goes in advance of

---

30. Adams, "Exegesis of Hebrews VI. 1f.," NTS 13 (1967), 378ff.

others. Here a military usage is prominent, denoting horsemen who go ahead of the army, or light troops who serve as guides or scouts. In the ancient Macedonian army there was a special corps known as "forerunners." (3) The term is used in other ways. It might refer to the first green shoot in the spring, or to the first green tree or flower, or to the first green figs. It might be used of a small boat that was a "forerunner" of the fleet. In Alexandria, where the ships of Italy and Rome were heavily loaded with grain, a "forerunner" or guide ship led the grain fleets out of the harbor. (4) The term is used metaphorically in the sense of "precursor." This meaning predominates from New Testament times onward, especially in Christian literature—the Old Testament prophets are described as "forerunners" of Christ, John the Baptist as a "forerunner," the Apostle John as a "forerunner" of the doctrine of the Logos, etc.

The author of Hebrews describes Jesus as "a forerunner on our behalf." He does not say "our forerunner" but "forerunner for us."[31] The thought intended is of Jesus the qualified high priest and His death which made eternal salvation possible (5:8-9). He has preceded His own in suffering, and is there behind the curtain for them. This, in turn, is not far removed from the figure of Jesus as a guide or scout, especially since He is represented as Pioneer (archēgos) in 2:10.

31. TDNT, VIII, 235.

HEBREWS SEVEN

Melchizedek
(7:1-3)

The subject of Christ's priesthood is now taken up again. At the close of the special digression (5:11—6:20), the name of Melchizedek is introduced a second time. It would be a mistake to think that Melchizedek is injected into the Epistle because the author had some strange compulsion to share his pet ideas on the subject. For the author, the question at issue is fundamental! Was Christ in any sense a priest? His conviction is that this cannot be answered apart from reference to Melchizedek. What the author stresses, then, as he proceeds, is the unchanging nature of Christ's priesthood—like Melchizedek's, it lasts *for ever*. The following statements, therefore, should be especially noticed: "he continues a priest for ever" (v. 3); "by one of whom it is testified that he lives" (v. 8); "the power of an indestructible life" (v. 16); "he holds his priesthood permanently, because he continues for ever" (v. 24); "he is able for all time to save ... since he always lives" (v. 25); "a Son who has been made perfect for ever" (v. 28). These central statements in chapter 7 explicate the principle, "Thou art a priest for ever, after the order of Melchizedek" (vv. 17, 21).

Two passages in the Old Testament speak of Melchizedek: Psalm 110:4, first cited in 5:6, and Genesis 14:18-20. Having already applied the former to Jesus, the author now goes back to the reference in Genesis and derives from it all that he wants to say of Melchizedek as a historical person. (See Additional Note.) **For this Melchizedek, king 1 of Salem, priest of the Most High God, met Abraham returning from the slaughter of the kings and blessed him; and to him Abraham appor- 2 tioned a tenth part of everything.** This is only the first part of the sentence which, as originally constructed, extends through verse 3. The main thought of the passage, stripped of its descriptive clauses, is **this Melchizedek . . . continues a priest for ever.** This is introduced with the preposition **for** *(gar),* connecting the beginning of chapter 7 with the close of chapter 6. The whole idea is that Jesus as high priest has entered into heaven and remains there because His priesthood, like Melchizedek's, is eternal.

The meeting of Abraham and Melchizedek, to which the author refers, took place following Abraham's rout of four kings in battle. Melchizedek, another local king who was also **priest of the Most High God,** greeted Abraham and blessed him; and in turn Abraham gave him a tenth part of the spoils of victory. The episode seems rather incidental in the Genesis narrative, but the author views it as a story filled with religious meaning. He goes on to explore it, attaching significance both to what the record says and does not say. He (Melchizedek) **is first, by translation of his name, king of righteousness, and then he is also king of Salem, that is, king of peace.** It is briefly noted that the Hebrew meaning of Melchizedek's name is **righteousness** (literally, "My King is Righteous") and also that Melchizedek was **king of Salem** (which means, **king of peace**). (Many authors identify Salem with Jerusalem, but the author makes no such point.[1]) Clearly, Melchizedek as a priest-king of righteousness and peace typifies the qualities that are characteristic of Messiah's kingdom (cf. Ps. 72:7; Isa. 9:6-7; Jer. 23:5; Rom. 5:1; Eph. 2:14, 15, 17). Already the author has noted the words addressed to the Son, "the righteous scepter is the scepter of thy kingdom" (1:8); and now he also obviously thinks of Messiah as Prince of Peace.

In the Genesis account nothing is said of Melchizedek's ancestry, nothing of his birth or death. Since these details are not supplied, the author finds significance in their absence. Expounding from the silence of Scripture, he says of Melchizedek: **He is without father or mother or genealogy, and has neither beginning of days nor end of life.** Of course, the author does not mean that Melchizedek was some kind of mysterious being who had no part in human history. On the contrary, Melchizedek was a real person. He was **without father or mother** *with respect to his priesthood.* To be a priest in Israel one had to be of the tribe of Levi. Melchizedek plainly did not meet this requirement, yet he was priest of God Most High. Motherless, fatherless, genealogy-

3

---

1. The identification of Salem with Jerusalem goes back as far as Josephus *(Antiquities* 1.10.2) and earlier. In the seventh scroll from Qumran Cave I (the *Genesis Apocryphon* 22, 13) an interpretive translation of Genesis 14 is given, which includes the statement that Abram "came to Salem, that is, Jerusalem." See Joseph A. Fitzmyer, " 'Now This Melchizedek . . .' (Heb. 7, 1)," CBQ 25 (1963), 313; CBQ 22 (1960), 281.

less, still he was a priest. Likewise, in contrast to Aaron, the prototype of Levitical priests, so far as the record goes, his years had no beginning, his life had no end (cf. Ex. 6:20; Num. 20:24-29). He was not of a priestly family, which means that his priesthood was based on personal credentials; and the fact that Scripture nowhere records his birth or death is taken by the author to symbolize a priesthood that is timeless. In these respects Melchizedek was one **resembling the Son of God.** It would be incorrect to say that Christ the Son was made like Melchizedek —and the author is very careful not to say this. Rather he says that Melchizedek was made like the Son of God, who, being eternal, existed before Melchizedek. But the point here concerns priesthood. So far as is recorded, Melchizedek had neither predecessor nor successor in his priestly office. It can be said of Melchizedek, then, that **he continues a priest for ever.** The parallel is striking. As Son of Man and as a historical person (like Melchizedek), Jesus had both a birth and a death; as Son of God, existing from eternity (1:2, 10-12; 9:14), He and His priesthood (like that of Melchizedek) are without beginning and without end.

The Greatness of Melchizedek *(7:4-10)*

It follows, then, that Christ's priesthood is like that of Melchizedek. The next stage of the argument is to establish the greatness of Melchizedek and thus demonstrate the superiority of his priesthood. The argument is fourfold.

1. Melchizedek received tithes from Abraham. **See how great he is,** **4** the command suggesting that there is a lesson here. **Abraham the patriarch gave him a tithe of the spoils.** Even Abraham **the patriarch—** the term is in the emphatic position in the Greek sentence and adds weight to the author's contention. Melchizedek possessed such dignity that even the illustrious Abraham, the head of the Hebrew nation and the greatest of great men, gave him a tenth part of the spoils. **Those** **5** **descendants of Levi who receive the priestly office have a commandment in the law to take tithes from the people, that is, from their brethren, though these also are descended from Abraham.** The Levites received tithes from the people and the priests in turn received "a tithe of the tithe" from the Levites (Num. 18:21-24, 26-28). The significance of Abraham's tithing can be seen when it is remembered that Levitical tithing was based on a legal obligation; tithes had to be paid in compliance with the law. But Abraham's act of tithing was voluntary and spontaneous, a tribute to Melchizedek's personal greatness. Besides, under the law the Levitical priests received support from **their brethren. But this man** (Melchizedek) **who has not their genealogy received tithes** **6**

from Abraham. The point is further enforced that Melchizedek by law had no right or claim to tithes, yet Abraham gave him a tithe. Abraham's action puts the Melchizedek type of priesthood in a different category altogether.

2. Melchizedek also showed himself superior by performing another priestly function: he **blessed him who had the promises.** God had promised to Abraham that all the world would be blessed through him (Gen. 12:3); yet Abraham, from whom so many blessings were passed down, was himself blessed by Melchizedek. Melchizedek, then, was 7 indeed in the honored position, for **It is beyond dispute that the inferior is blessed by the superior.** It is the place of a father to bless his sons (Gen. 27:1-29), a king a nation (2 Sam. 6:18-19), and so forth; so when a meeting took place between these two, Abraham was the lesser and Melchizedek the greater.

3. Melchizedek's priesthood takes precedence over the Levitical 8 priesthood because death has no hold over it. **Here tithes are received by mortal men; there, by one of whom it is testified that he lives.** The contrast is between **here** (referring to the traditional Jewish priesthood) and **there** (meaning the ancient Melchizedek priesthood).[2] In one instance the Levites receive tithes—as dying men who must give way to their successors; in the other, Abraham gave a tithe to one "whom Scripture affirms to be alive" (NEB). Melchizedek as a historical person doubtless died, but the sacred record does not register his death. As far as the record goes, he had no "end of life." From the standpoint of what is actually said in Scripture, Melchizedek lives.[3]

9 4. Melchizedek is greater because Levi paid tithes to him. **One might even say that Levi himself, who receives tithes, paid tithes** 10 **through Abraham, for he was still in the loins of his ancestor when Melchizedek met him.** "One might say" is an expression used by Greek writers to limit a startling statement and guard against misunderstanding. The **loins** refers to the place of generation and reflects Old Testament usage in passages such as Genesis 35:11 ("to come from the loins of"). The argument is rather subtle and the author himself indicates that it is not to be taken literally. Levi was Abraham's great-grandson and was yet unborn when Abraham paid tithes to Melchizedek. Nevertheless, Levi was, so to speak, in Abraham's loins and thus even Levi gave a

---

2. There may be in the words "here" and "there" a hint that the Epistle was written prior to A.D. 70.

3. "The true Priest never dies, and therefore is ever able to save..." (A. B. Bruce, *Hebrews*, p. 261). The implications of this are drawn out later in the chapter (vv. 23-25).

tithe to Melchizedek.[4] By so doing, Levi also (and with him all Levites) acknowledged the authority and superior position of Melchizedek.

The whole argument concerning Abraham and Melchizedek, and especially the reference to Levi, strongly suggest that the original readers of the Epistle had their roots in Judeo-Christian soil; and readers of the Epistle ever since have been struck by this. William Manson asks, "Why should the writer labour points like these unless he were writing to some over whom the official ordinances of Judaism, if not the hierarchy, still cast a spell?"[5]

The Significance of the New Priesthood (7:11-19)

Since Jesus is a priest like Melchizedek, two results follow: (1) the old Levitical priesthood, with its attendant Mosaic legislation, has been put aside; and (2) a new and better hope has been introduced, through which men draw near to God. These points are made explicit in verses 18-19, toward which the whole passage (11-19) moves. Indeed, the latter point, that through Christ men really have access to God, is the central idea of the Epistle. Everywhere, sometimes between the lines and sometimes stated boldly, this thought is present: *only the religion of Christ brings men to God.* This means, in turn, as the author reasons in verses 11-14, that the old Jewish system of worship was powerless and destined for replacement. Otherwise, there would have been no need for a new priestly order. **Now if perfection had been attainable** 11 **through the Levitical priesthood (for under it the people received the law), what further need would there have been for another priest to arise after the order of Melchizedek, rather than one named after the order of Aaron?** By **order** of priesthood, which the author now mentions once again, is meant not the acts or services of the priesthood but the persons serving in it. **If perfection had been attainable through the Levitical priesthood**—but the clear implication is that it was not. **Perfection** refers to a suitable relationship with God (v. 19), and the law was never able to bring that about. It could not adequately deal with sin (10:4; cf. 10:11), much less could it cleanse the conscience of the sinner (9:9).

The author's concept is quite like Paul's in his letter to the Galatians. "If," Paul reasons, "a law had been given which could make

---

4. The Biblical thought, as pointed out by Bruce, is that an ancestor is regarded as containing within himself all his descendants. Compare the references to Jacob and Esau (Gen. 25:23; Mal. 1:2f.; Rom. 9:11ff.), and especially the reference to Adam in Romans 5:12, where "all men sinned" is a way of saying "what happened when Adam sinned" (F. F. Bruce, *Hebrews,* p. 142).

5. William Manson, p. 113.

alive, then righteousness would indeed be by the law" (Gal. 3:21). The law could not give life, Paul says; and he goes on to say that it had a temporal function as a "custodian until Christ came" (Gal. 3:24). This, too, is how the author sees it, although he differs from Paul by drawing his phrases continually from a reservoir of sacerdotal vocabulary. Both agree that the law was only provisional, God having envisioned in ages past the "better things" in Christ.

Something, therefore, had to be done about this imperfect state of affairs; some change had to take place before the way could be open to the divine presence. And that change was revolutionary in character, 12 involving both priesthood and law. **For when there is a change in the priesthood, there is necessarily a change in the law as well.** When the author speaks of an inevitable **change in the law,** he is speaking of the whole Mosaic arrangement conceived of as sacrificial in essence. The law and the Levitical priesthood went together. One was integral to the other because on the basis of the priesthood the law was given. This is the meaning of the parenthetical statement in verse 11 (cf. NEB). Much of the law depended on the sacrificial system and could not operate without it. The priesthood was to the law what a foundation is to a building. Take away the foundation and the superstructure comes down with it. For the author it was axiomatic that if a new priestly order was established, that involved also a change of the old legal superstructure.

To prove his point that there had been in fact a change of priest-hood, from one order to another, the author focuses attention on Jesus' 13 earthly circumstances. **For the one of whom these things are spoken** (in Psalm 110:4) **belonged**[6] **to another tribe, from which no one has ever served at the altar.** Here the author maintains that Jesus was the fulfilment of the psalm. That psalm, the author affirms, has reference to Jesus who, according to physical lineage, could never have served at 14 the Jewish altar.[7] He as Messiah was of another tribe (Isa. 11:1-5; Mic. 5:2; Rev. 5:5), **For it is evident that our Lord was descended from Judah, and in connection with that tribe Moses said nothing about priests.** The facts of Jesus' human ancestry were well known in the

6. It is incorrect to infer from the perfect "belonged" (*meteschēken*) that Jesus in some way still has a share in the tribe of Judah. The perfect tense here is roughly equivalent to the aorist, stating only the fact that Jesus was descended from Judah.

7. In a well-known section of his writings, Josephus states that "no one should hold God's high priesthood except one who is of Aaron's blood," and further "that no one of another lineage, even if he happened to be a king, should attain to the high priesthood" (*Antiquities* 20.10.1). But what otherwise would be a difficulty for the author, he turns to his advantage: "So Jesus is not a Levite. How much better that He is not! Since He is not a Levite, this means that He is not bound to continue in the same old ritual routine."

early church (Rom. 1:3; Mt. 2:1-6), and it was equally well known that nothing was written in the Pentateuch about priests from Judah. Accordingly, if Jesus serves as high priest, two things stand out clearly: (1) He cannot as high priest wait at Jewish altars, for this service was limited to those who were of the tribe of Levi, and therefore, (2) the whole principle of priesthood, and the law itself, necessarily must be changed. And if these things are true, it is also true that the new priesthood is not only of a different order, but that it is of a different realm—heavenly not earthly, spiritual not material, eternal.

In verse 12 the author stated the incontestable fact that a change of priesthood implies a change of law. He now reasons further: **This 15 change becomes even more evident when another priest arises in the likeness of Melchizedek, who has become a priest, not according to a 16 legal requirement concerning bodily descent but by the power of an indestructible life. For it is witnessed of him, "Thou art a priest for 17 ever, after the order of Melchizedek."** The words of the psalm would have no meaning if they referred to the old priesthood. No Levitical priest could be a **priest for ever**—all were mortal. So the Scripture applies to another order of priesthood. The author's language, as he contrasts the priesthoods, is significant. The Levitical priesthood rested on law; the new priesthood is characterized by power. On one hand was a priesthood that was mortal and perishable, having to do with **bodily descent.** No matter what the man's disposition or the degree of his willingness to serve, he became a priest solely because of who his father and mother were. On the other hand, the new priesthood owes its existence to one in whom resides intrinsically "the power of a life that cannot be destroyed" (NEB).[8]

Thus Psalm 110 finds its fulfilment in Jesus; and with the introduction of the new priesthood both negative and positive results follow: **On the one hand, a former commandment is set aside because of its 18 weakness and uselessness (for the law made nothing perfect); on the 19 other hand, a better hope (cf. 6:18-19) is introduced.**[9] The term **set aside** *(athetēsis)*, as Deissmann has shown, was a technical term used in legal documents; the verb means "to declare as void," "to invalidate," "to abrogate," or "to disannul."[10] Here it is the Mosaic law, called the **former commandment,** that is cancelled, as sin is cancelled or made void by

8. The reference is obviously to Christ's triumph over death in resurrection.
9. The Greek word translated "introduced" *(epeisagōgē)* appears only here in the New Testament. In the papyri the verb is used as a technical term in marriage contracts, forbidding a man from "introducing" another woman into his house (Moulton-Milligan, p. 231). The term is used by Josephus *(Antiquities* 11.6.2) in reference to King Artaxerxes' "replacing" his queen Vashti with another wife.
10. Cf. Deissmann, *Bible Studies,* p. 228f.

Christ's sacrifice in 9:26. The fact that it is called a **former command-ment** indicates that at best it was only temporary and provisional. Although it had a distinct function, it could never bring God's purposes to full realization. "The Law brought nothing to perfection" (NEB). It made beginnings, taught basic principles, awakened impulses, fore-shadowed and pointed the way; but it was impossible for it to make available real fellowship with God. For this reason the Mosaic ma-chinery was weak and useless (cf. Rom. 8:3; Gal. 3:21, 23-25). Some-thing better had to be provided, something that was not a "law"—the author seems deliberately to avoid the use of the term—but a **hope,** where men no longer must stand off at a distance but **through which** they could obtain the goal of perfect religion and **draw near to God.** What is expressly stated elsewhere is alluded to here: all Christians are priests and individually have access to God (1 Pet. 2:5, 9; Rev. 1:6; 5:10). "That which was before (in a figure) the privilege of a class has become (in reality) the privilege of all."[11]

The Superiority of the New Priesthood (7:20-28)

20 The author's favorite text on Melchizedek (Ps. 110:4) provides still another argument on the nature of the new priesthood. **And,**[12] **when it was instituted, it was not without an oath.** Jesus' priesthood is perpetual and final, supported by heaven's unchanging oath (cf. 6:13-18). The author wishes it underlined that there is nothing destined beyond Christ's priesthood for the salvation of men because there is nothing better. The thought logically ties in with verse 22, that Jesus is the "surety" of the new covenant. That which intervenes is a kind of

21 parenthesis. **Those who formerly became priests** (meaning, of course, the Levites) **took their office without an oath.** The Aaronic order came into being due to a divine command (Ex. 28:1ff.), yet there was no oath. **But this one** (Jesus) **was addressed with an oath, "The Lord has sworn and will not change his mind, 'Thou art a priest for ever.'"** God does not take oaths lightly; and when God says, "I have sworn and will not change my mind," this means that the new order of priesthood is irrevocable. And if the new priesthood is something concerning which He will never have cause to change His mind, the implication is that in the old there were defects that had to be remedied. "The oracle insinuates that God had found the Levitical institute after trial un-

---

11. Westcott, p. 189.

12. The word "and" introduces an additional thought, as in verses 15 and 23. In these latter verses the RSV omission of "and," on stylistic grounds, somewhat blurs the author's progression of thought.

satisfactory; and as if weary of its law-made officials, and of their daily task of butchery and bloodshed, He swears a solemn oath saying: 'As I live, I will bring this fleshly system to an end.' "[13]

God's solemn oath was all-important; **This** (the oath) **makes Jesus** 22 **the surety of a better covenant.** Every word here is significant, forming the climax (in the Greek text) of the sentence begun in verse 20. **Jesus** stands at the end of the sentence for special effect. The verb used in connection with Jesus, translated **makes** (*gegonen*), is in the perfect tense, with the sense of "has made and is now making." The word **better** is a key word in the Epistle.[14] The idea of **covenant** is introduced but not developed. The author drops a hint of what will come in the next two chapters, and says no more. The term **covenant** stands for an "agreement" or "contract," and as viewed historically in the Old Testament is often used to denote a partnership relation between God and His people. (See Additional Note on 9:15). So the expression **better covenant** indicates not only the ascendancy of the new covenant but its ability to form the ideal partnership between God and man. It does what the former covenant could not do—bring men to God. And the author calls Jesus the **surety** of the better covenant. The word for **surety** is *enguos,* an interesting word that occurs nowhere else in the New Testament. It means the "guarantor" (NEB), the person who might stand good for a debt or the person who in a legal action might give bail for a prisoner.[15] Jesus Himself is the surety of the new covenant. He guarantees the new covenant. He pledges that it will not be abrogated. Just as God gave special assurance to Abraham in swearing an oath by Himself (6:13-18), Jesus stands good for the new covenant and is "blessed assurance" that it will not fall short like the old.[16]

Before rounding off the chapter, the author makes one further point to show the superiority of Christ's priesthood over its predecessor. His approach is along the lines of a contrast between the many and the one. **The former priests were many in number, because they were** 23 **prevented by death from continuing in office; but he holds his priest-** 24 **hood permanently, because he continues for ever.** The Levitical system recognized the importance of having a high priest at all times. But under that system, whose priests were mortal, a long line of succeeding priests was necessarily established. (The total number of high priests

---

13. A. B. Bruce, *Hebrews,* p. 273.

14. See p. 37.

15. See p. 130, n. 25.

16. Later Christ is spoken of as the "mediator" of the new covenant (8:6; 9:15; 12:24). He brought it into being, but here He also guarantees it. Westcott adds, "A surety for the most part pledges himself that something will be: but here the Ascended Christ witnesses that something is: the assurance is not simply of the future but of that which is present though unseen" (p. 191).

from Aaron to the fall of the second temple in A.D. 70, according to Josephus, was eighty-three.[17]) Christ, on the other hand, is one and abides through eternity. His priesthood, therefore, remains for ever. It is "perpetual" (NEB).[18]

25   **Consequently he is able for all time to save those who draw near to God through him, since he always lives to make intercession for them.** These words ascribe the highest measure of saving power to Jesus. He is able to do what the law could not do. He is the One through whom men **draw near** (cf. 4:16, Additional Note) **to God.** He has opened up the new and living way (cf. 10:19-22). His is a great (2:3) and eternal salvation (5:9). Uniquely qualified as priest, He is able to save "to the uttermost" (KJV, ASV), "absolutely" (NEB) or "for all time" (RSV). Differences exist among the translations at this point due to the various interpretations that are placed on the difficult Greek phrase *eis to panteles*. The phrase is found in Luke 13:11, where it is usually taken in the sense of "completely," "wholly." Understood in this way, the meaning here would be that Christ is able to deliver men from sin to the fullest degree possible, that He offers a perfect salvation that could not be gained under the old scheme of things. On the other hand, *eis to panteles* can have a temporal reference, meaning "for all time" or "for ever."[19] This fits well the context of the passage, for the author has been emphasizing all along that Jesus holds His priestly office in perpetuity. He does not offer daily sacrifices (v. 27), but **he always lives** in behalf of men. He lives in God's presence *for the purpose of interceding*—the construction of the Greek clause may be so rendered. "To all eternity He remains the introducer of men to God."[20]

The verb "intercede" *(entunchanō)* has a variety of meanings. It can mean "to light upon," "to fall in with," or "meet with"; "to converse with," "talk to," "appeal to," "petition" or "pray." It is used of lightning that strikes someone, of "meeting with" books and thus "reading" them,

---

17. *Antiquities* 20.10.1. The last of the high priests was "Phanasus" (one of several variant forms of his name). He was appointed by the Zealots in jest and mockery and was, Josephus says, "such a clown that he scarcely knew what the high priesthood meant" *(Jewish War* 4.156). The contrast of this type of high priest, and of the general degeneracy of the priesthood in the first century, with Christ the perfect high priest in the Epistle, is shameful and shocking.

18. The Greek term, *aparabatos*, is rare. Etymologically it refers to that which cannot be "overstepped" or "violated." It generally means "unchangeable," "immutable." Moffatt *(Hebrews,* p. 99) prefers here "non-transferable," but this sense is unattested. See the excellent article in TDNT, V, 742f.; cf. Moulton-Milligan, p. 53.

19. Moulton-Milligan supports the temporal sense, citing from the papyri an example of a man who sells his property "henceforth and forever" *(apo tou nun eis to panteles),* p. 477. Moulton-Milligan goes on to point out how well this sense fits with "always" *(pantote)* in the next clause of the verse.

20. Barclay, *Hebrews,* p. 88.

of visiting someone for a special purpose. It is commonly used in the papyri for "making a petition"; for example, "seeing that night and day I pray to God for you."[21] The term is infrequent in the New Testament and means "to appeal to" (Acts 25:24), "to plead against" (Rom. 11:2), or "to plead for" (Rom. 8:27, 34). In Romans (8:34), as well as in Hebrews, Christ is represented as interceding for His own. This He did while on earth (cf. Lk. 22:32; Jn. 17:6-26); and this He continues to do (entunchanein, present infinitive) in heaven (cf. 1 Jn. 2:1). Even in the heavenly state He lives not for Himself but for others. As priest He stands at the mid-point between God and man, representing strengthless believers at the throne.

In the last few verses of the chapter a summary is given, in which the author stresses his main points and raises new ones to prepare the way for the next stage of his argument. The Melchizedek type is put aside, attention now being given to the character of the true high priest and to the uniqueness of His sacrifice. **For it was fitting** (the same word as in 2:10) **that we should have such a high priest, holy, blameless, 26 unstained, separated from sinners, exalted above the heavens** (cf. 4:14; Eph. 4:10). The attributes listed refer both to Jesus' earthly career and to His heavenly session. As Son He had every right to appear in the presence of God; but in order to justly represent men and be an intermediary whom they could trust, He became incarnate and made the frustrations of earthly beings His own. He proved Himself **holy** toward God and **blameless** and **unstained** in relation to men—free from the slightest taint of imperfection that would have disqualified Him from His office. The law in Leviticus required the high priest to be unblemished in all physical respects (Lev. 21:16ff.), and the law required him to be distinguished above his fellow priests and the people in many other respects as well (Lev. 21:10ff.). In a much deeper sense the Christian high priest is **separated from sinners** and is "raised high above the heavens" (NEB).[22] The two expressions go together. The second denotes his celestial honor and authority, bringing to mind the earlier declaration in the Epistle, "he sat down at the right hand of the Majesty on high" (1:3). The first expression, employing the perfect tense in Greek, describes a fixed condition: Christ was and is separated from sinners. On earth His life, as the author has just said, was without sin; and in His exaltation He was removed from the region of sin, having dealt with sin adequately and finally (1:3; 9:28).

In naming all these traits, the author's language implicitly suggests

21. Moulton-Milligan, p. 219.
22. The author uses the plural "heavens" interchangeably with the singular (9:23, 24), as is often the case in other New Testament writings. In the Old Testament the Hebrew word for heaven is always plural.

a contrast between the moral and ethical perfection of Jesus and the outward purity of the Levitical priests. This contrast is made vivid in
27 the author's next statement: **He (Jesus) has no need, like those high priests, to offer sacrifices daily, first for his own sins and then for those of the people.** The law stipulated that the high priest must first offer a bull for his own sins and for the sins of his family; then he was to offer a goat as a sin offering for the people (Lev. 16:6ff.). This was to be done annually, on the Day of Atonement. But the author speaks of **daily** sacrifices offered by the high priest. In so speaking, it is not likely that he, who knows the Old Testament ritual so well, is inaccurate. He is quite aware of the yearly sacrifice made by the high priest, as is evident from 9:7, 25 and 10:1-3. When he speaks of **daily** sacrifices, then, the author is blending the high priest in with the whole sacrificial system. Josephus relates that on many occasions during the year the high priest involved himself with the other priests as they officiated— on the days of weekly sabbath, of new moon, of national festivals and annual gatherings of all the people.[23] The law instructed the priest that if he committed "sins unwittingly in any of the things which the Lord has commanded not to be done," he was to offer a young, unblemished bull to the Lord for a sin offering (Lev. 4:2-3). This was to be done to prevent guilt from being passed on to the people. Remembering other super-precautions of the Jews to avoid sin, it is probably correct to say that the later high priests *did* make daily offerings, just as the author says. Philo is in agreement, describing the high priest as one who "day by day offers prayers and sacrifices" for the people.[24]

The author especially wants to draw the lines of contrast between the daily sacrifices of Leviticalism and the one-time sacrifice of the Perfect High Priest. Christ, in celestial separation from sin, does not need to go through the routine of the Levitical ministry. He had no sins to atone for; and as for the sins of others, it is of course absurd to think of Him shuttling back and forth from heaven to deal with them. No, **he did this once for all when he offered up himself.** (The words *hapax* and *ephapax*, translated "once" and "once for all," are key terms that appear eleven times in the Epistle.[25]) The offering was presented to God a perfect offering—by its nature nonrepeatable, once for all time, something for the universe to see and pronounce as eternally satisfactory.

A final statement of contrast and summary brings the chapter to a
28 close. **Indeed, the law appoints men in their weakness as high priests,**

---

23. *Jewish War* 5.231.
24. *Special Laws* 3.131.
25. For *hapax* ("once"), see 6:4; 9:7, 26, 27, 28; 10:2; 12:26, 27. For *ephapax* ("once for all"), see 9:12; 10:10.

but the word of the oath, which came later than the law, appoints a Son as High Priest who has been made perfect for ever. Under the law men were appointed priests in weakness; as human beings, with all the limitations of men, they were "beset with weakness" (5:2). For them death was inevitable. But the Son, consecrated with an oath (Ps. 110:4) that came after the law, knows no human weakness. He has been made perfect for ever. This means that God has qualified the Son to come before Him in priestly action, and He has done this on the basis of the Son's suffering (2:10) and because of the Son's obedience (5:8-9). The Son, therefore, is the Perfect High Priest, His perfection being crowned and sealed by His exaltation to heaven. He is the only high priest capable of qualifying others that they, too, might come directly before God (7:19; 10:14).

Thus the author terminates his discussion of the order of Christ's priesthood. More indeed is to be said about Christ as high priest, but nothing more of Melchizedek. The author's proposition is proved. Although Jesus was descended from a tribe in connection with which nothing is said about priests (v. 13), He nevertheless is a priest. A new order of priesthood has arisen (v. 15), the Melchizedek type that replaces the old Aaronic order. Christ is priest like Melchizedek. He is priest "for ever," priest "for all time." Here at last is the *ideal* of priesthood. It is a priesthood based on personal greatness and not on legal requirements (v. 16). It is a priesthood that death cannot touch (v. 17). It is a priesthood that brings new hope, opening wide the doors of access to God (v. 19). It is a priesthood that never changes, and so Christ is always in God's presence to make intercession for man (v. 25). One word from Him is enough, or one look—just His being there—the very kind of high priest that humans require. Besides, as priest He is altogether pure and separated from sinners (v. 26); and what is more, He did not shrink from personal involvement and sacrifice. "He offered up Himself."

This grand thought is stated in verse 27 for the first time. Once struck, as someone has remarked, the note sounds on louder and louder. Later on, it is the thought that predominates: Christ as priest had something to offer—*Himself*. So by the time the author concludes his discussion on priesthood, he will have established two incontrovertible points: *Jesus the perfect high priest and Jesus the perfect sacrifice.*

Additional Notes

Melchizedek

V. 1. In addition to the passages in Hebrews, only two passages in the Old Testament mention Melchizedek. In the first (Gen. 14:18-20) the paths of Abraham and Melchizedek briefly cross in the King's Valley, when Melchizedek blesses Abraham and Abraham gives a tithe to the Canaanite who is both king and priest. In the second passage Melchizedek reappears after a long interval of silence in the sacred writings. In a few emphatic words it is divinely affirmed of a Davidic king, "You are a priest for ever after the order of Melchizedek" (Ps. 110:4). The background of this affirmation seems to be that David and his royal descendants, by conquest of Jerusalem, had become heirs of the priest-king prerogatives held by Melchizedek.

Coming out of the dim past, and because so little is known of him, Melchizedek has over the centuries been surrounded by an aura of mystery and awe. Conjectures have been abundant. In the rabbinic writings the prevalent opinion is that Melchizedek was the patriarch Shem, who survived the Deluge and outlived Abraham forty years. According to Jerome, this was the view of the Jews in his time; and it has been the view, more recently, of such men as Luther and Melanchthon. Others, similarly, have conjectured that Melchizedek was one of the other patriarchs: Ham, or a descendant of Japheth, or Job, or even Enoch reappearing on earth.

Both Philo and Josephus regard Melchizedek as a historical person. Josephus matter-of-factly relates the Genesis story, that Melchizedek hospitably received Abraham's men, blessed God for having delivered Abraham from his enemies, and received tithes from Abraham (*Antiquities* 1.10.2). Elsewhere Josephus describes Melchizedek as a "Canaanite chief," whose name means "Righteous King," who founded the city of Jerusalem, built a temple there, and officiated as "priest of God" (*Jewish War* 6.438). Philo, in contrast, resorts to allegory. He speaks of Abraham's gifts to Melchizedek and goes on to allegorize, explaining that "a tenth from all" means "from the things of sense, right use of sense; from the things of speech, good speaking; from the things of thought, good thinking" (*Preliminary Studies* 99). Melchizedek himself is compared with a king of peace (since Salem equals peace) who uses persuasion and gives directions by which one might travel life's voyage successfully (*Allegorical Interpretation* 3.78ff.).

It should be noticed that in all of this the Melchizedek in Hebrews has nothing in common with Philo's Melchizedek, except that both Philo and Hebrews make Melchizedek "king of peace" and interpret his name to mean "righteous king." In Hebrews Melchizedek is a type, not an allegory. The essential difference between the two presentations is that in Hebrews there are type and antitype, with a real, historical correspondence between them; in Philo there is allegory, and the application of this allegory depends largely on the fancy of the individual interpreter.

A few other conjectures may be briefly mentioned. Origen, followed by Didymus, thought that Melchizedek was an angel. In the early centuries of the church a number of orthodox Christians maintained that Melchizedek was none other than Christ in the flesh. But how, it was asked, could the incarnate Christ be made like Himself (7:3)? To avoid this difficulty, Hieracas, in Egypt, asserted that Melchizedek was the Holy Spirit, or at least in some sense a manifestation of the Spirit. About this time (the third century) a sect of the so-called Melchizedekians arose. Melchizedek, they affirmed, was not a man but a heavenly being, whose priesthood was superior to that of Christ. Christ's priesthood, they said, was only a copy of Melchizedek's, which was the original order. They, therefore, made their offerings "in the name of Melchizedek."

Of interest also are the later Jewish speculations that tie Melchizedek in with the archangel Michael. From one of the documents of the Dead Sea Scrolls (11Q Melchizedek) has come similar information, where Melchizedek is represented as having functions very much like those of Michael. Melchizedek is God's servant *par excellence,* who, with the aid of other angels, "executes the judgments of God against Belial and his spirits."[26]

It remains to be emphasized that the author of Hebrews does not engage in nonsensical conjectures about Melchizedek. He looks at his Old Testament with serious eyes and sees in it a real, human person. He sees in Melchizedek the union of the kingly and priestly offices, which was not only familiar in patriarchal times but was the ancient ideal. The connection between Melchizedek and Christ as type and antitype in the Epistle consists of the following points. Each was a priest (1) not based on physical descent—neither was of the tribe of Levi; (2) superior to Abraham; (3) whose beginning and end are without limits; (4) who was not only a priest, but also a king of righteousness and peace. The ancient ideal of priest-king, so long absent in Judaism, is seen as now restored in Christ.

"Without father..."

V. 3. "Without father or mother or genealogy." The Greeks and Romans used such language to describe the gods, or with reference to an orphan or illegitimate child. The older commentators, such as Chrysos-

---

26. M. de Jonge and A. S. Van Der Woude, "11Q Melchizedek and the New Testament," NTS 12 (1966), 301-26; cf. Joseph A. Fitzmyer, "Further Light on Melchizedek from Qumran Cave 11," JBL 86 (1967), 25-41. For a summary of views on Melchizedek, see O. Cullmann, *The Christology of the New Testament,* trans. Shirley C. Guthrie and Charles A. M. Hall (Philadelphia, 1959), p. 83ff. For recent studies on Melchizedek, see I. Hunt, "Recent Melkizedek Study," *The Bible in Current Catholic Thought,* ed. J. L. McKenzie (New York, 1962), pp. 21-33. For an extensive bibliography on the subject, see Spicq, II, p. 213f. See also TDNT, VI, 568-71.

tom, Oecumenius, and Theophylact, applied these terms to Melchizedek only secondarily. They explain that "without father" really refers to Christ with reference to His humanity, and "without mother" to Christ with reference to His divinity. But although it could be said that Jesus was "without father" in terms of His physical existence, it could not be said, literally, that He was "without genealogy." The author clearly is speaking of Melchizedek and of his qualifications as priest apart from credentials of ancestry.

Paramenein, "to continue in office"

V. 23. The KJV here reads: "And they truly were many priests, because they were not suffered to continue by reason of death...." The ASV reads similarly: "And they indeed have been made priests many in number, because that by death they are hindered from continuing...." "Continue" and "continuing" are renderings of the Greek infinitive *paramenein*.

Paramenein literally means "to stay beside," "to stand by" or "near." It is a term often used of slaves who stayed by their masters in faithful service. A common name for a slave was *Parmenōn*—"Trusty," a man who could be depended on for good service. *Paramenein*, therefore, came to be "a common euphemism for *serve*."[27]

This explains why the RSV and NEB render *paramenein* not simply as "continue" but as "continue in office." And even this could be improved, for the full thought is that Christ "continues to serve in His office" as high priest. Compare Philippians 1:25 and James 1:25, where the same verb *paramenein* is employed. Paul's desire is to "continue to serve" the Philippians. James, when he speaks of a man "who looks into the perfect law, the law of liberty, and perseveres [*parameinas*]," is describing a man who "continues to do" or "serve in" the law.

---

27. Moulton-Milligan, p. 487.

HEBREWS EIGHT

A Ministry in a Better Realm
(8:1-5)

Chapter 7 brings to a close part one (4:14–7:28) of the author's discussion of Christ as high priest. Jesus is a priest chosen and appointed by God and His priesthood is in no sense due to tribal descent. Part two on the new priesthood begins in earnest at 9:1. In this the main subject is the self-offering of Christ, with its enduring consequences. Other ideas, such as covenant and sanctuary, move in and out the discussion; for it is axiomatic with the author that no grasp of the significance of Jesus' offering is possible apart from a right understanding of covenant and sanctuary.

Chapter 8 is both a chapter of transition and a beginning of part two on the high priest. Broadly, chapters 5–7 offer a discussion of the personnel of the priesthood, chapters 9–10:18, the service of the priesthood, with chapter 8 acting as a bridge between them. Attention is now turned to the true sanctuary, which provides the author with an additional argument on the transcendent character of Jesus' role as priest. **Now the point in what we are saying is this.** These introductory words 1 can be taken variously. The margin of the American Standard Version reads: "Now to sum up what we are saying. . . ." This rendering is possible, though there is the difficulty that verse 1ff. is not a summary statement. The Revised Standard and New English Bible take the author as referring to the "main point" of what he is attempting to get across. (See Additional Note.) **We have such a high priest, one who is seated at the right hand of the throne of the Majesty in heaven** (cf. 1:3; 12:2). The author's **point** is that Jesus, having accomplished His work of sacrifice, is now enthroned in heaven, next to God Himself. He is

High Priest and His sitting suggests His kingly state: He sits royally in contrast to those sacerdotal drudges of the old system who stood offering their daily, ineffectual sacrifices (10:11). He sat down and is **2 a minister in the sanctuary and the true tent which is set up not by man but by the Lord.** The term for **minister** *(leitourgos)* is rare in the New Testament. Only here is it connected with Christ (elsewhere to the angels, 1:7), although in 8:6 the related word "ministry" *(leitourgia)* does refer to Christ's ministry. Lying behind New Testament usage is a long history of the term's being applied to anyone who served in public office at his own expense or who in any capacity did work for the state. The term later came to denote any type of ministry or service, including those with religious connotations. Here the author uses **minister** as the equivalent of "priest," as in Isaiah 61:6: "But you shall be called the priests of the Lord, men shall speak of you as the ministers of our God." He means that Christ is "the priest of the sanctuary." The **sanctuary** refers to heaven itself. It is called **true** because it is "real" and "eternal."[1] "This 'real sanctuary' belongs to the same order of being as the saints' everlasting rest of Chs. 3 and 4, the better country and well-founded city of Ch. 11:10, 16, the unshakable kingdom of Ch. 12:28."[2] The heavenly tent, where Christ ministers, has nothing to do with temporary, shadowy things. His ministry, then, is a superior ministry because it is done in a superior place.

The function of a high priest is to deal with men's sins by means of the required sacrifices. This has already been stated (5:1) and is now **3** restated by the author. **For every high priest is appointed to offer gifts and sacrifices.** This, of course, would include Jesus, since He, too, is a priest, belonging to a superior order. **Hence it is necessary for this priest also to have something to offer.** What that **something** is the author does not explain now. He writes as though he wishes his readers to ponder the question for a while, although he has already indicated the answer earlier (7:27) and will explain it more fully later on (9:14ff.). The important thing is that his readers remember that Christ had to make an offering, and that this offering has indeed taken place. (Jesus' death, to be sure, occurred on earth, but in the language of the Epistle His offering belongs to heaven and thus is of eternal significance.) The

1. The author's term, *alēthinos*, is perhaps best expressed by the two English words "real" and "eternal." *Alēthinos* is usually taken here to mean "real," "authentic," "genuine"; but the term seems to have a deeper sense, standing for that which truly is or that which is eternal. In John, *alēthinos* often means "true" in the sense of that which is "divine," as opposed to human and earthly reality, "divine" in the sense of "containing" or "dispensing revelation" (Jn. 1:9; etc.). See TDNT, I, 250.
2. F. F. Bruce, *Hebrews,* p. 163.

thought clearly is not that Jesus is still making His offering.³ In heaven He continues to intercede for men; He does not continue to offer "gifts and sacrifices."

Furthermore, the author reasons, Christ as high priest must minister in heaven, for **if he were on earth, he would not be a priest at all, since there are priests who offer gifts according to the law.** He could not be a priest on earth (or high priest) because that office was already occupied by the descendants of Levi. None but Levites could be priests (Num. 18:1-7). But Christ was of another tribe (7:13-14). As long as He was on earth, He could render no priestly service at all.

On earth Jesus was, so to speak, a layman. That, however, in the view of the author, serves only to emphasize the dignity of His heavenly priesthood. **They** (meaning specifically the earthly priests and by extension the earthly tabernacle) **serve a copy and shadow of the heavenly sanctuary.** In general terms it can be said that the author is speaking of two worlds. One world is the world of heaven, the only ultimately real world, made real because God is there. The other is the world of earth—vague, shadowy, and unreal. But the contrast of worlds is not conceived metaphysically. It is not essentially a contrast of reality and appearance. Rather it is a contrast that is viewed *temporally.*⁴ It is a contrast of type and antitype, a contrast of things in one age foreshadowing things of another. This is evident from the terms **copy** and **shadow,** which are to be taken together in the sense of "a shadowy outline."⁵ And of what are these a shadowy outline? Not heaven as ultimate reality, but **the heavenly sanctuary** (*epouraniōn,* literally, "the heavenly things"), the realm where Christ ministers. In 10:1 the author describes the law as "a shadow of the good things to come instead of the true form of these realities." In Colossians 2:17 Paul speaks of certain practices of the Jewish law as "no more than a shadow of what was to come" and adds that "the solid reality is Christ's" (NEB). The author speaks similarly here.

This dual-world language applies to and shows the difference between the old and new arrangements of worship. The old arrangement,

3. The tense of "to offer" (*prosenenkē*) is the aorist, pointing to a single sacrifice. The Phillips translation here is unfortunate: ". . . in these holy places this man has something that he is offering." The alternative rendering of the NEB obviates misunderstanding: "this one too must have had something to offer."

4. "The contrast which the Author of Hebrews has attempted to describe is not simply one between an earthly copy and a heavenly Reality. It is between an historical situation in the past and one which succeeded it *in time*" (R. Williamson, "Platonism and Hebrews," SJT 16 (1963), 419).

5. This is Moffatt's expression (p. 105), taking the two terms (*hupodeigma* and *skia*) as hendiadys. The word *hupodeigma* basically refers to an "example," "model," or "pattern"; by extension it can refer to a "copy" or "representation." The word *skia* means "shade" or "shadow," and by extension a "foreshadow."

being no more than a dim and imperfect outline, assured the existence of a more perfect form. Thus it was necessary, long ago, for special care to be taken in the construction of the tabernacle; **for when Moses was about to erect the tent, he was instructed by God, saying, "See that you make everything according to the pattern which was shown you on the mountain."** The quotation is from Exodus 25:40 (cf. Ex. 25:9; 26:30; 27:8; Num. 8:4; Acts 7:44), with the addition of the word **everything**—a form of the Old Testament citation found also in Philo.

Here, as throughout the Epistle, the author sketches his scenes by reference to the desert tabernacle instead of the temple in Jerusalem. He writes with a passion for the *ancient* order of things: the tabernacle, with its construction and furnishings, the priesthood, with its duties and requirements of membership, the law and its regulations for worship. Always he reverts to the foundations of Mosaism; for he believes that at their best, from their very inception, they fall painfully short of what true religion ought to be. He directs attention, then, to the building of the first tabernacle, not to a later temple. For while Solomon's temple was constructed according to the divine plan (1 Chron. 28:19), even so it was in essentials no more than a duplicate of the original erected under the careful eye of Moses. In this light, it seems equivocal to argue that the author of Hebrews has only a "book knowledge" of Judaism. That he characteristically goes to the Pentateuch for his presentation of the old religion is beside the question. Where else would he go to discuss the *Levitical* ritual? And what else would he consult to treat typically such important persons as Moses and Aaron?

One cannot infer, therefore, on the basis of the author's resorting to the desert tabernacle, that he had only a literary acquaintance with Judaism and that he knew nothing of—probably had never seen—the Herodian temple in Jerusalem. From this standpoint, nothing can really be decided about the race or geographical provenance of the author.

The building of the tabernacle in **everything** was according to the God-given **pattern.** It was to be modeled or patterned after the heavenly sanctuary. The word for **pattern** (*tupos*) means "a blow"; then, "the effect of a blow," as with an impression of a seal or a stamp made on a coin. It might also refer to an engraving, a carved figure or image, a general impression, a sketch or outline, a rough draft of a book, and so forth. A *tupos* was also a prescribed form to be imitated, an exact replica —children were called the *tupoi* of their parents. The pattern of the tabernacle given to Moses at Sinai might have been something visible to the eye, for the clause in the Hebrew text of Exodus 25:40 literally means "which you are caused to see." Perhaps Moses was allowed to see a copy of the pre-existing heavenly original; perhaps he saw something like a scale model of the sanctuary; or perhaps he saw in the sense of being able to conceive the pattern. This, accompanied by the necessary verbal directions, constituted the divine instructions[6] communicated to Moses.

A Ministry of a Better Covenant
(8:6-13)

The high-priestly ministry of Jesus is a superior ministry because it takes place in the heavenly realm. This is the gist of what is said in the opening verses of the chapter. Now the author adds another argument on the greatness of Jesus' ministry: it is superior because accompanying it is the new covenant which Jesus Himself mediates. **But as it** 6 **is** (the new high priest not being on earth), **Christ has obtained a ministry which is as much more excellent than the old as the new covenant he mediates is better.** Wherever the author mentions Jesus and compares Him with others, He is always associated with the **better** things. (The terms "better" and "eternal" go together in the Epistle, terms that in themselves furnish an apologetic for the absoluteness of the Christian religion.[7]) The thought is much like that of 7:22. There Jesus is presented as "the surety of a better covenant," here He is the Mediator of the better covenant.

The readers of the Epistle were quite familiar with the term "mediator" (mesitēs). It is a word that was used in daily commerce, for often someone had to function as an "arbitrator" of business transactions. He was one who stood in the middle, mesitēs being derived from mesos, meaning "in the middle." He had to be able to stand on neutral ground and as a go-betwen bring the two contracting parties together. In the old covenant the person who performed this service was Moses, as is implied in Galatians 3:19. In the new covenant Jesus is Mediator and far transcends Moses (cf. 9:19; 12:21). He serves both as Guarantor (7:22) and Mediator (cf. 9:15; 12:24). He stands in the middle between God and man, the ideal representative for both parties; and by His presence He not only mediates the new covenant but pledges the fulfilment of it.

Christ Jesus, then, is the One who has negotiated the new covenant.

---

6. The verb used for "instructed" is chrēmatizō. It is used especially for divine warnings or revelations (11:7; Mt. 2:12, 22; Acts 10:22; etc.). Of particular interest here is Josephus' use of the term in connection with Moses. He relates that Moses did not continue to go up to Sinai to receive communication from God, but rather "entered the tabernacle and there received responses (echrēmatizeto) to all that he asked from God" (Antiquities 3.8.8).

In other NT passages chrēmatizō means "to bear a name" or "be called" (Acts 11:26; Rom. 7:3). Moulton-Howard-Turner (II, p. 265) argues that these are two entirely distinct words, the one derived from chrēsmos ("oracle"), the other from chrēma ("business").

7. See Introduction, p. 37.

And the new covenant is superior to the old precisely because, the author says, **it is enacted on better promises.** That is, the new covenant, no less than the old one, was enacted ("legally secured," NEB) by divine authority. The language is juridical, appropriate to covenants. What the **better promises** in the new covenant are the author proceeds to explain (vv. 10-12).

The very existence of a new covenant argues the failure of the old.
7 **For if that first covenant had been faultless, there would have been no occasion for a second.** The old law in itself was, as Paul states, "holy and just and good" (Rom. 7:12). But it was weak and useless (7:18), not able to accomplish the purpose of true religion. It could not bring men into permanent fellowship with God.

At its best, the old covenant was a temporary expedient that sooner or later had to give way to something better. This was obvious even in the time of the prophet Jeremiah. In the sixth century B.C., Jeremiah saw that the nation of Judah was destined to fall to the Babylonians. Judah had sinned, it had broken its long-existent covenant with God, and God would allow its enemies to overrun it. But this would not be the end. "There is hope for your future, says the Lord, and your children shall come back to their own country" (Jer. 31:17). The old covenant would be no more, but God would make a new covenant with His people.

This is what Jeremiah envisioned in the long ages past, and the author of the Epistle seizes on the deep tones of that oracle. Even in Old Testament times, a change of the old order of things was contem-
8 plated. **For he finds fault with them when he says: "The days will come, says the Lord, when I will establish a new covenant with the house of Israel and with the house of Judah."** The quotation, which here fills up five verses, is from Jeremiah 31:31ff. and is cited at length to prove the superiority of the new covenant and its provisions. The author, in characteristic fashion, stresses that the oracle is divine. It is God who is represented as speaking, it is God who finds fault with His people. Both the covenant, since it could not perfect religious fellowship, and the people of the covenant, who were stiff-necked in their disobedience, were at fault. An entirely different kind of covenant was
9 needed—**not like the covenant,** God says, **that I made with their fathers on the day when I took them by the hand to lead them out of Egypt.** The new covenant was not to be the same thing warmed over, a reiteration of impotence and futility. The former covenant had failed. The entire history of the Old Testament can be summed up as the perpetual failure of Israel to live up to the terms agreed upon in the covenant. God was willing. And He was fully able to keep His part of the bargain, as shown by His deliverance of Israel from the Egyptian

slave pens. But "they did not continue in my covenant, and so I paid no heed to them, says the Lord."

The oracle continues, "This is the covenant that I will make with the house of Israel after those days, says the Lord." The new covenant is to be with the house of Israel and with the house of Judah (v. 8), that is, with the new people of God among whom the distinction between Israel and Judah no longer held. The covenant God had in mind, as the continued quotation shows, contains three special blessings and improvements over the first covenant. **10**

1. The new covenant is inward and spiritual. "I will put my laws into their minds, and write them on their hearts, and I will be their God, and they shall be my people." When God made a covenant with Israel at Sinai, He promised them that they would be His special people. "If you will obey my voice and keep my covenant, you shall be my own possession among all peoples; for all the earth is mine, and you shall be to me a kingdom of priests and a holy nation" (Ex. 19:5-6; cf. Ex. 6:7). To the same people He later said, "I will walk among you, and will be your God, and you shall be my people" (Lev. 26:12). Yet that covenant, based on mere externals, lacked spiritual power and depth. Written on tables of stone, it could not affect the inner man where the covenant feelings of loyalty and love must arise. To guarantee that allegiance, God would have to set His laws in the minds of His people and inscribe them on their hearts.

2. The new covenant is a covenant that is both individual and universal. "And they shall not teach every one his fellow or every one his brother, saying, 'Know the Lord,' for all shall know me, from the least of them to the greatest." This statement of promise logically follows the previous one. God's laws in the new era are to be received within, and this implies a personal and individual knowledge of God. In the new covenant all were to be "taught by the Lord" (Isa. 54:13; Jn. 6:44-45). As God would write His laws on men's hearts, so God Himself would be the teacher of His people. Under the old covenant all people did not know God's law. No one but the trained expert, the scribe or the priest, could know the endless minutiae of regulations concerning offerings and sacrifices.[8] But in the new covenant the knowledge of **11**

---

8. "Exact knowledge of God was at once necessary and difficult. It was so difficult, that the rise of a class like the scribes, whose business it was to interpret the law, became inevitable; it was so necessary, that a man could not be legally righteous without a minute acquaintance with the contents of the statute book.... This it was which made the legal yoke grievous. It was not enough to be a good man; you must likewise, as touching the positive precepts of the law, be blameless. And it was so difficult to be ritually blameless, that one might know God essentially very well, even as a prophet knew Him, and yet be in Divine things an *ignoramus*, from the point of view of the priestly code. For this incongruous state of matters abrogation was the only remedy" (A. B. Bruce, *Hebrews*, p. 301).

divine matters would not be the private possession of a particular class. No longer would there be distinction between layman and priest. The knowledge of God would be accessible to all alike—to the poor as well as to the rich, to both the unlearned and the learned, to the least and to the greatest.

3. The new covenant is a covenant that makes gracious provision
12 for sin. **"For I will be merciful toward their iniquities, and I will re-member their sins no more."** The **for** is important, showing that forgive-ness of sins is the basis of the blessings previously mentioned. Indeed, forgiveness of sins, as the author later emphasizes, is the very heart of the new covenant (10:16-18); for real forgiveness was, above all, what the first covenant lacked (9:9; 10:1-2; 10:11). It was able to deal with certain ritual offenses, but how could it effect purity of heart and life? The old system, in effect, separated religion from life. A man could be right in ceremony and wrong in heart, or right in heart and wrong in ceremony. Such artificiality! And such superfluity in dealing with sin! In the new covenant, instead of "a reminder of sin year after year" (10:3), God remembers sin "no more at all" (10:17, NEB). Because of Christ's once-for-all sacrifice (7:27), God's forgiveness is final.

But in the author's view, the prophecy of Jeremiah involved even more. It was for him the total proof from Scripture that time had run
13 out on the Sinaitic covenant. **In speaking of a new covenant he treats the first as obsolete. And what is becoming obsolete and growing old is ready to vanish away. A new covenant** implies, of course, that God regards the former as old. (The word **first** forms an inclusion with the word "first" in verse 7; **first** is also a hook word with 9:1.) With the speaking of the word **new,** in Jeremiah's time, the warning was given that the Mosaic law and Levitical priesthood were about to cease their work. And if they were obsolete in Jeremiah's time, how much more so at the time the author writes. (Nothing can be deduced here as to whether the temple was still standing when the author wrote. Not the destruction of Jerusalem but the inauguration of the new covenant spelled the end to the old.) All those past years, little by little—inevitably—the legal system was decaying and was destined to pass from view. Here the author does not pause to explain the precise point *when* the old covenant disappeared, but he leaves it to be inferred from what he has previously said (1:2; 7:18-22; 8:6-7) and from the theme of the Epistle as a whole.

Chapter 8 is a continuation of the author's treatise on Jesus' priest-hood. All of what has been said before on this subject can be sum-marized in one chief point: Jesus as high priest in the new age performs His service in the real, heavenly sanctuary. No shadows here, no scenes of crude sacrificial rites. They pertained to the old sanctuary, a sanctuary of boards and stones and animal skins. A sanctuary is a real sanctuary only if God is there. And that is precisely what makes the heavenly sanctuary, where Christ ministers, the real one. From this it follows that Christ's priestly service, performed in the presence of God, outranks that of His predecessors. His service belongs by nature to the eternal order. As He Himself is eternal, His place is rightfully in heaven and there He perpetually ministers.

Proportionate to Jesus' greater ministry is the superiority of the new covenant. That superiority is clearly seen when the two covenants, the new and the old, are placed side by side. The old covenant was at fault because it could not bring men close to God; and this, along with sin on Israel's part, destined its abolition. A new covenant, new in quality or kind, would have to be made, even as the prophet Jeremiah foretold. And this new covenant would be a better covenant because it would afford its adherents better promises. The new covenant would be written on the heart, establish a full and universal knowledge of God, and remove forever the burden and guilt of sin.

Additional Notes

Kephalaion, "the point"

V. 1. In the KJV the opening statement of the chapter reads: "Now of the things which we have spoken *this is* the sum. . . ." The translation is inexact, making the clause point back to what has been said, although the tense of the participle *(legomenois)* is present and should be translated "what we are saying." This use of the present participle would seem to argue that *kephalaion* (literally, "belonging to the head") has reference to the "chief point" that is being made. William Manson, following A. B. Bruce and others, prefers to translate *kephalaion* as "the crown" of the argument.[9] This has the advantage of throwing the emphasis forward, which fits the context well. Nairne translates: "Here is the climax of the argument."[10]

Mesitēs, "mediator"

V. 6. Here for the first time the author applies the word "mediator" *(mesitēs)* to Christ. Earlier, in 6:17, he used the verb *mesiteuō* with reference to God's having "interposed" or "guaranteed" His word with an oath. Later, he speaks again of Christ as "mediator" (9:15; 12:24); and it is significant that in all three passages in the Epistle, "mediator" is connected with "covenant." Paul uses the word "mediator" *(mesitēs)*

9. William Manson, p. 123.
10. Nairne, *Epistle to Hebrews,* p. 80.

twice: to refer to Moses the mediator of the old covenant (Gal. 3:19), and to Christ, the "one mediator between God and men" (1 Tim. 2:5).

The term *mesitēs* is derived from *mesos,* which means "middle" or "in the middle." In ancient times the *mesitēs* might have many functions. He might serve as an "umpire," as a "negotiator" to secure peace between two feuding parties, as an "arbiter" in legal transactions, as a "witness" or "guarantor" of the execution of an agreement, as a "guarantor" who would provide bail with his own funds for someone else, and so forth.[11]

The author of Hebrews draws attention to Christ as Mediator in order to show His supremacy over Moses. Yet the theme of Christ as Mediator of the new covenant fits in well with his overall presentation of Christ as priest and of the adequacy of His one-time sacrifice. And as Moffatt remarks,[12] he deliberately ignores the common beliefs of his time in numerous angels as mediators, of the intercession of departed saints on behalf of men on earth, and the like. For the author, and for Paul, there is only one mediator.

---

11. See TDNT, IV, 598ff.; Barclay, *A New Testament Wordbook,* p. 85ff.
12. Moffatt, *Hebrews,* p. xxxix.

HEBREWS NINE

The Tabernacle
(9:1-5)

The author now calls the attention of his readers to the arrangements for worship under the old covenant. He describes the tabernacle and its furnishings for one main reason: to show the inadequacy and ineffectiveness of its services. The term "covenant" implies a right relationship between God and His people. But what the author seeks to establish, by giving a detailed list of costly articles in the tabernacle, is that even all these could not offer man this right relationship. On the contrary, he sees in these arrangements barriers to fellowship between God and man, hindrances that symbolize a complete breakdown of covenant relationship. In the final analysis, then, worship in the old regime was an exercise in futility—a conclusion which when reached causes the author to push ahead in succeeding lines to the uniqueness and finality of Christ's sacrifice.

Now even the first covenant had (past tense, since the new covenant 1 has arrived) **regulations for worship and an earthly sanctuary.** The statement connects with the previous chapter. There the author had spoken of the two covenants; and now he speaks of the first covenant, of its sanctuary and service. (The word for **covenant** does not appear in the original text but has been interpolated by the translators, as the sense demands.) The **sanctuary** refers to the tabernacle as a whole, with its two separate compartments. Under the old system there were indeed divinely appointed procedures for worship, but that worship was done in a place that was earthly and material and physical. The term used here is *kosmikos*, "belonging to the world," in contrast to the heavenly sanctuary not made with hands (vv. 11, 24).

163

There follows an inventory of the furnishings in the two chambers of the tabernacle. An inventory of the furniture—how fatiguing to the modern mind! But the author's description shows that even such costly furnishings, the very best that could be, were still "of this world" and **2** destined to vanish away. **For a tent was prepared, the outer one, in which were the lampstand and the table and the bread of the Presence; it is called the Holy Place.** The author's information concerning the tabernacle is drawn chiefly from Exodus 25—26. In the preparation of the material sanctuary nothing was done in a slipshod manner; for God had cautioned, "See that you make everything according to the pattern" (8:5). The outer division of the tabernacle, entered from the east, was twice the size of the inner; and since the two compartments were separated by a curtain, the author speaks of them as two distinct tents. Inside the tent-sanctuary the only source of light was **the lampstand,**[1] which was placed next to the south wall. It was a golden lampstand with seven arms; its lamps were never allowed to go out. Opposite the lampstand, on the north wall of the outer tent, stood **the table** with its **bread of the Presence.** Known also as "showbread," it was the bread that was to be set continually before the Divine Presence. There were twelve loaves in all, one for each tribe, which were arranged in two rows of six. Fresh loaves were brought each sabbath into the sanctuary, and there the old loaves were eaten by the priests (Lev. 24:5-9). The table itself was made of acacia wood plated with gold. Only into the Holy Place were the priests allowed to enter; they were excluded from going into the inner shrine.

The author proceeds to describe the most sacred part of the **3** tabernacle. **Behind the second curtain** (so called to distinguish it from the curtain at the entrance) **stood a tent called the Holy of Holies. Holy of Holies** is a literal translation of the Hebrew expression which means "Holiest" or "Most Holy." The inner room is pictured as having **4** two items of furniture, **the golden altar of incense and the ark of the covenant.** There has been considerable disagreement among interpreters concerning the meaning of the Greek term *thumiatērion.* It is here translated **altar of incense,** which is its most probable meaning in this passage; but older versions understood it as designating the golden censer that was used by the high priest on the Day of Atonement (Lev. 16:12). (See Additional Note.)

On mentioning the **ark of the covenant,** the author pauses to describe it in some detail. It was a chest made of acacia wood, about four feet long by almost two and a half feet high and wide (Ex. 25:10ff.).

---

1. "Lampstand" is correct, not "candlestick." In all cases, in both Old Testament and New Testament, the rendering should be "lamp" and "lampstand."

It was covered on all sides with gold and it contained a golden urn holding the manna, and Aaron's rod that budded, and the tables of the covenant. Tables of the covenant, of course, refer to the Ten Commandments, which were divinely dictated to Moses and placed in the ark (Ex. 25:16, 21; 40:20; Deut. 10:2-5). The urn or jar is not said to be golden in the Hebrew text but is so described in the Septuagint. According to the Pentateuch, the jar of manna was to be kept "before the Lord" (Ex. 16:33). Aaron's rod also was to be laid "before the testimony" (Num. 17:10), the rod's transformation symbolizing the priestly prerogatives of Levi above all challengers. From the first, therefore, these sacred memorial objects were associated with the ark and some time later undoubtedly were placed in the ark for safe keeping. As to their subsequent history, nothing is known. Perhaps they were lost or destroyed when the ark was captured by the Philistines in battle (1 Sam. 4:1-11). Later, in the time of Solomon, it is said that "there was nothing in the ark except the two tables of stone which Moses put there at Horeb" (1 Ki. 8:9).

Above it (the ark) were the cherubim of glory overshadowing the 5 mercy seat. The cherubs were composite creatures, sphinx-like, with faces of human beings, bodies of animals, and wings of birds. They were made of gold and were all of one piece with the top of the ark (Ex. 25:18-20). Placed at each end of the ark, they were positioned in such a way as to face each other, with their wings overshadowing the mercy seat. In Genesis 3:24 the cherubim are pictured as guardians of the way to the tree of life, and so here as guardians of the ark and of the Divine Presence. When the author speaks of them as cherubim of glory, he is using glory as a periphrasis for God—glory in the sense of the Divine Presence, the Shekinah. The New English Bible makes this clear by translating, "the cherubim of God's glory."

The protective wings of the two cherubim provided the place where, symbolically speaking, God dwelled among His people (Ps. 80:1; 99:1). This place in English is known as the mercy seat; the term itself comes from the translation of William Tyndale, who followed Luther's rendering of the Hebrew word that means "covering" or "lid." It is appropriately called mercy seat since the Greek word hilastērion (found here and in Rom. 3:25) denotes a place of propitiation or expiation. It was thus the holiest place of all, the place where blood was sprinkled on the Day of Atonement that made possible reconciliation between men and God. But, the author says, Of these things—of the Holy Place and the Most Holy Place, and of their furnishings—we cannot now speak in detail. That is, the author refrains from exploring further the typical significance of these details. He feels that he must move on to discuss the true tabernacle in heaven and its perfect sacrifice. But again it is important to ask why the author would even to this extent refer to the worship of the tent-sanctuary if he were not writing to a circle of friends who had either a knowledge of or a lingering attachment to the old cultus.

The Tabernacle Ritual
(9:6-10)

In pressing toward his goal, however, the author finds it necessary to describe briefly the tabernacle ritual. He first speaks of the ordinary
6 priests as they discharge their assigned duties. **These preparations** (the furnishings of the tabernacle) **having thus been made, the priests go continually into the outer tent, performing their ritual duties.** The outer portion of the tabernacle was in daily use. Here the priests entered, morning and evening, to trim the lamps on the lampstand and to offer incense on the altar of incense (Ex. 27:20-21; 30:7-8). In addition, on each sabbath the priests went into the Holy Place to renew the bread of the Presence. But no matter how often they went in and out, the priests could only go so far: they could never go into the immediate Presence of God.

The worship in the outer compartment is of no special importance to the author's scheme, except to point up the insufficiency and spiritual dearth of the old regime. But the service of the inner sanctuary, the
7 author believes, is of real and lasting significance. **Into the second only the high priest goes, and he but once a year.** The occasion referred to is the Day of Atonement (Lev. 16), the one great day when all sin and uncleanness before the Lord were relieved. **Once** does not mean "one time," but rather refers to the one day in the year when the high priest could go into the inmost chamber. According to Leviticus 16:12-16, he entered at least three times on that day, first with the incense to cloud the mercy seat, then with the blood of the young bull to make expiation for his own sins, and then with the blood of the goat to make expiation for the sins of the people.

So sacred was this place that the high priest himself dared not enter it without the protection of sacrifice—**not without taking blood which he offers for himself and for the errors of the people.** Errors is the translation of *agnoēmatōn*, a term that can refer to offenses in general, but ordinarily suggests "sins of ignorance" (NEB). On the Day of Atonement provisions were thus made for sins committed inadvertently, acts of wrong done through weakness or ignorance (see my comments on 5:2).[2] With the mention of the **blood**, which was sprinkled

---

2. According to rabbinic tradition, however, a man's forgiveness on the Day of Atonement was not unqualified. For example: "If any says, 'I will sin and repent, I

on the mercy seat by the high priest, the author begins to develop a theme that looms large in succeeding verses.

In all of this the author sees the working of divine providence. **By this the Holy Spirit,** the author of the law and the ordinances of **8** worship, **indicates that the way into the sanctuary is not yet opened.** The **sanctuary** is the heavenly one (cf. 9:11, 24), metaphorical terminology for the higher realm of the Divine Presence. The language is anticipatory, looking ahead to 10:19-20. There Jesus (or rather His sacrifice) is pictured as opening up the fresh and living way through the curtain. But until that sacrifice, the veil remained. There was no unencumbered access to God: the layman could not enter the tabernacle at all; the priest could go only into the first room; and the high priest, even when he went into the second room, could enter only once a year and then only by means of blood. **As long as the outer tent is still standing** is a further explanatory clause in reference to the barriers that existed in the ancient ritual. When the ordinary person came with his sacrifice, as the outer curtain was opened, he could catch a glimpse of the interior of the Holy Place but never of the Most Holy Place. His view, and by implication his way, was entirely cut off **as long as the outer tent** was **still standing.** This, too, the author holds, represents more than meets the eye; for, he says, it **is symbolic** (literally, "a parable") **for the present 9 age.** The expression is not easy to understand. Possibly his "parable" is that **the outer tent,** restricting as it did man's approach to God, symbolizes the old dispensation up to the coming of Christ, that is, that it stands for the pre-Christian era as seen from the vantage point of the origin of these arrangements. The King James understands it this way and translates "the time then present." On the other hand, the English Revised Version renders "the time *now* present," with which the American Standard and Revised Standard versions are in essential agreement. It is possible to take the clause as referring to the tabernacle set-up as a whole and translate, "this is a figure pointing to the present age" (cf. NEB). If the clause is understood in this way, the author would be saying that the earthly tabernacle, in which the Jewish ritual was centered, could not be seen as it really was—inferior and imperfect—until set in contrast with the new order inaugurated by the sacrifice of Jesus. Yet the former view seems to have several points in its favor. First, the simplest construction is to take the relative pronoun **which** with **outer tent** and to allow **outer tent** its usual meaning instead of standing for the tabernacle as a whole. Second, if in the author's view "world to come" and "age to come" (see comments on 2:5 and 6:5) refer to the Christian world-order, then it seems that **the present age** should refer

---

will sin and repent,' to him God grants no occasion to repent. If he says, 'I will sin, and the Day shall atone,' the Day will not atone for him" (Mishnah, *Yoma*, 8:9).

to the Old Testament period. Third, this appears to fit in better with
the remainder of the verse and results in a contrast between the present
age (the transitory, old covenant) and the time of reformation (the
new covenant).

The contrast now comes into clearer focus. According to this
arrangement, that of the old, gifts and sacrifices are offered which cannot perfect the conscience of the worshiper. The beginning of the
clause, "according to which" (kath hēn, the word arrangement being
supplied by the translators), is a feminine construction and connects
with "parable," which is also feminine. The thought is that as the
outer tent parabolizes a system tainted with imperfection, so gifts and
offerings made in it could never confer the spiritual blessing needed.
The one signal failure of animal sacrifices pertained to conscience. A
man might obtain external perfection, but not internal (cf. 9:14; 10:1;
on "perfect," see the comments on 2:10). This is a truth which the author
feels is self-evident, that no heap of legal ordinances can heal the conscience or bring the worshiper near to God. The whole ancient system
10   was at fault. And what a futile system it was that could deal only
with food and drink and various ablutions! The Levitical code contained
many instructions with reference to clean and unclean foods (Lev. 11;
Deut. 14:3-21). There were also laws as to drink (Lev. 10:9; Num. 6:2-3).
There were numerous laws on washings. There were washings for the
high priest (Lev. 16:4, 24), washings for the priests (Ex. 30:18-21; Lev.
8:6), washings for the Levites (Num. 8:6-7), washings for lepers and
unclean persons (Lev. 14:8-9; Num. 19), and washings of garments and
vessels (Lev. 6:27-28). "So many washings," the author would say, "and
nothing made clean!" One senses a feeling of contempt for these petty
matters—what to eat, what to drink, what to wash—things grossly material in nature. Ordinances of the flesh and not of the conscience, they
had to do with mere regulations for the body that were only temporary,
imposed until the time of reformation.

Such externals were never intended to last, for the time would
come for a reconstruction of religion, when a complete overhaul would
be due, when all that was defective could be put in perfect working
order. The author's term for this is reformation, a word that means "to
straighten what has fallen from its original position." It was a term used
for correcting errors, for repairing something that had been broken, or
for setting a fractured limb. The expression time of reformation is a
description of the Christian age from an Old Testament standpoint. It
is as though the people of the old covenant, aware of its inadequacy,
looked forward eagerly to a new day when all things out of order would
be put right. This day dawned, as the first words in the next verse

indicate, when Christ came. Man's sense of moral guilt, unaffected by a mass of sacrificial rites, could now be thoroughly dealt with in Jesus.

Christ's Redemptive Ministry
(9:11-14)

The nature of Christ's high-priestly ministry and of His sacrifice is now pointedly contrasted with the ministry of the old covenant. In reference to the old system of sacrifice, as stated in verses 11-12, it is superior in four respects: (1) it is an offering made by Christ entering through "the greater and more perfect tent"; (2) it is an offering that Christ made with "his own blood," not the blood of goats and calves; (3) it is an offering that thus secured not an annual but an "eternal redemption"; (4) it is an offering, therefore, that need be made only "once." **But when Christ appeared as a high priest of the good things** 11 **that have come, then through the greater and more perfect tent (not made with hands, that is, not of this creation) he entered once for all** 12 **into the Holy Place, taking not the blood of goats and calves but his own blood, thus securing an eternal redemption.**

The long sentence, with its meandering clauses opening up fresh conceptions, should be read as a unit. For the author the climax of all came **when Christ appeared.**[3] This was the focal point of the entire Old Testament, the one great event that changed everything. He came on the scene of human history to do the work of a high priest, a work for which, as the author has already demonstrated, He was eminently qualified. And now that He has come, **good things** also **have come.** This, of course, is the natural consequence. The author's words express the theme and tone of his whole writing—*good things in Christ.*

The Christian high priest entered into the presence of God **through the greater and more perfect tent.** The language need not be pressed, as though there were a division of the heavenly sanctuary into two parts, and Christ had to move through one before proceeding to the other. (See Additional Note.) No such impression is intended. The author once again is speaking in highly figurative terms that bring to mind his previous description of Jesus as the great high priest "who has passed through the heavens" (4:14). And since it is the **more perfect tent,** it is not a tent made by human skill; that is, it does not belong to the physical order of creation. In words employed previously it is "the true tent which is set up not by man but by the Lord" (8:2).

---

3. The clause does not refer to a particular appearance of Christ, say, at His baptism or at the beginning of His preaching ministry. The aorist participle, *paragenomenos,* sums up the entire course of His life from earthly advent to heavenly ascension as high priest.

The earthly high priest entered into the holiest through **the blood of goats and calves;** the heavenly High Priest came "through" His own blood. The Revised Standard translates here **taking . . . his own blood,** a loose and misleading translation. The Levitical high priest did indeed carry the blood of sacrifice with him when he entered the Holy of Holies, but the author skillfully avoids saying this of Christ. Instead he says that Christ entered "through" *(dia)* His own blood, that is, by virtue of His own shed blood—because He Himself was the victim—He was able to enter the heavenly sanctuary. Little wonder that He was able to gain admission! What a contrast between "a brute beast slain involuntarily, without foreknowledge, and without capacity to consent to, or appreciate the reason of, its dying" and "a holy, loving Man, who laid down His own life deliberately, freely, devotedly, animated by an eternal spirit of goodness."[4]

The effective action of Christ's sacrifice appears in the words, **securing an eternal redemption.**[5] By the presentation of animal blood the high priest of Israel obtained for himself and for the people an annual redemption; by the offering of Himself Christ gained an everlasting redemption. His sacrifice took away the sins of the whole world and inducted men into an unending age of grace. And because it is an eternally valid sacrifice, it can never be repeated. Repetition implies inadequacy—what else could that long series of slaughtered beasts teach? But the sacrifice of Christ was a thing thoroughly done, an offering truly **once for all.** (See comments on 7:27.)

Christ's sacrifice as eternal is now vindicated. Why is Christ's redemption absolutely final and acceptable in perpetuity? The author 13 proceeds to explain: **For if the sprinkling of defiled persons with the blood of goats and bulls and with the ashes of a heifer sanctifies for** 14 **the purification of the flesh, how much more shall the blood of Christ . . . purify your conscience from dead works to serve the living God.** Here two different types of purification are referred to: the blood of goats and bulls, and the ashes of a heifer. The first is a general reference to various sacrifices, including those of the Day of Atonement. The second is in reference to impurity brought about by touching a corpse, by entering a house with a corpse in it, or by touching a human bone or grave (Num. 19). A red, unblemished cow, which had never borne the yoke, was slaughtered and burned; its ashes were kept in a clean

---

4. A. B. Bruce, *Hebrews,* p. 332.

5. The action of the participle is simultaneous with the previous verb "entered." If the participle is translated "having secured" (which would be a literal rendering of the Greek tense), it would suggest that the redemption preceded the entering. But the securing and the entering was one act—to enter was to secure. The NEB well translates: "And thus he has entered the sanctuary once and for all and secured an eternal deliverance."

place outside the camp. In case of any defilement incurred by touching a dead body, the unclean person was sprinkled with a mixture of the ashes and fresh water. This "sanctification" restored to the unclean person his external purity, thus enabling him to participate once again in the religious observances of the tabernacle.

The author does not pause to debate or argue these points. The efficacy of shed blood is assumed. For him, and apparently for his readers, it is enough that these matters are clearly prescribed in the Old Testament. In fact, it is on the basis of these incontrovertible procedures that he establishes his argument. The argument is twofold. If the blood of goats and bulls and the ashes of a heifer cleanse, how much more the blood of Christ?[6] And if the animal sacrifices of the old arrangement cleanse the flesh, how much more shall Christ's blood cleanse the conscience? (For "dead works," see the comments on 6:1; for "living God," see the comments on 3:12.) Only Christ's blood can remove the stains of inward guilt and effect the full forgiveness of sins promised in the new covenant.

But there is more as to why the blood of Christ has permanent atoning significance. Speaking of Christ, the author says: **who through the eternal Spirit offered himself without blemish to God.** Three things in particular stand out: Christ offered *Himself;* in offering Himself He made a *perfect* sacrifice; and He offered *through an eternal spirit.* Christ's sacrifice was not the slaughter of a reluctant victim, but a deliberate act, a sacrifice of heart and will in obedience to God (Phil. 2:8). His sacrifice was also a spotless sacrifice—spotless not in the outward sense, but in the inward and moral sense, an indispensable requirement of a spiritual sacrifice.

Christ's sacrifice, too, was presented **through the eternal Spirit.** What does this rather obscure expression mean? The article is absent in the Greek, and the words literally say "through eternal spirit." By printing "Spirit," many translations strongly suggest that the Holy Spirit is meant. But this is improbable, for elsewhere the author specifically says "Holy Spirit" (3:7; 9:8; 10:15). Here, however, he refers to Christ's own spirit or spiritual nature, to the region of spirit, to the eternal order of things. This can be seen by a comparison of verses 13 and 14, where it is obvious that **flesh** and **spirit** are in contrast. **Conscience** (v. 14) is also a part of this contrast. The old sacrifices, being fleshly in nature, could cleanse only the flesh; the new sacrifice is able to cleanse the conscience because it belongs by nature to the domain

---

6. This is the author's one point in connection with "the ashes of a heifer." The Epistle of Barnabas (8:1ff.), however, allegorizes and makes the young cow typify Jesus.

of eternal spirit.[7] In other words, the author conceives the sacrifice of Jesus as that which is essentially spiritual. It was not simply a blood-shedding, with no expression of spirit. It was a free, willing sacrifice of a person. And as an eternal sacrifice, it was something beyond space and time. Although His death took place on earth, yet, in significance and value, it really took place in the eternal order. "The act performed by Jesus in offering Himself may, as an historical event, become old with the lapse of ages; but the spirit in which the act was done can never become a thing of the past."[8]

The Mediator of the New Covenant
(9:15-22)

The last verse (9:14) is a climax to the author's argument as to the significance of the sacrifice of Christ. From this it would seem easy for the author to move on to his practical exhortations to faithfulness which begin at 10:19. Indeed, there is a close correspondence of ideas in 10:19ff. with what the author has just stated. This can be seen by a casual reading of the two passages. But since the author does not turn immediately to exhortation, it must be assumed that there is some reason for his delay. Most likely it lies in his determination to make sure that his first readers, whom he has already castigated for their mental sluggishness, truly comprehend the significance and necessity of Jesus' death. That was something that almost invariably required explanation wherever Christ was preached. If He was the Messiah promised in divine Scripture, why did He have to die? This would be the question of the inquiring Jew and even of many knowledgeable Gentiles; and this is the question that the author previously has dealt with (2:5-9). He now adds that the death of Christ was necessary in order to

15 inaugurate the new covenant. **Therefore he is the mediator of a new covenant** (see the comments and Additional Note on 8:6). To be sure, the direct effect of His priestly sacrifice is to establish such a covenant, for the oracle of Jeremiah looked to the time when men's sins would be remembered no more (8:12). Thus the offering of Christ's own blood as an adequate atonement inevitably involved the bringing in of a better covenant.

The old covenant being unable to provide "eternal redemption," there had to be some kind of arrangement made for those sins; and the author says that **a death has** indeed **occurred which redeems them from**

7. "In the old covenant purely earthly and corruptible things were offered in the sphere of *sarx* [flesh]; here, however, there offers Himself One who comes from the sphere of *pneuma* [spirit] and possesses the *pneuma*, so that brings a salvation that lasts beyond the *sarx* [flesh]" TDNT, VI, 446.
8. A. B. Bruce, *Hebrews*, p. 339.

the transgressions under the first covenant. That is, the death of Christ was retroactive in its consequences, cancelling the sins of a former age that were left untouched by a mass of legalistic sacrifices (cf. 10:4). And all of this was for the purpose that those who are called (including people under both covenants) may receive the promised eternal inheritance (cf. 6:17). The connection between "the call" and "the inheritance" is definite, as is evident in 11:8. Those who are called brings to mind the author's earlier designation of Christians as those "who share in a heavenly call" (3:1). The promised eternal inheritance likewise goes back to facts already established: that God's rest was promised to His people long ago; that the Israelites failed to gain this rest because of unbelief; and that, therefore, God's rest remains for His people to enter (3:7—4:11). But the author here speaks of this rest in terms of a promised inheritance, which he is now able to characterize as eternal—as eternal as the covenant itself (13:20); as eternal as redemption and salvation (9:12; 5:9); as eternally valid as the offering of Christ, which is "a spiritual and eternal sacrifice" (9:14, NEB). The full thought is, as becomes clear in what follows, that Christ had to die before the inheritance could be received.

The Greek word for "covenant" is *diathēkē;* the term also means "testament" or "will." (See Additional Note.) It is important to realize this, for otherwise the English reader will not grasp the main thoughts of the passage. In verse 15 the author speaks of a "covenant," in verses 16-17 of a "will," and then in verses 18-20 he returns to the idea of a "covenant." The one word *diathēkē* is used throughout, for actually the author is playing on the double meaning of the term. For where a will 16 is involved, he says, the death of the one who made it must be established. For a will takes effect only at death, since it is not in force as 17 long as the one who made it is alive. It now becomes apparent why the author, momentarily, ceases to think of a new covenant and begins to speak of a new testament or will. He has just spoken of an "inheritance" (v. 15); and, of course, an inheritance is not received without a will. In the case of a will, though not in that of a covenant, a death must occur—the death of the one who makes the will. So by this device the author shows how the death of Christ is not incongruous with His position as Mediator of the new covenant. Rather, it is His death that conveys the inheritance of salvation.

The principle that has been illustrated generally (vv. 16-17) is now made specific by reference to Sinai. The author now reverts to the usual Biblical sense of *diathēkē* as "covenant." Hence even the first 18 covenant was not ratified ("inaugurated," NEB) without blood. Even then, when the covenant was so imperfect and when the shedding of blood might have seemed so unnecessary, it was essential that death

19 take place. Death and covenanting are closely conjoined. **For when every commandment of the law had been declared by Moses to all the people, he took the blood of calves and goats.** The passage referred to is Exodus 24:3-8. The author's narration varies somewhat from the Old Testament account, omitting some details and adding others. The Exodus text does not mention the offering of goats, but the words "and goats" were probably not in the original text of the Epistle. (See Additional Note.) The **water and scarlet wool and hyssop** also are not mentioned in Exodus, but they were doubtless used, being associated with sacrifice in general. **Water** was used to dilute the shed blood. **Hyssop** is mentioned several times in the Bible, although the references suggest different species of plants. Hyssop was used, with cedarwood and scarlet, in the ceremonial cleansing of lepers (Lev. 14:4-7). It was also used for the sprinkling of the blood of the Passover lamb (Ex. 12:22) and in the rite of the red heifer (Num. 19:6, 18; see comments on v. 13). **Scarlet wool** was tied around the stems of hyssop to make a shaker for the sprinkling of blood. Making use of these things, Moses took the blood of calves **and sprinkled both the book itself and all the people,**
20 **saying, "This is the blood of the covenant which God commanded you."** The quotation is from Exodus 24:8, which reads, "Behold the blood of the covenant. . . ." The form of the quotation ("This is" instead of "Behold") perhaps is influenced by the words of Jesus concerning the new covenant at the institution of the Supper (Mt. 26:28). There is no reference in Exodus to the sprinkling of the book. But if Moses sprinkled the people and read to them out of "the book of the covenant" (Ex. 24:7), it is natural that he would sprinkle the book as well, especially since according to the law almost everything is cleansed by blood (v. 22).

Yet the inauguration of the Sinaitic covenant was not the only
21 occasion when blood was sprinkled. The author points to another. **And in the same way he** (Moses) **sprinkled with the blood both the tent and all the vessels used in worship.** It is not to be thought that this happened at the time of the dedication of the covenant (certainly the author does not say this), for the tabernacle was not then in existence. On the contrary, it is likely that the consecration of the tabernacle took place at the same time as the consecration of Aaron and his sons (Ex. 40:9-15; Lev. 8). In the Pentateuch no mention is made of the anointing of the tabernacle and its furniture with blood, but only an anointing with oil. But in the consecration of Aaron and his sons, both oil and blood were used (Lev. 8:30), a fact which makes it not unlikely that both were used at the erection of the tabernacle. This inference is justified not only from the author but from Josephus (*Antiquities* 3.8.6) as well, who states that the tabernacle and its vessels were consecrated with "fragrant oil" and "with the blood of bulls and of goats."

The dedication of the covenant and of the tabernacle are but two instances that could be cited to demonstrate an almost universal principle. **Indeed,** the author states, **under the law almost everything is purified with blood.** Almost, but not all—the exceptions, such as cleansing by fire or water (Num. 31:21-24), were rare; but the general rule was that everything used in the worship and every worshiper had to be purified by blood. The author rounds it all off by saying, **and without the shedding of blood there is no forgiveness of sins.** The Greek text says simply "forgiveness," but in context it is clear that "forgiveness of sins" is meant. Here the author is stating an uncontested maxim, that sins can be forgiven only where there is the death of a victim. The rule appears as one of the many Levitical requirements and explanations (Lev. 17:11)—"it is the blood that makes atonement, by reason of the life." An apparent exception to this is found in Leviticus 5:11-13, where the law provided that in a circumstance of poverty a bloodless sin offering, a tenth of an ephah (about two-thirds of a bushel) of fine flour, could be presented for forgiveness.

The Finality of Christ's Sacrifice (9:23-28)

The author has shown, both from the standpoint of a will and from that of a covenant, the necessity of Jesus' death. His last statement, "no blood shed, no forgiveness," opens the way for him to restate the fact of His death and its lasting effects. **Thus it was necessary for the copies of the heavenly things to be purified with these rites** (referring back to the rites of vv. 18-22). The language is similar to that of 8:5, where the imagery of two worlds is employed; on one hand the unreal world of shadows and copies, and on the other the real world that is spiritual and heavenly. The author reasons that if animal sacrifices cleansed **the copies**—the tabernacle and everything related to it—then **the heavenly things themselves** had to be cleansed **with better sacrifices than these.** These words must not be pressed to mean that heaven itself or something in heaven (Satan, wicked angels, evil, etc.) was defiled and required purification. The author is speaking poetically and metaphorically.[9] His meaning is that as men on earth could approach God only after the offering of blood, so God is now accessible to sinful men because of the sacrifice of Christ. The thought is practically equivalent

---

9. The good common sense of A. B. Bruce here deserves notice. Speaking of this verse, he says: "For my own part I prefer to make no attempt to assign a theological meaning to the words. . . . I believe there is more of poetry than of theology in the words. For the writer is a poet as well as a theologian, and on this account theological pedants, however learned, can never succeed in interpreting satisfactorily this Epistle" (*Hebrews*, p. 366).

to what is said in the next verse, that Christ entered heaven itself to appear before God on man's behalf. The plural, **sacrifices,** is used in order to fit the analogy and can refer to nothing other than the one sacrifice of Christ which infinitely surpassed in value all that had been offered before.

In language that is reminiscent of verses 11-12, the author con-
24 tinues: **For Christ has entered, not into a sanctuary made with hands, a copy of the true one** (cf. 8:2), **but into heaven itself, now to appear in the presence of God on our behalf.** The sanctuary is identified for the first time as being heaven itself. The point is that since this sanctuary is not a man-made but a spiritual one, the sacrifice made must be in keeping with the dignity of the heavenly place, a sacrifice whose requirements can be met only by Him who possesses eternal attributes. Having made that sacrifice and having entered the heavenly realm, He appears before God (literally, "before the face of God"). He is face to face with God, representing wayward men (cf. 7:25; Rom. 8:34; 1 Jn. 2:1). And Christ appears in heaven indefinitely onward, **now**—the author says as with a sigh—"now, at long last" (cf. 1:2).

The remaining verses of the chapter magnify a theme already introduced, which the author now purposes to rivet in the minds of his readers. This theme is, *Christ offered Himself once and once only*
25 (cf. 7:27; 9:12). **Nor was it to offer himself repeatedly, as the high priest**
26 **enters the Holy Place yearly with blood not his own; for then he would have had to suffer repeatedly since the foundation of the world.** Two things are implied here: (1) that Christ has always existed, and (2) that Christ's sacrifice reaches backward and deals with the sins of past generations (v. 15). The offering made by Christ was distinctly unlike those of the Levitical high priests, for they, with the blood of fresh sacrifices, went in and out year after year. But Christ remains perpetually in the presence of God, neither coming nor going; otherwise He would have to suffer from the time of creation. That is, as sin entered into the world from the beginning, if Christ's sacrifice had not been entirely adequate, it would have been necessary for Him to die successively from the founding of the world. Either He would have had to die again and again for each sin, or He would have had to die again and again for each sinful generation. But this would be nonsense. Christ died once, as the author goes on to say, just as all men die once; and that in itself is a commentary on the effectiveness of His atonement. **But as it is, he has appeared once for all at the end of the age. At the end of the age** is equivalent to the "last days" (1:2) or the final period of the world's history (cf. 1 Cor. 10:11; 1 Pet. 1:20). This is when Christ came, and the *when* is instructive. He did not enter earth's early history and suffer repeatedly. He came "at the climax of history" (NEB), after

many generations had passed away—another evidence that His offering was once for all. The purpose of His coming in human form was **to put away** ("cancel" or "abolish," as in 7:18, where the same word is used of cancelling the "former commandment") **sin by the sacrifice of himself.**

An illustration is now drawn from the common experience of men, as a further thought on the one time sacrifice of Christ. **And just as it is appointed for men to die once, and after that comes judgment, so Christ having been offered once to bear the sins of many, will appear a second time.** The translation is not as forceful as it could be (cf. the NEB). The point is that as men die once, so Christ offered Himself once (cf. 10:10, 12, 14). And **it is appointed** that men should **die once,** not simply that men will die. The word **appointed** (from *apokeimai*) means, literally, "to lie," or "to be laid aside." In the secular papyri the word is often used of something that is "stored up" at home, at the granary, etc. In other New Testament passages (Lk. 19:20; Col. 1:5; 2 Tim. 4:8) it has the sense of "laid up." So here death is **appointed** or "laid up" or "reserved" for man—death awaits man.[10] The idea of judgment here is almost incidental, serving as a parallel to Christ's second appearance, although it is returned to later (10:27, 30; 12:23). The phrase **to bear the sins** may mean to bear the consequences (punishment) of sins for others, as in Numbers 14:33, or it may mean to bear away the sins of others (in the sense of "put away," as in verse 26).[11] The thought is similar to that of John 1:29, where the Lamb of God either "takes away" the sin of the world or "takes" the sin of the world upon Himself. The whole expression **to bear the sins of many** echoes the language of Isaiah 53:10-12, a messianic "Servant Song" that meant much to the early church. **Many** does not limit the atonement, as though Christ did not die for all, but indicates the large number graciously provided for by the one sacrifice (cf. 2:9-10; Mk. 10:45; Rom. 5:15).

Christ became flesh to take away sin; but when He comes again it will **not** be, the author adds, **to deal with sin but to save those who are eagerly waiting for him.** His first coming was sin-oriented. In His earthly mission He was pressed down with sin, not with His own sins but with the sins of the many; He was occupied with the whole world's guilt. Now He has put away sin and is forevermore separated from sinners. And to His second advent the redeemed **eagerly** look (Phil. 3:20; 1 Thess. 1:10; 2 Tim. 4:8). In both comings alluded to, Christ is depicted as Savior. When He came the first time, He came as a sin-bearer. When He comes a second time, He comes to save those who are watching for

---

10. See TDNT, III, 655.

11. Deissmann's considerable note (*Bible Studies,* p. 88ff.) argues for the latter meaning in 1 Pet. 2:24; but on the same verse Beare (p. 123f.) and Selwyn (p. 180), among others, argue for the former.

Him, to those who hold on to their hope (cf. 3:6; 6:11, 18). After His first coming, no other sacrifice for sin is needed; and in His coming again nothing else will remain but for Him to gather the fruits of His sacrifice.

Additional Notes

The table and the bread

V. 2. "The table and the bread of the Presence" is hendiadys for "the table of the bread of the Presence." Thus the NEB correctly translates "the table with the bread of the Presence."

Thumiatērion ("altar of incense") and its location

V. 4. This verse has been the subject of much discussion in the past. The problem posed is twofold: (1) the meaning of the Greek word *thumiatērion*, (2) the specific location of the *thumiatērion* within the tabernacle. The Greek term can be taken to mean either "censer" or "altar of incense," the word itself indicating no more than something on which or in which incense is placed. The KJV and ERV, following the LXX, the Latin Vulgate and the Syriac Peshitta, rendered *thumiatērion* here as "censer"; the ASV, RSV and most of the recent versions choose the other alternative and translate "altar of incense."

Of the two possible meanings, "altar of incense" is definitely to be preferred. The writer of Hebrews most probably is *not* referring to a "golden censer." Nowhere in the Old Testament is a censer mentioned as part of the furniture of the Holy of Holies. Further, it is not likely that the reference is to Aaron's censer which was used on the Day of Atonement (Lev. 16:12-13). This censer was of no special importance; and even if it had been, it could not have been kept in the Holy of Holies, for the high priest had to use it to carry coals from the altar as he entered the Holy of Holies. The author, then, appears to be referring to the "altar of incense." Support for this interpretation of the term comes from the writings of Philo and Josephus, and also from the Greek versions of Symmachus and Theodotion. More significant, however, is the very great importance of the incense altar for the Jewish religion. It was a very important article among the furnishings of the tabernacle. It seems incredible that the author of Hebrews, in describing the tabernacle and its contents, would fail to make mention of it.

These are the reasons for believing that the author is speaking here of the altar of incense.

The other aspect of the problem concerns the position of the *thumiatērion* in the tabernacle. According to Exodus 30:6 the altar of incense was to be placed "before the veil that is by the ark of the testimony," that is, in the Holy Place; yet apparently the author of

Hebrews locates it in the Holy of Holies. What explanation can be given for this? Has the author made a mistake by putting the altar in the wrong place? In response it can be said that the author could hardly have been ignorant of something like the altar of incense. Surely he was well acquainted with its function, that incense was to be burned on it morning and evening as "a perpetual incense before the Lord" (Ex. 30:7-8). To have burned this incense within the veil would have necessitated repeated entries into the Holy of Holies, entries which were altogether forbidden (Lev. 16:2). So the altar stood in a position immediately "before the veil" (Ex. 40:26), thus allowing the smoke of the burnt incense to penetrate the inner compartment.

On the Day of Atonement the Jewish high priest was required to make an annual expiation on the horns of the incense altar "with the blood of the sin offering" (Ex. 30:10). This ceremony connected in a tangible way the altar of incense with the Holy of Holies. This fact, along with the proximity of the incense altar (next to the veil) to the Holy of Holies, seems sufficient to account for the author's description. Instead of saying "in which were the golden altar of incense and the ark of the covenant," he speaks of the inmost compartment as "having the golden altar of incense." Whether the form of the expression in itself is enough to account for the difficulty, at least it can be allowed that "having" (echousa, v. 4) is a more general expression than "in which" (en hē, v. 2) and may mean "belonging to," that is, in the sense of the altar "belonging to" the Holy of Holies (so A. B. Bruce, Westcott, Davidson, Peake, Nairne, Hewitt, etc.). Compare the RSV of I Kings 6:22, a verse which, however, was not in the LXX, the text used by the author.

"The priests go continually"

V. 6. By using the present tense, "the priests go continually," the author is not speaking of what takes place in his own time. He is describing the procedures which were followed in the tabernacle ritual; thus nothing can be inferred about the existence of the temple at the time of his writing. The present tense of the verb is the historical present.

Food and drink regulations

V. 10. The food and drink regulations here may well be a clue to the problem and background of the entire Epistle. Certain Jewish-Christians quite possibly were holding to the Mosaic law (and even contending for its superiority?) because they could not bring themselves to accept the freedom of Christian conscience in these matters.

The reading of 9:11

The difference between "the good things that have come" (RSV) and the "good things to come" (KJV, ASV) is the result of variant readings in the manuscripts. The text of the RSV has superior attestation, supported by P[46], B, D, 1739, etc.

"The greater and more perfect tent"

V. 11. The views have been many on "the greater and more perfect tent." Some have said that the expression stands for the whole world; others that it represents the visible heavens through which Christ passed as He went to the throne of God; still others have said it refers to the angelic abode; or to God's people, the church. But such views seem strained and unnatural. The early expositors, both Greek and Latin, explained the "tent" as a reference to the fleshly body of Christ. If the phrase is understood in this way, Christ's humanity becomes the means of qualifying Him to serve as high priest in the heavenly sanctuary. But how could the author, when speaking of Christ's body, say "not of this creation," especially when earlier (ch. 2) he had contended that His fleshly nature was the same as that of other men? And how would such a view fit here? The passage would appear strange indeed if Christ were tent and priest and victim.

A. Vanhoye, followed by J. Swetnam, has revived an older view, that the tent refers not to Jesus' fleshly body but to His glorified body.[12] This view has the advantage of not conflicting with the qualifying phrase, "not of this creation," for Christ's resurrected, glorified body was different from His earthly body. Yet there remains the problem of explaining how Christ passed "through" His glorified body.

It is better to think that the author is here employing imaginative language dictated by the parallelism of earthly and heavenly high priest. It seems unnecessary to inquire further as to the meaning of "the greater and more perfect tent."

Diathēkē, "covenant"

V. 15. The word for "covenant" *(diathēkē)* has already appeared several times in chapters 7 and 8, and is used frequently in chapter 9. *Diathēkē* is a very common term in the LXX (occurring 270 times), but is not found so often in the New Testament. Of its 33 occurrences, 17 are in this Epistle.

The basic idea of "covenant" is "contract" or "agreement"—an agreement that is entered upon by two contracting parties. It might denote an agreement between friends (1 Sam. 23:18), between husband and wife (Mal. 2:14), between tribes (1 Sam. 11:1), between king and nation (2 Chron. 23:3), etc. But the word "covenant" is also the unique

---

12. Albert Vanhoye, "'Par la tente plus grande et plus parfaite...' (He 9, 11)," *Biblica* 46 (1965), 1-28; James Swetnam, "'The Greater and More Perfect Tent.' A Contribution to the Discussion of Hebrews 9, 11," *Biblica* 47 (1966), 91-106.

word in the Old Testament for the special "agreement" or "relationship" between God and His people. At Sinai God gave the people His covenant; neither He nor they were to forget that covenant (Deut. 4:13, 23, 31). The heart of the covenant was expressed in the words, "Now therefore, if you will obey my voice and keep my covenant, you shall be my own possession among all peoples . . . and you shall be to me a kingdom of priests and a holy nation" (Ex. 19:5-6; cf. Jer. 7:23; 31:33).

In the New Testament it is significant that the word *diathēkē* is used for "covenant." This is a word that suggests that God lays down the conditions of the covenant. It is the ordinary word for "will" or "testament," and, of course, a person who makes a will lays down the conditions of that will. (The word *sunthēkē*, not *diathēkē*, was used by the Greeks for the making of a contract in which both parties were on equal footing.) The New Testament concept, therefore, is always that of God making His covenant available by His gracious, saving activity.

Hebrews contributes immeasurably to the idea of God's new covenant with His people. Jesus is the Mediator of the new covenant (8:6; 9:15; 12:24). As the old covenant was ratified with blood (9:18-22), so it is the blood of Jesus that establishes the new covenant (9:12-14; 10:19, 29; 12:24; 13:12, 20). This makes forgiveness of sins possible (9:14-15; 10:17-18); and, of course, it was precisely because the old covenant could not provide forgiveness of sins (10:4) that it had to be abolished (8:7, 13).

In 9:16-17, the word *diathēkē* is translated "will." Here the author plays on the two senses of *diathēkē* as "covenant" and "will" in order to illustrate the necessity of Jesus' death in the making of the new covenant. For further reference, see G. E. Mendenhall, *Law and Covenant in Israel and the Ancient Near East* (Pittsburgh, 1955); also TDNT, II, 104ff.

The reading of 9:19

"The blood of calves and goats" is read by the KJV, ASV, and RSV. The NEB, however, simply reads "the blood of the calves." It is questionable whether "and goats" (Greek, *kai tragōn*) belongs in the text. P[46], followed by Aleph[c], K, L, and others, omits the words, which results in precise agreement with Exodus 24:5. Zuntz argues that the addition of the words is due to the influence of verse 12, which mentions both "goats and calves."[13]

---

13. Zuntz, p. 55.

HEBREWS TEN

The Last Word on Animal Sacrifices (10:1-4)

The author is now coming toward the end of his discussion on priesthood and sacrifice. Eighteen verses yet remain. In these he brings together his main ideas on the meaning of Christ's death and adds the profound thought that Christ's sacrifice was a free, voluntary expression of *will* in accordance with the will of God. The author begins by referring to the defects of the Levitical law, stating that **the law has but 1 a shadow of the good things to come instead of the true form of these realities.** This idea is first hinted at in 8:5. The **good things** spoken of are the good things in Christ, such as the better sacrifices and better hope, eternal redemption and the eternal inheritance. These are the good things **to come** from the standpoint of a person who lived under the old law, not from the Christian point of view (cf. 9:11). Of these good things the law had but a **shadow** *(skia)*, but with the coming of Christ the shadow gave way to the **true form** *(eikōn)* of real things. The terms *skia* and *eikōn* express the comparative worth of Leviticalism and Christianity. The *skia* is a dark outline, faint and indistinct, like an artist's first sketch of a picture; the *eikōn* is the image itself, an exact representation, as an artist's finished portrait with all the colors in it. The words are well-chosen, expressing the supremacy of the Christian religion over its Jewish counterpart.

Because the law is only a shadow, the author maintains **it can never, by the same sacrifices which are continually offered year after year, make perfect those who draw near.** The sacrifices probably refer to those on the Day of Atonement, although the complete circle of sacrificial rites may be included. That these sacrifices had to be made

183

year after year shows that they were ineffective; they could not really cleanse or **make perfect. Those who draw near** denotes the worshipers (cf. 7:25; see Additional Note on 4:16).

No amount of repetition can transform a shadow into a reality.
2 If repetition could avail, **would they** (the Levitical sacrifices) **not have ceased to be offered?** The posing of the question supplies the answer: for **if the worshipers had once been cleansed, they would no longer have any consciousness of sin.** The thought is the same as is found in 9:9. **Once,** in effect, means "once for all" (so NEB), since the Greek perfect tense is used and expresses results still existing. If the worshiper had been cleansed once for all, he would no longer be apprehensive about sin. This implies a single offering for sin which could effect a one-time cleansing of the conscience.

Instead of cleansing, the continual slaying of animals brings to
3 mind the opposite, since **in these sacrifices there is** actually **a reminder of sin year after year.** The Jew might see in the annual atonement a day on which his sins were removed, but the author sees in it the very opposite. So far from remitting his sins, all that the sacrifices did was to remind him that he was still a sinner. There was a remembrance of sin and not a satisfactory atonement. What a wide chasm between the two! The contrast of remembrance of sin under the old covenant and no more remembrance of sin in the new covenant (8:12) is characteristic of the contrast of inferior and superior written in large letters throughout the Epistle.

Now, finally, the author says bluntly, as with one bold stroke, what all of his ingenious and prolonged arguments amount to: that
4 **it is impossible that the blood of bulls and goats should take away sins.** The proposition is stated as being self-evident, at least to every person with spiritual discernment. What possible connection is there between human guilt and the death of senseless creatures? It simply cannot be that sin of conscience can be removed by the slaughter of animals.

The Perfect Sacrifice
(10:5-10)

In referring to the offering of "bulls and goats" (v. 4), the author seems to be thinking particularly of the Day of Atonement. But since so many animals were killed in the course of one year, his thought might well extend to all sacrifices. At Passover time in Jerusalem, for example, "it was a boast of the sons of Aaron to wade up to their ankles in (sacrificial) blood."[1] The number of lambs slain ran into many thou-

---

1. Jeremias, p. 44.

sands, although Josephus' number of 255,600 is a gross exaggeration.[2] Of such animals slain, the author would say: "Look at all those sacrifices and all the blood shed! And to what purpose?"

The inherent impotency of the old ritual required a new sacrifice, the free and purposeful self-sacrifice of Jesus. This is now demonstrated in a passage of elevated beauty and grandeur. **Consequently (because 5 all the previous sacrifices were ineffectual), when Christ came into the world, he said. . . .** The words describe Christ's descent into the world from His heavenly home and provide a context for His quotation of Psalm 40: 6-8. The author is fond of the Psalms, to which he has appealed at various times (Ps. 2, 45, 95, 110, etc.) for final proof of his message. The psalm is conceived of as being a kind of conversation between the eternal Son and God the Father, with the Son as the speaker.

The quotation runs: **"Sacrifices and offerings thou hast not desired, but a body hast thou prepared for me; in burnt offerings and sin offer- 6 ings thou hast taken no pleasure. Then I said, 'Lo, I have come to do 7 thy will, O God,' as it is written of me in the roll of the book."**

Psalm 40 combines a hymn of thanksgiving for deliverance with a prayer for help. In the heart of the psalm there stands the pledge to do God's will rather than offer formal sacrifices. As such it is a marvelous expression of the prophetic truth, "to obey is better than sacrifice" (1 Sam. 15:22). But as seen by the author, it expresses an even higher truth: that instead of the useless Levitical rites, only the personal sacrifice of Jesus can suffice in dealing with sin because only it fulfils the will of God.

The words, **a body hast thou prepared for me,** follow the Septuagint, in keeping with the usual preference of the author. The Hebrew text, however, literally reads, "ears hast thou digged for me," which apparently means that God has given man ears to hear that he might obey Him. The Septuagint translators dealt freely with the text by substituting the whole ("body") for the part ("ears"), resulting in the meaning that instead of God's equipping man with ears, He made or prepared for man a body. With either text the author's argument is not essentially different, for his main point is that there is an inner relation between Jesus' sacrifice and God's will.

It is the Son who says to the Father, **"Lo, I have come to do thy will, O God."** Originally, the psalmist spoke these words of himself, having read about obedience **in the roll of the book**[3] of God's law

---

2. Ibid., p. 57. Josephus' number is given in his *Jewish War* 6.424.

3. The Greek for "in the roll of the book" is *en kephalidi bibliou. Kephalis* (literally, "little head") denotes the extremity of anything—the tip of a shoe, the foot of a table, etc. It also refers to the head or knob of a stick on which a manuscript was rolled. Here the knob stands for the roll and is so translated.

(e.g., Deut. 6:5). But the author finds a fuller meaning than was obvious when these words were first spoken. To him they can refer to none other than Jesus who, during all His stay on earth, did God's will as it was written of Him in **the book** (cf. Mt. 5:17; Lk. 24:44).

Following his quotation of the psalm, the author reasons as to its implications, both past and present. **When he said above** (in the quo-
8 tation), **"Thou hast neither desired nor taken pleasure in sacrifices and offerings and burnt offerings and sin offerings" (these are offered accord- ing to the law)**—the words of the quotation are those of the Son, as is
9 clear from what follows—**then he added, "Lo, I have come to do thy will."** In His preincarnate state Christ knew that the sacrifices of the old order were not adequate, and He knew that something would have to take their place. So He decided to intervene personally and give Himself. He said, "Lo, I come. . . ." And consequently, **He abolishes the first** (the worn-out, legalistic, sacrificial system) **in order to establish the second** (the new, free, loving sacrifice of Christ).

The author concludes his remarks on the psalm by laying stress on
10 the divine will. **By that will** (through Christ's obedience to God's will) **we have been sanctified through the offering of the body of Jesus Christ once for all.** Sanctification is a ceremonial concept (see comment on 2:11). Under the Jewish law an unclean person was cleansed or sanctified by ritualistic means before he could approach God in worship. The idea here is similar. Jesus offered His body on the cross, and because of this offering men can now have fellowship with God. In this sanctification the will of God is of supreme importance. Burnt offerings and sin offerings were not really the will of God—and thus Jesus had to come! His offering was the final will of God on sacrifice, a perfect sacrifice because it was the perfect fulfilment of the divine will. In that offering God took delight, and forgave sin.

The Exalted Christ
(10:11-18)

It remains for the author to show from the Old Testament that the sacrifice of Jesus was a one-time sacrifice, eternally effective. This he does by taking notice of two passages, Psalm 110:1 and Jeremiah 31:33-34. The first passage, to which reference has already been made (1:13; cf. 1:3; 8:1), speaks of Messiah's being invited to sit at God's right hand. Attention is now drawn to this passage in a contrast of the Levitical priest and the great High Priest. The contrast is lucid and vivid, like two portraits painted by a master artist. The Jewish priest is
11 first pictured. **Every priest stands daily at his service, offering repeatedly the same sacrifices, which can never take away sins.** Each word con-

tributes to the effect. **Every** suggests that many priests over the years were needed, itself a mark of inadequacy (cf. 7:23). **Every priest stands**—always the posture of the priest in the tabernacle—as though waiting to do some further work. **Daily** indicates that there was no end to the routine. **The same sacrifices**—ever the same, the same animals offered at the same place at the same time in the same way. All this was done **repeatedly,** on and on, indefinitely. And to what effect? Of no value whatever, a string of zeros; for those sacrifices could **never take away sins.** "This combination of *ever* and *never* is very pathetic. . . . Ever, ever, at work; never, never, never doing any real good."[4]

The other person pictured is the Priest-King on the throne. **But 12 when Christ had offered for all time a single sacrifice for sins, he sat down at the right hand of God.** This priest, too, had something to offer (8:3), and what a magnificent offering it was! Because of that single offering, so well done and so acceptable, He sat down at God's hand; He is seated for ever a priest (7:17) because no other sacrifice is required.

He who on earth humbled Himself is now exalted in heaven, there **to wait until his enemies should be made a stool for his feet.** The words **13** complete the quotation in substance from Psalm 110:1. No particular application is made of them, other than their adding to the grand picture of Christ's universal dominion (cf. 1 Cor. 15:24-28). Positioned at God's right hand, Jesus is in a place of unrivaled honor. Indeed, the language indirectly affirms divinity. But His exalted position suggests also that His work of sacrifice is finished. The thought, already made unforgettable, is stated one more time: **For by a single offering he has 14 perfected for all time those who are sanctified.**

The argument of the passage is clinched by a final reference to Jeremiah 31, a passage that also makes way for the exhortation to follow. But only the highlights of the prophetic oracle, previously quoted in chapter 8, are given. The text of Jeremiah 31:33ff. is viewed as being divinely inspired and written especially for those in the Christian era (cf. 1 Cor. 10:11). **And the Holy Spirit also bears witness to us; for 15 after saying, "This is the covenant that I will make with them after 16 those days, says the Lord: I will put my laws on their hearts, and write them on their minds," then he adds, "I will remember their sins and 17 their misdeeds no more."** This oracle was introduced earlier to show the displacement of the old covenant by the new. Now it is quoted to establish the proposition that with the new covenant came forgiveness

---

4. A. B. Bruce, *Hebrews*, p. 381. The quotation is from a brilliant passage in which Bruce sees the contrast as a picture of "The Sacerdotal Drudge and the Priest upon the Throne." Bruce's highly descriptive style has had a marked influence on the vocabulary of virtually all of the subsequent English commentaries. I gladly register my debt to him, here and throughout my study of the Epistle.

18 of sins—and this means no further sacrifice. For **Where there is forgiveness of these, there is no longer any offering for sin.** Repeated remembrance of sins means repeated sacrifices; absolute forgiveness means that satisfactory atonement has been made. There is every reason, then, for the author to call this a *new* covenant.

Draw Near
(10:19-25)

With 10:18 the doctrinal exposition of the Epistle comes to a close. The author will indeed embellish here and there some of his leading thoughts, much like an artist who puts the last touches to a painting nearly finished. But from now on, he will seek to drive home the practical implications of his formal argument, that his readers may grasp the sense of responsibility and privilege that goes with the new covenant. If there are no true advantages in Judaism, if forgiveness of sins and the cleansing of conscience come only in the new order of religion, if Christ has made it possible to have perfect fellowship with God, then clearly it is the duty of the Christian to be firm and unswerving in his faith. That, the author feels, is what Christianity is all about—and that is why he has reasoned so long about the relative merits of the old and the new.

Except for several outbreaks of exhortation previously made, all of the author's doctrinal elaborations have really been preliminary to his final, extended appeal for perseverance (10:19—12:29). This appeal now

19 begins. **Therefore, brethren, since we have confidence to enter the sanctuary by the blood of Jesus....** The first few lines of the exhortation are very much like 4:14-16 (cf. Eph. 3:12), except that here mention is made of the sanctuary and of the sacrifice of Jesus, themes as yet undeveloped in the earlier passage. He addresses his readers as **brethren** (cf. 3:1; 13:22), identifying himself with his readers as recipients of special grace. **Confidence** or "boldness" was the need of the hour—a free, open attitude toward God (see comment on 4:16) here connected with entrance into His Presence. In the Jewish period the sanctuary was screened off from the worshiper. There was always a dividing wall, there was always a barrier that kept men at a distance. Now, however, the way is opened **by the blood of Jesus**, on the grounds of His perfect offering.

20 This way is **the new and living way which he opened for us through the curtain, that is, through his flesh.** The terms modifying way are meaningful. The way is new *(prosphaton)*, a word that very often means "fresh," like fresh grapes, fresh olives, fresh fish, fresh water, etc. The term also refers to some event that has recently happened. The two

conceptions coalesce. The **new way** has been recently made accessible and is perennially "fresh." The **way** is likewise a **living way** because it brings life from God. It is a **way** not scattered with dead sacrifices, but made accessible by the living Christ (cf. Jn. 14:6), who Himself cleared the path. He **opened it up,** for the verb *enkainizō* can be used in the sense "to make a way that was not there before" (TDNT, III, 454). The implied contrast "is not between a new, unfrequented path, and an old one, familiar and well-trodden; but rather between a new way and no way at all."[5]

So now the way **through the curtain** into the place of God's throne is forever opened. In speaking of **the curtain,** the author is once again using symbolic language. In the earthly tabernacle the veil which hung between the outer and inner compartments served as a reminder that the way to God's presence was as yet unrevealed. But a great transformation was wrought by the sacrifice of Jesus. This is what the author is pointing to when he says **through his flesh.** The author identifies **the curtain** with **his flesh** that his readers might better visualize the necessity of Jesus' death. As entrance into the inner shrine could only be gained through the veil, so for Christ entrance before God could not be had except through the veil of His flesh. His own death, so to speak, stood between Him and His way of approach to God. The cross, then, was a matter of divine necessity, and the access thus gained cost much.

The way of free access is not the only privilege of the Christian. He has also **a great priest over the house of God** (cf. 4:14). A new priest **21** is in charge of the sanctuary, one who is truly qualified to introduce men to God; and because He is there, a gracious reception is assured to all the members of God's house (cf. 3:6).

Then follows a stimulating appeal in triplicate, each part beginning with "let us" (vv. 22, 23, 24), and each part emphasizing first faith, then hope, and then love. **Let us draw near with a true heart in full assurance 22 of faith.** The boldness of tone is in keeping with the absoluteness of the Epistle—Christianity is the best of all possible religions. The exhortation is, as in 4:16, to draw near in worship and service to God's gracious throne where abundant help can be secured. The implication is that it should be done now. The approach is to be made with the attitude of **a true heart.** It is not to be like the Old Testament priest who came before God externally perfect but with a dead heart. It is to be an entrance of sincerity, an experience of the inner man, and above all an entrance without doubt or hesitation. Such an attitude of heart inevitably involves **full assurance of faith** (a full faith, like a full hope,

---

5. A. B. Bruce, *Hebrews,* p. 395.

6:11), without which there can be no confidence in the unseen realities within the veil. Of this kind of faith the author speaks later when he says that "whoever would draw near to God must believe that he exists and that he rewards those who seek him" (11:6).

The right to draw near to God assumes that certain conditions have been met. These include, according to the author, **our hearts sprinkled clean from an evil conscience and our bodies washed with pure water.** The first clause is shortened. Its full sense is that men's hearts are sprinkled with the blood of Christ and thus are cleansed from dead works (cf. 9:14). The sprinkled heart discerns the significance of Christ's sacrifice, and effects inward relief. The language is once again liturgical, an analogy being drawn from the ceremonial cleansing with blood required for the Jewish priests (Ex. 29:21; Lev. 8:30). Since the same ceremony required that the priests be bathed in water (Ex. 29:4; Lev. 16:4), the author naturally thinks of the Christian counterpart where water is employed. That he is referring to baptism seems unquestionable; for in the New Testament baptism is described in terms of a washing (Acts 22:16; Eph. 5:26; Tit. 3:5), although the stress is on the inner and not the outer cleansing (cf. 1 Pet. 3:21). Taken together the sprinkling of the heart and the washing of the body stand for the process of conversion, containing allusions to repentance and baptism.

23   The second aspect of the exhortation is given in the words **Let us hold fast the confession of our hope without wavering.** The exhortation, although applicable to all Christians, is not an ordinary one. The words are strong and urgent, suggesting that underneath the surface lurks the peril of apostasy. The author has already spoken to his readers along these lines, pleading with them that they "hold fast" in Christ (3:6, 14; 4:14). Here he speaks of their hope (cf. 6:11, 13-20; 7:19), and of their confession of hope. This is not their confession that they have a hope, but their confession of the things that they believe in against a mocking, skeptical world. **Hope** here stands for the Christian religion because of the hopes it inspires. Their hope is to be maintained no matter what the obstacles, **for he who promised is faithful** (cf. 11:11). God will not fail them (13:5). His words are unalterably true (6:18). Therefore, they are to be constant in their hope, allowing it to bend neither to one side nor the other.[6]

To faith and hope is now added love, which forms the third branch of the exhortation. Faith, hope, and love receive weighty emphasis in Paul (1 Cor. 13:13; 1 Thess. 1:3), and apparently were the subjects of much early Christian instruction. The author still speaks in the first

---

6. This is the force of the Greek word *aklinēs* ("without wavering"), for the term means "bending to neither side," "unswerving," "steady."

person. **Let us consider how to stir up one another to love and good** 24
works. A more literal translation would be, "Let us consider one another
for [with a view to] the provocation of love and good works." That is,
"Let us consider one another to stir up to love and good works." The
point is not to "consider how" but rather to "consider one another" and
thus be able to stimulate one's brother to love and practical goodness.
The word for **stir up** is *paroxusmos* (cf. the English "paroxysm"), which
means "to spur on" or "incite" to either good or bad. Christians **consider
. . . one another** mainly by taking into account the circumstances and
weaknesses of others, in order to lend them support. Christians also
consider . . . one another, as the structure of the Greek sentence makes
clear, by **not neglecting to meet together** (next verse).[7]

Love for others cannot be shown in separation. In none of their
affairs, and especially in spiritual matters, can Christians regard themselves as isolated digits. Thus they must not fail to meet together for
worship and mutual encouragement: **not neglecting to meet together,** 25
as is the habit of some, but encouraging one another. There is a vital
connection between the expressions **meet together** and **encouraging one
another.** The thought is not so much that they were to encourage one
another to meet together, but that they were to meet together where
such encouragement was available in the assembly. A chief function of
public worship, according to Paul, is the edification of all who come
together (1 Cor. 14:26ff.). But how can men be edified when they absent
themselves from the assembly? The question clearly was in the back of
the author's mind.

There is a question of considerable importance here as to the exact
connotation of the participle *enkataleipontes* ("neglecting"). Ordinarily
the verb means "to leave behind," "leave in the lurch," "abandon." So it
can be argued here that they were breaking ranks from the group, that
they were not just "neglecting" but were "abandoning" or "deserting"
the worship meetings of the saints. They were *apostatizing.* But if the
author is talking of apostasy, how could he say **as is the habit of some?**
In view of the latter expression, it seems preferable to translate **not
neglecting to meet together.** But because the author writes, **Let us**
consider . . . one another and **encouraging one another,** there can be
little doubt but that he saw that neglect of the assembly would in time
lead to the utter desertion of the faith.

No hint is given as to why they were absenting themselves. Perhaps
some were quitting the services because they felt that the Christian

---

7. "Do not keep apart by yourselves in secret," says the Epistle of Barnabas (c. A.D.
130), "as if you were already justified, but meet together and seek out the common
good" (4:10). For further references on Christians meeting together, see Harnack,
I, p. 434f. See also TDNT, VII, 843 (n. 15).

gatherings were generally uninspiring and unattractive, especially when set beside the extravagance of the Jewish ritual. It may be that some had become Christians thinking to obtain magical favor, just as they might patronize the mystery cults; and having obtained the favor, they withdrew.[8] Or it is slightly possible that some, with visions of their own intellectual grandeur, discounted even the need of common worship; disdaining the ties and responsibilities of brotherhood fellowship, they determined to be a congregation all their own. What would appear more probable, however, is that some had begun to give in to pressure from the outside.[9] These Christians had already suffered much, as is clear from 10:32ff. They had known fear and hardship and personal abuse, but that was in the early days. Since then time had worn on, and the journey had become difficult. So the question was being raised, Is Christ and Christianity really worth all these struggles? Some apparently had answered in the negative and had given up. Some perhaps had gone so far as to return to the relative safety of synagogue worship. In view of the context of the passage, a reconstruction along these lines seems to fit the historical circumstances; yet it is no more than a plausible reconstruction.

Instead of wavering in their faith, then, the readers are urged to meet together for mutual edification, and this **all the more as** they **see the Day drawing near.** What is the day whose near approach can be seen? The main views can be summarized:

1. It is said that **the Day** refers to the day of Christian worship, in particular to the day which elsewhere is called "the first day of the week" (Acts 20:7; 1 Cor. 16:2) and "the Lord's day" (Rev. 1:10). But the very fact that in other passages it is so designated argues that **Day,** without further qualification, is used here in a different sense. Too, it should be remembered that verse 25 deals with exhortation *in* the assembly, not exhortation *to* the assembly.

2. It is said that **the Day** refers to the destruction of Jerusalem in A.D. 70. A number of older commentators especially held this view, since they associated "The Epistle to the Hebrews" with Jewish Christians who lived in or near Jerusalem. Jesus had spoken to His disciples of His coming in destruction and judgment on the city, and He had given them certain signs that would warn of its imminent overthrow

---

8. "At first and indeed always there were naturally some people who imagined that one could secure the holy contents and blessings of Christianity as one did those of Isis or the Magna Mater, and then withdrew" (Harnack, I, pp. 434-35). Here Harnack, as he speaks of Heb. 10:25, lists several reasons why early Christians withdrew from their public meetings.

9. "Many . . . were actuated by fear of the authorities; they shunned attendance at public worship, to avoid being recognized as Christians" (Ibid., p. 435).

(Mt. 24). These signs were external, having to do with the social and political alternations that led up to the Judean catastrophe. As such they were signs that could be *seen* by discerning people. In this light **as you see the Day drawing near** would point to the visible signs of Jerusalem's fall. If, on the other hand, the Epistle was written to Christians outside of Palestine, how could they **see** the coming signs of Jerusalem's destruction?

3. It is said that **the Day** refers to "the day of the Lord," to the day of final judgment when Christ comes again. This interpretation is generally held in most recent commentaries and translations (RSV, NEB, TEV, etc.). **The Day** would thus directly tie in with the subsequent reference to judgment and Christ's second appearance (v. 37), and it would correspond with 9:28 and numerous other passages in the New Testament that speak of the Last Day. The day is spoken of as **drawing near** in the same sense that Paul affirmed, for example, that "the night is far gone, the day is at hand" (Rom. 13:12; cf. 1 Thess. 5:4; Phil. 4:5; Js. 5:8). If it is asked how they could **see** the Day of Christ approaching, the answer lies in such passages as 2:9. If through faith the readers could see (Greek verb, *blepō*) Jesus crowned with glory and honor, they also through faith could see *(blepō)* the approach of His coming and His Day.

A Further Warning Against Apostasy (10:26-31)

Because that great Day draws near, Christians are exhorted to attend to the needs and responsibilities of social worship. If they do not, the consequences are grave indeed. This the author now proceeds to show. **For if we sin deliberately after receiving the knowledge of the 26 truth, there no longer remains a sacrifice for sins.** Thus begin the ominous lines of a passage similar to, but even more severe than, the warning in 6:4-8. There, as here, the danger is one of complete apostasy from the Christian faith. It is clear that the author is not speaking of mere human weakness or inclination to sin. He is fully aware that men are beset with weaknesses, and he has assured his readers that in Jesus Christ as High Priest they have one who is able to help them in their temptations and bear gently with them even when they go astray (2:18; 4:16; 5:2). Rather than inadvertent sin, the author is speaking of the sin of presumption, sinning "with a high hand" (see comment on 5:2). **Deliberately** is positioned as the first word in the author's sentence, adding a vivid touch. What the author has in mind is a deliberate rejection of truth after truth has once been received, an extinguishing of light that has already shone in the heart, a conscious preference for the dark. He speaks not so much of an act of sin but of a state of sin, for the force of the verb is repeated action—"if we go on sinning," "if we continue to sin," "if we persist in sin" (cf. TEV, NEB). That is, if enlightened men persist in "departing from the living God" (3:12), if they wilfully abandon Christ and repudiate His covenant (v. 29), there is for them no way of forgiveness. The Mosaic religion cannot be resorted to, for the author has proved that no sacrifice there is of any value. If the one sacrifice of Christ is rejected, what then? "The once-for-all nature of Christ's sacrifice is like a two-edged sword. On the one hand, it is so effective that it does not need to be repeated (7:27), but, on the other hand, it cannot be repeated, even if needed."[10] Defection from Christianity, therefore, brings final doom.

The Mosaic law was firm; "disobedience met with due retribution" (2:2, NEB). Under the new law, for those who apostatize there remains 27 only **a fearful prospect of judgment, and a fury of fire which will consume the adversaries.** The terror of the expectation is brought out by a more literal rendering of the words, "a certain fearful expectation of judgment" (ASV); for the indefinite "a certain" leaves it somewhat open to the reader's imagination to fill in the gruesome details of that judgment. God's judgment on the wicked is often pictured as coming in fire (Isa. 66:15-16; Zeph. 1:18; 2 Thess. 1:7-10; cf. Heb. 12:29; Rom. 2:8; for the whole expression, cf. Isa. 26:11). The words **fury of fire,** if literally translated, would be "jealousy [zeal] of fire," suggesting that the divine anger in fiery judgment is like the flaming heart of a jealous lover.

God's fierce anger against apostates is not without justification. This, the author reasons, on the basis of the law laid down in Deuter-28 onomy 17:2-7. **A man who has violated the law of Moses dies without mercy at the testimony of two or three witnesses.** The reference is to the sin of idolatry and its punishment as a capital offense. The parallel of the Jews forsaking the true God and Christians forsaking the living Christ is significant. If a man who violated Moses' law died without 29 mercy, without the right of appeal or reprieve, **How much worse punishment do you think,** the author asks, appealing to his readers' sense of judgment, **will be deserved by the man who has spurned the Son of God, and profaned the blood of the covenant by which he was sanctified, and outraged the Spirit of grace?** The argument follows the lines of 2:1-4 and 12:25. The penalty of judgment is worse, of course, inasmuch as Jesus is greater than Moses (3:1-6) and His new covenant greater than the old (8:6—10:18).

That the whole passage concerns blatant rebellion and apostasy becomes even clearer from the enormity of the sins depicted. To

---

10. Buchanan, p. 171.

apostatize is (1) to spurn and trample under foot the Son of God,[11] to "hold him up to contempt" (6:6), knowing all the while that He is the Son of God. To apostatize is (2) to count the blood of the covenant, by which is meant the blood of Christ (9:15-22; 13:20), common like any blood—the very blood which the apostate has been cleansed by, that blood which is God's only means to make men holy. To apostatize is (3) to blasphemously insult the Holy Spirit. The Spirit is here called **the Spirit of grace** (contrasted with Moses' law, v. 28; cf. Jn. 1:17) "to bring out the personal, gracious nature of the power so wantonly insulted."[12] What greater crime can be imagined than to despise God's Son, regard His sacrifice as no more than an ordinary death, do outrage to His gracious Spirit, and all of this by one who once acknowledged Jesus as Lord?

It should not be thought that God will regard such conduct lightly. Indeed, the nature of His character makes retribution certain. **For we know him who said, "Vengeance is mine, I will repay."**[13] **And again, "The Lord will judge his people."** The two quotations are from the Song of Moses in Deuteronomy, the first from 32:35 and the second from 32:36 (cf. Ps. 135:14). Each, in its original context, refers to God's readiness to vindicate His people against their enemies. Here, however, the words are applied more generally, making certain that God's retributive judgment will fall on His unfaithful people as well. **30**

The somber passage is brought to an end with one last word of warning: **It is a fearful thing to fall into the hands of the living God.** The form of the expression brings to mind a statement of David, who, looking to God to do right, said, "Let us fall into the hand of the Lord, for his mercy is great" (2 Sam. 24:14). To the believer it is a wonderful thing to be left in the hands of God. But to the unbelieving apostate, of whom the author speaks, to be at the disposal of God's punitive justice can only be "a terrifying expectation of judgement" (v. 27, NEB). **31**

---

11. The verb *katapateō* ("to trample under foot," "deny," "despise") "denotes contempt of the most flagrant kind" (Moffatt, *Hebrews*, p. 151). It is used in the New Testament of salt paths that are trodden underfoot (Mt. 5:13), of seed sown that is trampled down (Lk. 8:5), etc. In the writings of the Greeks it is often used of laws or oaths that are trampled down, i.e., disobeyed or unkept.

12. Moffatt, *Hebrews*, p. 151.

13. The quotation corresponds exactly with neither the LXX nor the Hebrew text (MT), although in part it is like both. The MT reads, "Vengeance is mine and recompense"; the LXX, "In the day of vengeance I will recompense." It appears that the author, and Paul (cf. Rom. 12:19), either were quoting the Deuteronomic statement as popularly known or were dependent on a form of the text whose precise wording is not extant today. See the article by George Howard, "Hebrews and the Old Testament Quotations," NovTest 10 (1968), 208-16; cf. Peter Katz, "The Quotations from Deuteronomy in Hebrews," ZNW 49 (1958), 219f.

Do Not Draw Back
(10:32-39)

The tone of this section is similar to that of chapter 6. There, after the author portrays the irrevocable doom of apostates (6:4-8), he speaks in soothing terms and assures his readers that he expects only the best of them. His confidence there is based on their deeds of practical goodness and brotherly love (6:9-12). Now the appeal to his readers is that

32 they be worthy of their glorious past. **But recall the former days when, after you were enlightened, you endured a hard struggle with sufferings.** Reference to **the former days** implies, as is indicated also in 5:12ff., that the people addressed have been Christians for some time. How long, and what the specific circumstances of hardship were, are not known. If more details were available, much helpful light might be cast on the original readers of the Epistle. What apparently happened, however, was that shortly after they had entered the Christian way, when they were **enlightened** with the new light of Christ, a period of persecution set in. But they had stood courageously, even though they had suffered

33 many things, **sometimes being publicly exposed to abuse and affliction, and sometimes being partners with those so treated.** A striking term is used to describe the insults that were theirs—*theatrizō*, to be made a "theatrical display," "held up to shame," to be made a "public show" (NEB).[14] The term is taken from the practice of arraigning and punishing criminals before a crowd assembled in the theater. It is not to be taken literally here, as though a reference to the exposure of Christians to wild beasts. A figurative sense is rather required. They were held up to public scorn, taunted and jeered at, and even physically kicked about and abused.

Not only did they suffer like this, but they became partners with

34 those who were so abused. **For,** the author says, **you had compassion on the prisoners, and you joyfully accepted the plundering of your property.** They had actively ministered to the needs of their afflicted brothers. Christians imprisoned in ancient times had to be visited and fed. This was a never-to-be-forgotten obligation (13:3; Mt. 25:36, 39, 43-44); and that they had in fact done so is clear from this passage (perhaps alluded to in 6:10). They had not only met their losses with calm detachment but had even **joyfully accepted** (cf. Acts 5:41; Rom. 5:3) the plundering of their goods. Their belongings either had been confiscated by civil authority or simply had been looted by the mob in

---

14. Cf. the use of *theatron*, "spectacle," in I Cor. 4:9, where the apostles are compared to "men condemned to death in the arena, a spectacle to the whole universe" (NEB).

a time of riotous persecution. In the midst of these trials they had rejoiced, as Jesus had taught His disciples to do (Mt. 5:12), knowing full well that they had a better possession and an abiding one. Others could rob them of their goods, but they could not take away their treasures laid up in heaven (Mt. 6:20).[15]

Having inspired them with memories of past accomplishments, the author's appeal becomes even more direct: **Therefore do not throw** 35 **away your confidence, which has a great reward. Throw away** is the opposite of "hold fast" (3:6, 14; 10:23). **Confidence** describes that bold attitude toward God, that firm assurance with which one approaches the throne of grace (4:16) and enters into the sanctuary (10:19), a confident outlook based on the sacrifice of Christ. For the Christian it involves also the unashamed confession of his faith, and as such is to be held on to (3:6) and not cast away as worthless. Indeed, there attaches to it, if retained, a great reward (cf. 11:26; 6:10).

What was needed was further spiritual exertion: **For you have** 36 **need of endurance, so that you may do the will of God and receive what is promised.** Considerable emphasis is placed on doing the will of God. Their human wills might run counter to His will; still they were not to compromise that will in their lives. The implication perhaps is that they might, in the words of 1 Peter, have to "suffer according to God's will" (1 Pet. 4:19; cf. 2:15; 3:17); and if so, they must will to do His will and persevere. The exhortation reminds one of the argument in chapter 4: reach out, press forward, do not fail, as the Israelites did, to gain the promised inheritance.

But how long would it be before the promise was realized? The question was not academic, not at least for the readers who had already suffered and were to suffer again for His name. The author responds by citing the Old Testament: "**For yet a little while,**[16] **and the coming one** 37 **shall come and shall not tarry.**" The quotation, which is concluded in the following verse, is taken largely from Habakkuk 2:3-4; the first line of the quotation (the "little while") is apparently from Isaiah 26:20. (The form of the quotation is close to that of the LXX. See Additional Note.) In effect, the author's answer to the question of how long is: "Be patient. The time is not long. Isaiah says it will be 'a very little while'; and Habakkuk says that the Coming One will not delay."

---

15. Of these harassed yet cheerful Christians Robinson has observed: "No doubt their eschatology was a help to them.... But it should always be a mark of the spirit of the Christian that he should own nothing, outside himself, to which he cannot say goodbye with a smile" (Robinson, p. 151).

16. The expression in Greek (*mikron hoson hoson*) is unusual, literally meaning "a little, how very, how very." It should be translated "a very little while."

38   The quotation from Habakkuk continues: **But my righteous one**[17] **shall live by faith, and if he shrinks back, my soul has no pleasure in him.** Paul's use of these words (Rom. 1:17; Gal. 3:11) is somewhat different. He argues from this passage that the one grand justification principle of lost men is faith, that the righteous man is made righteous by faith and thus shall live. The author of Hebrews reflects more of the original sense of Habakkuk. The ancient prophet began his oracle by asking, "O Lord, how long shall I cry for help, and thou wilt not hear?" (1:2). He was anxious to learn why a righteous God permits His own people to be trampled under foot by the heathen oppressors. God answers that He is still sovereign and that in His own time He will bring down the wicked. In the meantime, however, "the righteous man shall live by his faithfulness." Israel, if it put its trust in the Lord, would receive its reward.

The author is thus able to make full use of Habakkuk. The conditions in Habakkuk are much the same as those in Hebrews. The impatient prophet cried out to God, "How long?" The readers of Hebrews wondered, similarly, about the duration of their struggles. Perhaps their state of aimlessness and spiritual retardation had been partially induced by their own frustration over the Lord's delay. Likewise, as in Habakkuk the vision was surely to come, so in Hebrews it is an assured matter that the Coming One will come and not tarry long. And if in Habakkuk's time the righteous man could be saved by his faithful and tenacious clinging to God, fidelity and fortitude are even more required of the righteous man to whom the author directs his appeal.

The passage is now brought to its end on a clear note of hope and optimism. The author cannot believe that his readers will defect.

39 Identifying himself with them, he speaks reassuringly, **But we are not of those who shrink back and are destroyed, but of those who have faith and keep their souls.** The Greek word for **shrink back** is *hupostolē*, used only here in the New Testament. The verb is *hupostellō*, a word which comes out of a rich background.[18] It first means "to draw in" or "contract," as someone might furl a sail or a dog tuck his tail. It then

---

17. The note struck by "my righteous one," as Moffatt (*Hebrews*, p. 157f.) observes, echoes on and on through the following passage: "Abel . . . received approval as righteous" (11:4); "Noah . . . an heir of . . . righteousness" (11:7); "through faith . . . enforced justice [or, righteousness]" (11:33); "discipline . . . yields the peaceful fruit of righteousness" (12:11); "the spirits of just [or, righteous] men made perfect" (12:23).

18. Besides its use in the previous verse, *hupostellō* in Gal. 2:12 describes the timid conduct of Peter. After important Jews came from Jerusalem, he "slunk away from" and no longer ate with Gentiles. Cf. the use of *hupostellō* in the middle voice in Acts 20:20, 27.

means "to draw back," "abstain from" "avoid," "cover," etc. Sometimes it is used of a person "who has stuck at nothing." This is very close to the thought here. The Epistle's readers were not to be quitters but were to persevere in faith.

Chapters 9 and 10 are rather lengthy chapters that require a summary. The central theme that is developed in the chapters is the superior ministry of Christ's priesthood over that of the Levitical high priest. In 9:1-10 the author describes, first, the furnishings of the desert tabernacle, and, second, the religious services conducted in the tabernacle. As to its furnishings, they were elaborate and costly, especially those items of the inner shrine that were overlaid with gold. Why mention the furniture? Because every item was as good as it possibly could be— in any *earthly* sanctuary.

But the beauty of those items could not guarantee an effective worship. Always, under the old arrangement, there was the curtain that hid the presence of God from the worshiper. Even the high priest could enter behind the curtain only once a year, and then only by means of blood. How inferior and imperfect that old system was, with its separating curtain. But now Christ has opened the curtain (10:19-20), and the exhortation is that Christians should "draw near with a true heart in the full assurance of faith" (10:22).

In contrast to the earthly tabernacle, there is the tabernacle "not made with hands" (9:11). Into that tabernacle, the heavenly one, Christ entered on the merits of His own blood. What a difference He makes as the victim—what a difference between the blood of a nonthinking beast and the blood of One who gives Himself as a loving, rational, free sacrifice! His blood, therefore, secured not annual but eternal redemption; and His sacrifice in significance belongs to the eternal order. This is the gist of 9:11-14, the few verses that may well be the most central verses in the author's theme. In these verses the word "Christ" is the key word that begins the inclusion in verse 11 and concludes the inclusion in verse 14.

In the references that follow, references to the new covenant, to Christ's entrance into heaven, to the law of shadows, and so on, one thought predominates—Christ offered Himself once and once only. It is not a new thought (cf. 7:27; 9:12) but a thought which the teacher by repetition seeks to din into the ears of his hearers. Christ has entered into the heavenly sanctuary, and the fact that He stays there shows the efficacy of His sacrifice. He does not go in and out to deal with sin. He died once, just as all men die once. When He comes again, He comes as Savior and not as victim.

What remains on Leviticalism may well be summarized in the

author's dictum, "It is impossible that the blood of bulls and goats should take away sins" (10:4). The law, a shadow, could never perform the function of the substance (10:1). This required, therefore, a new sacrifice that was the perfect fulfilment of God's will (10:5-10).

Then follow the exhortations to the readers to draw near with full faith and not to cast away their confidence. They could not give up now. They had gone too far for that. True, the storm had burst on them early, but they had weathered it bravely. Why should they give up the voyage now, when it was nearly done?[19] Indeed, they should not; and the author is persuaded that they would not. He is sure that they are not men who shrink back but are men of faith.[20]

Additional Notes

The KJV on 10:23

The KJV reads here "profession of our faith." The translation cannot be justified, for the Greek text reads "hope" and not "faith." Instead of "profession" modern English usage, of course, would require "confession."

The form of the quotation in 10:30

The quotation, "Vengeance is mine . . . ," differs somewhat from the LXX but is in exact agreement with the form of the quotation found in Romans 12:19. It is one instance in the Epistle where a quotation is closer to the Hebrew text than to the LXX. The Targum of Onkelos renders the clause, "Vengeance is before me, and I will repay." The agreement between Paul and Hebrews is explained by some on the basis of their common knowledge of this targumic paraphrase; others prefer to say that this was simply the form of the quotation in popular use.

The reading of 10:34

The KJV reads, "For ye had compassion of men in my bonds." The RSV reads, "For you had compassion on the prisoners." The difference in translation is due to different readings in the Greek text. In a case of this kind the reading that is most likely to be original is the reading that can best explain the origin of other readings. This reading is *desmiois* (translated "prisoners"), supported by such authorities as A, D, 33, 1739, etc. *Desmois* ("bonds") is the reading of P[46] and others. A few old Latin MSS read *desmois autōn* ("their bonds"), while other MSS (including Aleph and many later MSS) read *desmois mou* ("my bonds"). The translation of the KJV, based on later MSS, has con-

---

19. The words are an adaptation of Moffatt, *Hebrews*, p. 153.
20. The word "faith" is an important hook word that ties together 10:39 and 11:1.

tributed to the view that Hebrews was written by the apostle Paul (cf. Col. 4:18; Phil. 1:17).

The form of the quotation in 10:37-38

The quotation of Habakkuk 2:3-4, with slight variations, is from the LXX. The chief differences are as follows: (1) The text of Hebrews, by the addition of the definite article *ho*, is made to point more specifically to the Messiah as "the coming one"; while the LXX reads "coming he will come," that is, "he will surely come." (2) The author of Hebrews, as he quotes, transposes the last two clauses of Habakkuk 2:4. (3) The author inserts the emphatic *mou* ("my"), the quotation thus reading "my righteous one shall live by faith." It is of importance to add that the author's use of the quotation is very much in the same spirit as the LXX. While the Hebrew text of Habakkuk refers to a vision of deliverance that will not tarry, the LXX speaks of a personal deliverer: "If he is late, wait for him; because he will surely come, he will not delay." The author thus makes use of a passage which, most probably, was already understood messianically. Paul's use of the same Habakkuk passage (Rom. 1:17; Gal. 3:11) suggests this.

HEBREWS ELEVEN

A Description of Faith
(11:1-3)

Hebrews 11 stands in Scripture as the great faith chapter. An enthusiastic appeal for steadfastness, it brings the reader into the "enchanted land"; for it partakes of the realm of which it speaks, the realm of the spiritual and eternal.

It may be that this discourse was at one time a masterful sermon on faith, prepared and delivered by the author on another occasion. If so, its form was to state the nature of faith and simply illustrate faith with a number of well-chosen examples from people of the past.[1] It may be that the author had found various occasions to speak on this theme to Christian assemblies, a theme to which he now once more addresses himself in urgent circumstances.

Or it may be that this is all idle speculation. It is beyond question, however, that though the chapter is primarily hortatory, still it fits logically into the argument of the whole Epistle. The first readers of the Epistle had their roots deep in history, and on that history the author bases his appeal. His appeal as it develops, however, gradually is transformed into an implicit argument: he points to men of faith in the old covenant that he may renew loyalty to the new. He uses what is precious and sacred to enforce the very lessons he has been seeking to get across—his readers will best imitate the religion of their fathers

---

1. Michel (p. 371), locating this type of preaching in circles of Hellenistic Judaism, points to similar examples of heroes appealed to in Wisdom of Solomon 10; Ecclesiasticus 44–50; 4 Maccabees 16:16-23; Philo, *On the Virtues* 198ff. and *On Rewards and Punishments* 1ff.; 4 Ezra 7.105ff. Also cf. the speech of Stephen (Acts 7:1-50); 1 Clement 4:7ff.; 7:5ff.; etc.

not by falling back to Judaism but by holding on to Jesus as Savior and Lord.

The great chapter on faith, however, is frequently misread. "Faith" here does not mean precisely what it means in the writings of Paul. To him faith is the act of personal commitment and trust in Christ, a principle that effects salvation as opposed to the vapidness of the Mosaic legalism (Rom. 3:27-28; 5:1; Gal. 2:16). For the author of Hebrews, — however, faith is essentially trust or confidence in God. (In Hebrews God is the prime object of faith, whether expressed or not; Christ is "the pioneer and perfecter of our faith" [12:2].) Faith in chapter 11, then, is faith in God, primarily faith in all His declarations, whether past (v. 3) or future (vv. 7, 8, 10, 13, etc.). At times "faith" shades into "faithfulness" (cf. the close of chap. 10): faith is the opposite of falling back, it is the staying power, it is the courageous spirit that enables a man to choose hardship and duty over ease and safety. Thus in the long chronicle of heroes given here, the author stresses three characteristics particularly in the lives of men of faith: their unfaltering trust in God, their vision of the invisible, and their power to press on in hope.[2]

1   The author begins with a description of faith. **Now faith is the assurance of things hoped for, the conviction of things not seen.** This is not, of course, a theologically exact definition; for the words which follow are not so much a definition of what constitutes faith as a description of what faith does in men's lives. But what is the meaning of the author's opening statement on faith? It is nearly impossible to propose a certain translation of these words. It is especially difficult to determine the meanings of two words. The first word is *hupostasis* ("assurance"). It refers literally to something that stands under, of a foundation or substructure of a building. Then, among other things, it denotes a plan or purpose of something, a coming into existence or origin of a thing, the substance or real nature of a thing. It is also used of something on which a hope is based, and from this derives the sense of "confidence" or "assurance." The author has already used *hupostasis* both in the sense of "real nature" (1:3) and in the sense of "confidence" (3:14).

The other difficult word here is *elenchos*. It is a term from the law courts. It refers to an argument of disproof or refutation; it is used of cross-examining someone with a view to establishing evidence. It refers also to the basis on which a person is convicted; thus most of the translations read here "evidence" or "conviction." But the difficulty of these two words, *hupostasis* and *elenchos*, does not concern their wide range of meanings. The problem is rather their specific connotations here. Is

2. In this chapter "faith" is very much related to "hope." See TDNT, VI, 207f.

hupostasis "substance" or "assurance"? Is it the basis of hope, that which "gives substance to our hopes" (NEB)? Or is it the absolute confidence in these hoped-for realities? And is *elenchos* to be taken as parallel with *hupostasis*, in some way limiting or defining it? And what is the meaning of *elenchos*? If it is a legal term used for *objective* evidence, can it also be used to refer to *inner* conviction or persuasion?

A good case can be made for taking **faith** as the "substance" or "ground" or "reality" **of things hoped for.** Moulton and Milligan cite examples from the secular papyri and maintain that *hupostasis* refers to "something that *underlies* visible conditions and guarantees a future possession."[3] Finding one example in particular that refers to "deeds of property,"[4] they suggest the translation here, "faith is the *title-deed* of things hoped for." This compares favorably with other passages that speak of the Holy Spirit as the "first fruits" or "guarantee" of the Christian's eternal inheritance (Rom. 8:23; 2 Cor. 1:22; 5:5; Eph. 1:14).[5]

Since the time of Erasmus, Luther, and Tyndale, **faith** has been generally understood as **the** confidence or **assurance of things hoped for.** On this side it is argued that if faith gives reality to things hoped for, then these things are reduced to a subjective illusion. Surely things hoped for have an existence independent of faith—faith cannot bestow on them their reality.[6] There is, besides, the general impression that "the writer wishes to show," as Moffatt has it, "not the reality of these unseen ends of God—he assumes these—but the fact and force of believing in them with absolute confidence."[7]

But in what sense is **faith** the **conviction** of unseen realities? The thought would seem to be that as, for example, the eyes prove certain facts in the visible world, so faith enables one to act with a view to facts in the higher, invisible realm. The two clauses of verse 1, with their key words **assurance** and **conviction,** are probably to be taken together, forming one declaration: **faith is the** full **assurance** and inner

---

3. Moulton-Milligan, p. 660.

4. "Wives shall add copies of their marriage contracts to their husbands' deeds of property" (P. Oxy., II, 237, 8, 26 (A.D. 186). "It should be noted that *hupostasis* is not the possession of land as such but the document which guarantees its actual possession" (H. Köster, TDNT, VIII, 580).

5. Spicq (II, p. 337) decidedly holds this view and takes *hupostasis* in the sense of "anticipated possession" or "objective guarantee." Köster associates *hupostasis* more with the philosophical background of Middle Platonism and takes it (as in 1:3) to refer to reality: faith is the reality of what is hoped for. Köster adds "that the reality of what is hoped for is presupposed and faith is equated with it" (TDNT, VIII, 587).

6. It is possible, however, for faith to give present reality to things future.

7. Moffatt, *Hebrews*, p. 160.

conviction that gives men the power to stake their lives on unseen realities.[8]

The author proceeds to illustrate his statement on faith. But before doing so, he speaks generally of the men's faith concerning which he will
2 speak in detail in the rest of the chapter. **For by it** (this kind of faith) **the men of old received divine approval.** The translation **men of old** (RSV, NEB) is to be preferred, since "elders" (KJV, ASV) is susceptible to misunderstanding. The author's reference is, of course, to the men of renown of whom he is about to speak, to the "fathers" (1:1) who lived in past ages, from the time of Abel onward. These men, on account of their faith, received witness borne to them by God and stand immortalized in Scripture.

About to relate in historical sequence the actions of faith-filled
3 men, the author pauses and begins at the beginning of things. **By faith,** he says, **we understand that the world** (*aiōnas,* "ages" or "worlds," cf. 1:2) **was created by the word of God.** The existence of the world is a fact substantiated by experience, and that it has been "fashioned" or "created"[9] in some inexplicable way is a natural deduction of the human mind. But that it has all come into being **by the word of God** is a theory unsupported by empirical evidence. The Genesis account attributes this to the action of God. God spoke, and it was so. "By the word of the Lord the heavens were made, and all their host by the breath of his mouth" (Ps. 33:6). Thus the conception, **that what is seen was made out of things which do not appear,** comes only through faith (cf. Rom. 1:20). It is because of faith and by means of faith that a true understanding of the created order is gained. Behind everything there is an unseen force that is not subject to the investigations of science.

Faith in the Old World
(11:4-7)

4 The roll call of **the men of old** now begins. **By faith Abel offered to God a more acceptable sacrifice than Cain.** The text reads, literally, "a more sacrifice"—more excellent, more adequate, more acceptable, and so forth—or "a greater sacrifice" (NEB). Whether its superiority consisted in what was offered or the manner in which it was offered, is not stated. The author does state, however, that Abel's sacrifice was made

---

8. Linguistically, there still are problems, for *elenchos* is as yet unattested in the sense of inner conviction. Arndt-Gingrich says of *elenchos,* therefore, "perhaps *inner conviction*" (p. 248).

9. The Greek verb here is *katartizo* which, among other things, means "to put in order," "equip," "make," or "create." What the author states here, however, is not so much that the world was created out of nothing but that creation cannot be explained by material means.

in faith—which would indicate that anyone who worships God must worship in faith.

Abel's worship got results, for, as the author goes on to say, **through it he received approval as righteous, God bearing witness by accepting his gifts.** Divine testimony was borne to Abel, for the Genesis record reads, "And the Lord had regard for Abel and his offering" (Gen. 4:4). God accepted his gifts, and this meant that in God's sight he was **righteous** (cf. Mt. 23:35; 1 Jn. 3:12). With faith Abel was pronounced a righteous man; without faith (as presumably in the case of Cain) no acceptance would have been granted him.

But Abel's death was not the end. **He died,** it is true, **but through his faith he is still speaking.** How does Abel speak? In one of two senses, either (1) through the record of Scripture calling for the avenging of his death, or (2) through the continuing force of his example of faith. In favor of (2) are the profiles of faith in Hebrews 11. Abel died as the first of all martyrs. He was a righteous man, a man of faith. His sacrificial offering made through faith inspires and encourages and still speaks to men. But in favor of (1) is the context of Genesis 4. There God speaks to Cain, saying, "The voice of your brother's blood is crying to me from the ground." Abel's blood cried for vengeance. After death he still (through the permanently recorded words of Scripture) speaks as though not dead.[10] In support of this is the further reference to Abel's blood in 12:24, where it is said that Christ's blood "speaks more graciously than the blood of Abel."

A second example of faith, this one also from very early times, is set forward. **By faith Enoch was taken up so that he should not see death; and he was not found, because God had taken him.** The Old Testament record on Enoch is quite brief: "When Enoch had lived sixty-five years, he became the father of Methuselah. Enoch walked with God after the birth of Methuselah three hundred years, and had other sons and daughters. Thus all the days of Enoch were three hundred and sixty-five years. Enoch walked with God; and he was not, for God took him" (Gen. 5:21-24). Over the centuries many popular traditions came to be associated with the man who "walked with God." He was said to be a preacher of repentance, a special communicant with God who mediated hidden mysteries, a master of learning, of nature and of history, and so on. But the author refrains from speculations of this kind. He derives his information solely from the Old Testament,

5

---

10. It is possible to take the present tense, "he speaks" (*lalei*), as a historical present (where the present tense is used for vividness to express a past action). In this case the text would read: "he died, but through his faith he spoke." That is, Abel's death at that time cried for vengeance. This makes good sense, but it ignores the fact that in Hebrews *lalein* is always used in reference to a divine utterance. The point is that Abel, through the divinely uttered Scripture, speaks today.

where what is implied in the Hebrew text (Gen. 5:24) is expressly stated in the Septuagint, that Enoch did not die like other men but was "translated" (*metetethē*, "conveyed from one place to another," as in Acts 7:16).

So unusual was Enoch's transference that no one else in the Old Testament, except Elijah (2 Kg. 2:11), had this experience. Enoch's special favor in this regard is explained as follows: **Now before he was taken he was attested as having pleased God.** Again the author is quoting from the Old Testament. The Hebrew text reads, "Enoch walked with God." The translators of the Septuagint, thinking that such an expression compromised God's separateness from man, loosely rendered that Enoch "pleased God."

The stress throughout is on faith, for this lay at the heart of Enoch's being **attested** (in the divine word) as well pleasing to God. Thus the author naturally glides into his next statement, which serves as an
6 expansion of his previous description of faith (v. 1). **And without faith it is impossible to please him. For whoever would draw near to God must believe that he exists and that he rewards those who seek him.** The first statement allows no exceptions, that if someone pleases God he must have faith. Anyone who pleases God must draw near (used here in a way characteristic of the Epistle, 4:16; 7:25; 10:22) to God, and no one can draw near unless he believes that God really exists and that He does reward those who seek Him. Enoch had this sort of faith; and in being removed from earth, his faith was richly rewarded. And if Enoch was so blessed, such blessings, the author wishes to drive home, are left open to others as well.

It is the nature of faith to live in hope and to look toward things
7 not seen. Noah is a remarkable illustration of this. **By faith Noah, being warned by God concerning events as yet unseen, took heed and constructed an ark for the saving of his household.** Noah's faith proved itself in positive action. This is significant not only here but in the other representatives of faith portrayed in the chapter. Being divinely warned[11] of a flood that no one could anticipate, he took God at His word. He began the preparation of an ark on dry land, long before the threat of clouds and high water appeared; and this he did because he was moved with godly fear.[12] **By this** (the exhibition of his faith) **he**

---

11. The term is *chrēmatistheis* (cf. 8:5; 12:25), used regularly in the New Testament for a divine communication or instruction. See p. 157, footnote 6.

12. Instead of "moved with godly fear" (ASV), the NEB translates "took good heed" (so practically the RSV). The verb *eulabeomai* (cf. its related substantive form, *eulabeia*, in 5:7; 12:28) carries with it the idea of concern, respect, and reverence. It is distinct from *phobeō*, which usually denotes quaking fear. Faith is not afraid (cf. 11:23, 27) but faith does have a respectful regard for God and His word. This respectful regard is what Noah had, and it led to his obedient faith.

condemned the world and became an heir of the righteousness which comes by faith. The thought on condemnation here is similar to that in Matthew 12:41, meaning that Noah's faith stood out in strong contrast to the unbelieving world. His conduct condemned theirs. Thus Noah became an **heir** (used here in the sense of actual possession; on "heir" cf. 1:2, 4, 14; 6:12, 17; 11:9; 12:17) to that righteousness that results from faith. He **became** righteous by building the ark. "Noah did this; he did all that God commanded him" (Gen. 6:22).

The Faith of Abraham
(11:8-12)

Attention is now directed to Abraham, the great patriarch. In contrast to the others mentioned so far, the Book of Genesis makes express mention of Abraham's faith. "And he [Abraham] believed the Lord; and he reckoned it to him as righteousness" (Gen. 15:6). Abraham became among the Jews the classic expression of faith. Ezra prayed: "Thou art the Lord, the God who didst choose Abram and bring him forth out of Ur of the Chaldeans and give him the name Abraham; and thou didst find his heart faithful before thee . . ." (Neh. 9:7-8). The New Testament also holds forth Abraham's faith (Rom. 4:1-3; Gal. 3:6-9; Js. 2:21-23). It was natural, then, for the author to spend considerable time in recounting his exploits. In addition, the experiences through which Abraham passed were remarkably like the circumstances of the original readers of the Epistle. Abraham had received a call to go forth, and they had been summoned to go forth to Jesus outside the camp, taking His stigma. Abraham had wandered about in Canaan, finding no certain home; they, too, as strangers and passing travelers on earth, had to look to the eternal city.

By faith Abraham obeyed when he was called to go out to a place 8 **which he was to receive as an inheritance; and he went out, not knowing where he was to go.** In the region of Mesopotamia, at Ur of the Chaldees, the call first came to Abraham (Gen. 11:31ff.); and to that call there was an immediate response. The participle **called** (*kaloumenos*) is in the present tense, suggesting that no sooner was the call given than it was obeyed. "He obeyed the call while . . . it was still sounding in his ears."[13] He tore himself loose from his own country, his family and his friends, venturing out on the call of God. "It was, therefore, no attractive account of Canaan which induced him to forsake Mesopotamia, no ordinary emigrant's motive which moved him, but mere faith in God's promise."[14] That he went out not knowing his destination—his

13. Westcott, p. 360.
14. Dods, p. 355.

faith was tested by the unknown—underscores the magnitude of his trust.

9 The faith of Abraham showed itself also in patient endurance. **By faith he sojourned in the land of promise, as in a foreign land.** Even when Abraham reached the land where God led him, he did not possess it. For the rest of his life, though in promise it was his, he lived in the country "like a foreign visitor hastening on his way."[15] At the time of his death his only possession in the land was the plot of ground that kept the bones of his wife (cf. Gen. 23:3-20; 25:7-10). In Canaan he moved about, with a true pilgrim heart, from place to place, **living in tents with Isaac and Jacob,** who were **heirs with him of the same promise** (Gen. 26:3; 28:13).

The author's mention of Isaac and Jacob brings to mind the long years over which Abraham's wandering was spread. Though **in the**
10 **land of promise,** he established no permanent home. **For he looked forward to the city which has foundations, whose builder and maker is God.** There is little difference in meaning between **builder** and **maker;** the phrase is merely rhetorical.[16] There were many cities in Canaan; but Abraham, living with "conviction of things not seen" (v. 1), "expectantly waited"[17] for the eternal city. This city, contrasted with tents, has immovable foundations. Altogether unlike this life (cf. 13:14), it is a permanent city, planned and built by God Himself. For this city, a higher and heavenly home, Abraham had inward longings.

The author next makes a momentary reference to the faith of
11 Sarah, and then returns to speak of Abraham. **By faith Sarah herself received power to conceive, even when she was past the age, since she considered him faithful who had promised.** The introduction of Sarah has been thought difficult to explain. Why Sarah, who laughed to herself when she learned that she would give birth in her old age (Gen. 18:9-15)?[18] Some, therefore, suspect the words "and Sarah herself" to be a primitive insertion into the text, and suppose that Abraham was

---

15. The words are those of Seneca (*Epistle* 120.19) as he, in good Stoic fashion, describes the attitude of detachment necessary for the good life. For the Christian outlook as that of a pilgrim, see Additional Note.

16. The word *technitēs* ("builder") means an "artificer" or "craftsman," a "skilled workman." The word *dēmiourgos* ("maker"), which originally signified "one who works for the people," also means a "skilled workman." Metaphorically, it stands for "author," "maker," "creator"; in the Greek classics it is often used of a lesser deity (thus "demiurge").

17. The verb is *ekdechomai,* which here, as often in the New Testament, conveys the idea of waiting with anticipation (cf. Js. 5:7; Acts 17:16). The English translation "he looked forward to" conveys this meaning, but is somewhat ambiguous since it is often taken to mean "he looked toward." The point is not that Abraham looked toward the heavenly city but that he expectantly waited for that city.

18. Yet Abraham also laughed when the marvelous announcement was made to him (Gen. 17:17).

the original subject of the verbs in verse 11. (See Additional Note.) Apparently, however, the author is viewing Sarah not just at the time when she received news of her conception, to which she quite naturally responded with unbelief, but later after she had had time to adjust to the news and overcome her incredulity. The words **Sarah herself** suggest this—that her faith won out over her earlier unbelief. This victory she was able to gain because she considered God trustworthy.

Both Sarah and Abraham, then, were united in believing that God would work the impossible. **Therefore from one man, and him as good** 12 **as dead, were born descendants.** The **one man** is in contrast to the **many** descendants mentioned later in the verse. Sarah no longer had the power to conceive and Abraham no longer had the power to beget (Rom. 4:19). Yet the certainty of God's promise set aside these obstacles, and their descendants became **as many as the stars of heaven and as the innumerable grains of sand by the seashore** (Gen. 15:5; 22:17; cf. Isa. 51:2).

Homeland of the Faithful
(11:13-16)

What follows is not a digression from the main theme. It is rather a pause expressing the author's deepest feelings on the Christian's true home. It is a pause written with a sigh, for nothing is so clear to the author as the unalterable fact that God's people are wanderers in a foreign territory. Urged on by personal conviction, the author emphasizes the importance of faith and shows that faith sees beyond present, material circumstances. Faith takes long views.

These (in particular, Abraham, Isaac and Jacob) **all died in faith,** 13 **not having received what was promised.** Living in faith, they also died in faith. In faith they stood the last test, even though they had not seen the actual fulfilment of God's promises. Yet, on the other hand, they had seen. Through the eye of faith they had seen the working-out of God's promise to bless the world through them; and **having seen it, they greeted it from afar** (cf. Jn. 8:56). Firmly convinced that God's promise would be fulfilled, they gladly welcomed it from a distance. On the strength of this conviction they continued to live as in a foreign land, **having acknowledged that they were strangers and exiles on the earth.** The confessions made by the patriarchs were, no doubt, confessions in conduct, for they lived as nomads in the land of promise. But their confessions were also verbal. To the sons of Heth, as he mourned over the death of Sarah, Abraham said: "I am a stranger and a sojourner among you" (Gen. 23:4). And when Pharaoh asked Jacob about the number of his years on earth, Jacob replied in terms of his life and the lives of his forefathers as a "sojourning" (Gen. 47:9). These Old Testament verses were without doubt on the mind of the author as he wrote, as well as, perhaps, the statement of the psalmist who says of himself: "For I am thy passing agent, a sojourner, like all my fathers" (Ps. 39:12).

Such words prove to the author that men like this were conscious 14 that they had no real place on earth. **For people who speak thus make it clear that they are seeking a homeland.** A homeland is one's native country, the place of one's origin. The acknowledgment of the patriarchs that the land in which they lived was not their own made it clear that 15 they were headed for another land. **If they had been thinking of that land from which they had gone out, they would have had opportunity to return.** At any time during their lives they could have returned to Mesopotamia, the place of their nativity. **But as it is,** with a pilgrim 16 outlook, **they desire a better country, that is, a heavenly one.** On earth, they set their hopes and aspirations on heaven. **Therefore God is not ashamed to be called their God.** They were not ashamed of Him and He was not ashamed of them. This He showed by identifying Himself as "the God of Abraham, the God of Isaac, and the God of Jacob" (Ex. 3:15; cf. Mt. 22:32). That He was truly their God is shown, further, by His generous provisions for them, **for he has prepared for them a city.** This city, God's own city (cf. v. 10), was the goal of their quest— the only real city they ever knew, the home of the heart's full desire. Though they were away from it, they looked in its direction and were even homesick for it. Men like this, the author wishes to stress, God does not blush to acknowledge.

The Faith of Abraham, Isaac, Jacob, and Joseph (11:17-22)

Attention is directed once again to the faith of Abraham, and this time, in the words of Philo, to "his greatest action which deserves re- 17 porting."[19] **By faith Abraham, when he was tested, offered up Isaac, and he who had received the promises was ready to offer up his only son.** Isaac was the **only son** (see Additional Note) of promise (Gen. 21:12). Twice this verse makes reference to the offering of Isaac, which helps in grasping the meaning of that sacrifice as understood by the author. The word translated **offered** is in the perfect tense, while the expression **was ready to offer up** is in the imperfect.[20] The imperfect

19. Philo, *On Abraham* 167.
20. This is the Conative or Tendential Imperfect in the sense of "he was attempting to offer," "he was ready to offer." For other examples of this in the New Testament, cf. Lk. 1:59; Mt. 3:14; Gal. 1:13, 23; etc.

tense vividly portrays unfinished action: Abraham was in the act of offering Isaac when God intervened. The perfect tense expresses the idea that the demands in the sacrifice were fully met, and that, from an ideal standpoint and as far as Abraham was concerned, the offering was a completed action.[21]

The strain on Abraham's faith was severe. Already it had triumphed over Sarah's barrenness and Abraham's own physical impotence. Already it had endured the long years of waiting until the time came for God to give them a son. Now Abraham is called upon to give up that son **of whom it was said, "Through Isaac shall your descendants be named."** 18 The task was doubly difficult. Not only was this son the beloved one, but in this son were centered all the hopes and promises that God Himself had made. How was it possible that God could make the promise and then sever at the roots the one tender shoot through which that promise was to be forwarded? How could the promise and the command stand side by side? The brilliance of Abraham's faith is that, in all of this, he left it up to God. It was God's problem. God had promised. God had commanded. He would obey. **He considered** (reasoned, calcu- 19 lated in his mind) **that God was able to raise men even from the dead.** What an unexpected command this was! Yet Abraham thought it through. In faith he was able to say to the young men that accompanied him, as they neared the place of sacrifice, "Stay here ... I and the lad will go yonder and worship, and come again to you" (Gen. 22:5). He reasoned that God would raise the dead rather than allow one iota of His word to fail. And in this respect Abraham was right, for **figuratively speaking, he did receive him back.**[22] Isaac, bound on the altar, was as good as dead; but when the heavenly voice stopped in midair the downward thrust of Abraham's knife, Abraham received his son back from the dead. No greater test of trust, or greater reward, could have been given.

---

21. Moffatt (*Hebrews*, p. 176) believes, however, that the perfect tense is to be taken here aoristically, that is, simply as a past tense.

22. Philo (*On Abraham* 172ff.) graphically tells the story of Abraham and his son as they ascended the mount. "They walked with equal speed of mind rather than body along the short straight road ... and came to the appointed place. And then, while the father was collecting stones to build the altar, the son, seeing everything else ready for sacrifice but no animal, looked at his father and said: 'My father, behold the fire and the wood, but where is the victim?' To anyone else who knew what he was about to do, and was hiding in his heart, these words would have brought confusion and tearfulness and he would have remained silent through extreme emotion, and thus given an indication of what was going to happen. But Abraham admitted no swerving of body or mind, and with visage and thought alike unmoved he said in answer to the question, 'Child, God will provide Himself a victim, even in this wide desert ... but know that to God all things are possible, including those that are impossible or insuperable to men.' And as he said this, he hastily seized his son, and laid him on the altar. ...."

Following Abraham come Isaac, Jacob, and Joseph, whose faith also is worthy of notice. Each instance of faith is summarily treated and in each a single incident is chosen in order to show that these men, 20 as they approached death, looked in faith to things as yet unseen. **By faith Isaac invoked future blessings on Jacob and Esau.** Genesis 27:1-40 relates Isaac's blessing of his two sons in his old age. Thinking Jacob to be Esau, Isaac pronounced the blessing upon Jacob. Later, however, after learning of his mistake, he persistently refused to change the blessing, apparently recognizing the action of God's overruling providence. His faith thus enabled him to look to the future fulfilment of the divine promises.

21   Jacob, also, exhibited similar faith. **By faith Jacob, when dying, blessed each of the sons of Joseph, bowing in worship** to God **over the head of his staff.** Isaac was tricked into granting the blessing to the younger son; but Jacob, when blessing the sons of Joseph, purposefully chose to bless the younger son Ephraim (Gen. 48:14-20). This he did in faith; and in blessing his grandsons, two generations removed from him, he demonstrated that he, too, had faith concerning future things. The last clause of the verse, **bowing in worship over the head of his staff,** refers to an earlier incident recorded in Genesis 47:29-31. Jacob, with the prospect of death before him, made Joseph swear that he would bury him not in Egypt but in the burial place of his fathers. There is a difference here between the Septuagint and the Hebrew text of Genesis 47:31. The latter reads, "And Israel bowed himself upon the bed's head," instead of the reading given by the author in agreement with the Septuagint. But the problem is no more than one of vowel-points (which were added much later), for the same Hebrew word can be either "staff" or "bed." The consonants in the Hebrew are MTH. If pronounced *miṭṭah,* the meaning is "bed"; if pronounced *maṭṭeh,* the meaning is "staff."

Verse 21 relates two incidents in Jacob's life in inverted order. The most probable explanation for this is that the author wished to tie together the two blessings given by Isaac and Jacob. The inverted order results also in bringing in close connection Jacob's instructions con- 22 cerning his body with similar instructions given by Joseph. **By faith Joseph, at the end of his life, made mention of the exodus of the Israelites and gave directions concerning his burial.** At the close of his life, Joseph's mind was set on the future fulfilment of God's promises. To his brothers he said, "God will visit you, and bring you up out of this land to the land which he swore to Abraham, to Isaac, and to Jacob"; and in full faith he commanded, "you shall carry up my bones from here" (Gen. 50:24-25). This command was kept; for when the Israelites left Egypt they carried Joseph's mummy with them (Ex. 13:19), and he was finally laid to rest in the land of promise at Shechem (Josh. 24:32).

The Faith of Moses
(11:23-28)

The author now moves from the age of the patriarchs to the time of Moses. Of Moses he will speak in some detail, since his name is practically synonymous with the old dispensation and since his faithfulness has already been alluded to (3:2ff.).[23] Several instances of Moses' faith are cited, but the author begins by relating the brave conduct of his parents. **By faith Moses, when he was born, was hid for three months** 23 **by his parents.** The Hebrew text of the Old Testament mentions only the faith of Moses' mother (Ex. 2:2ff.); but the text of the Septuagint, which is followed by the author, speaks of the faith of both parents. This might be inferred from the Hebrew for, obviously, without joint action, the babe could not have been kept in hiding and thus spared. The decision of Moses' parents to do this is explained on the grounds that **they saw that the child was beautiful** (cf. Acts 7:20) and that, in spite of the penalty, **they were not afraid of the king's edict** (given in Ex. 1:22). The faith of Moses' parents allowed them to perceive in the appearance of the child a token of God's distinctive purpose for him in regard to the nation.

Moses' own faith is shown to be even more remarkable. **By faith** 24 **Moses, when he was grown up, refused to be called the son of Pharaoh's daughter.** Josephus[24] hands down a tale of this refusal, as though it came early in life. He reports that Moses, while still a babe, was offered his crown by Pharaoh; that Moses responded by throwing it to the ground and stomping on it. But the author of Hebrews disdains such exaggerations. He is emphatic in stating that Moses' choice was due neither to childish ignorance nor youthful impetuosity, but to the decision of a responsible adult. A decision deliberately made, it was also a decision of self-renunciation, which meant **choosing rather to share** 25 **ill-treatment with the people of God than to enjoy the fleeting pleasures of sin.** This choice was made by Moses after, in the words of Exodus, "he went out to his people and looked on their burdens" (Ex. 2:11). What faced him was a crisis decision: whether to remain in the eyes of men "the son of Pharaoh's daughter," or to throw in his lot with the despised people of God. He could not be both an Egyptian and an Israelite. On one hand was all the splendor of Egypt, with its rare

---

23. In 3:2-6 Moses' faithfulness is freely granted in order to prove, by contrast, the superiority of Jesus and by implication the superiority of His religion.
24. *Antiquities* 2.9.7.

treasures and its magnificent heritage; to be in Pharaoh's palaces and to possess perhaps even the throne, to be in a position of power and in a place of privilege and refinement—all the things (the author describes them as **the fleeting pleasures of sin**) an ancient empire could offer. On the other hand were poverty, contempt, and affliction; for Israel at this time was a nation of slaves, groaning under its heavy load, with broken spirits and vanished hopes, hemmed in inexorably to daily abuse.

Yet Moses, by faith, recognized these people to be the people of God. He deliberately chose to travel with them the dangerous way rather than to continue in ease. He saw, by faith, that to continue in ease would be **sin** and further, that the **pleasures of sin** give no lasting

26 satisfaction. **He considered abuse suffered for the Christ greater wealth than the treasures of Egypt.** Moses, like Christ, was not ashamed of his brothers (cf. 2:11-12). He became one with them, suffering **abuse . . . for the Christ.** This expression is meaningful and especially important for the readers of the Epistle. The author is sure that abuse is always associated with Christ, that to be a Christian is even to expect such abuse (13:13); and he is sure, as he looks at Moses, that it has always been that way. This the readers need to keep in mind. Moses suffered in Egypt the same reproach that Christ was later to bear; his suffering was even, it might be said, a prefiguring of Christ's suffering. Moses was able to do this because he had an uncommon awareness of true values: **he looked to the reward.** The verb for **he looked** is *apoblepō* which here can bear its basic meaning—"to look away from all other objects to look only at one."[25] Moses did this. He fixed his eye on one goal, and the force of the imperfect tense here suggests that he kept on looking to the heavenly reward (cf. 10:35; 11:6).

27 **By faith he** (Moses) **left Egypt, not being afraid of the anger of the king.** In this, again, Moses' faith stood out decidedly. It was faith, the author says, mounting in Moses' heart, that caused him to leave Egypt and go to Midian. At this point a difficulty emerges. According to Exodus 2:11-15, Moses fled from Egypt after killing an Egyptian and on learning that others knew what he had done. But here it is said that he left Egypt, "not being afraid of the anger of the king." To alleviate the difficulty, some interpreters make the statement refer not to Moses' initial departure to Midian but to his later and final departure when he left Egypt at the head of the Israelite nation. But if this be the correct interpretation, the author has misplaced some of his events, for it makes the Passover (v. 28) come after the Exodus (v. 27). It would seem better to think that the author does not interrupt his chronological sequence

25. In 12:2 the author uses *aphoraō*, another verb which means "to look away from other things to look at one." See my comment on that passage.

and, in addition, to think that his knowledge of Moses' life was not so inadequate as to lead him to make a blunder about Moses' departure from Egypt. As the records stand, the one in Exodus and the other here, the two are not irreconcilable. Subsequent to his murder of the Egyptian, Moses naturally feared for his own personal safety; but concerning his choice to serve God rather than Pharaoh, he had no fear. It is of his choice to serve God that the author speaks, and so he says that Moses left Egypt by faith. Indeed, the text indicates that the author had even more in his mind, saying of Moses, **for he endured as seeing him who is invisible.** This means that Moses was strong, that he steadied himself against the course of the stream. Acts 7:25 indicates that Moses envisioned himself as a deliverer of God's people. Yet even when these people were not ready to welcome his leadership, and against all temptations to the contrary, Moses was resolute in his purpose. His flight from Egypt did not mean abandonment of his plans to deliver his people; and all during his long stay in the desert at Midian, as he contemplated the unseen, Moses was still persevering toward his goal.[26]

Still another manifestation of Moses' faith is brought forward. **By faith he kept the Passover and sprinkled the blood, so that the Destroyer of the first-born** (whether of man or of beast [Ex. 12:12]) **might not touch them.** In this feast of **the Passover** all the Israelite nation participated, but it was Moses who instituted it. The kind of faith alluded to is similar to that of Noah, for in each instance careful obedience to a divine command was the only means of escape from oncoming destruction. By the sprinkling of blood on the lintels and doorposts of their houses (Ex. 12:7, 22), Israel declared itself as God's people and its first-born were passed over unharmed.

Faith Displayed at the Exodus and at Jericho (11:29-31)

The following examples well illustrate the power of faith to do impossible things. **By faith the people crossed the Red Sea as if on dry land; but the Egyptians, when they attempted to do the same, were drowned.** A shift is now made to the faith of the people, yet this would have been nothing without the faith of Moses. It was he who said, "Fear not, stand firm, and see the salvation of the Lord" (Ex. 14:13); and it was Moses who commanded the people to move forward toward the

---

26. The aorist *ekarterēsen* ("endured") could refer simply to Moses' fixed intention as he left Egypt, but it could also refer to his forty years at Midian, during which time "he had to learn that God's work must be done in God's way and not in his own" (Peake, *Heroes and Martyrs of Faith*, p. 136).

water. Still, it was the people who responded positively by committing themselves to the sea. They showed their faith by obeying Moses' command, and thus they all passed through the sea on dry land. The greatness of the people's faith stands out in strong relief against the fate of the Egyptians, whose attempt to cross over was an act of presumption.

The author continues to demonstrate that faith is able to work

30 amazing wonders. **By faith the walls of Jericho fell down after they had been encircled for seven days.** It is noticeable that Israel's desert wanderings of forty years are passed over. Those years, however, loom large in the author's mind as years of rebellion and unbelief (3:16-19), as barren as the desert which Israel traversed. But at Jericho a truly remarkable faith was once again exhibited. To assemble the people for a march around the city, to encircle the city once each day for six days and seven times on the seventh day, to require the blowing of the rams' horns and the loud shouts of the people—these were unusual procedures for the capture of a city. But Joshua and the people carefully followed the divine instructions—a characteristic mark of faith—and the walls of the city came crashing down (Josh. 6:1-21).

Faith, likewise, is all that can account for another happening at

31 Jericho. **By faith Rahab the harlot did not perish with those who were disobedient, because she had given friendly welcome**[27] **to the spies.** It may be thought surprising that a woman of loose conduct, designated a harlot,[28] would be appealed to as an example; but James also goes back to Rahab to confirm the principle that faith is dead without works (Js. 2:25-26). **Those who were disobedient** refers to the inhabitants of Jericho who, though they had learned of the wondrous power of Israel's God, nevertheless failed to yield themselves to Him (Josh. 2:9-10). By contrast, Rahab confessed to the spies whom she aided that their God "is he who is God in heaven above and on earth beneath" (Josh. 2:11). Such faith, and this from a Gentile, brought about the preservation of herself and her household.

Other Examples of Faith
(11:32-38)

Because of the limitations of time and space, the author cannot go

32 on detailing examples of faith in the annals of the Jewish nation. **And**

27. "Friendly welcome" is the idiomatic equivalent of the Greek *met' eirēnēs* ("with peace"). The Hebrew *shālōm* ("peace") is the ordinary word for a greeting.
28. Codex Sinaiticus and a few other text-authorities read *hē epilegomenē pornē*, "the so-called harlot," in an attempt to tone down the author's language.

what more shall I say?[29] His mind is filled with a multitude of examples that he could cite, but he must shorten his list and speak more generally. **For time would fail me to tell of Gideon, Barak, Samson, Jephthah, of David and Samuel and the prophets.** The abbreviated list begins with six names, which may be grouped in three pairs of two. At this point the author, instead of following a strict chronological order, seems to choose names which, for one reason or another, are stamped on his memory. **Gideon** is mentioned first, probably because of his heroic action (by faith) with his three hundred men against an overwhelming number of Midianites (Jg. 7). Next is **Barak** who, along with the prophetess Deborah, led Israel in victory over Sisera and the Canaanites (Jg. 4–5). **Samson** was the mighty warrior who killed a thousand Philistines with the jawbone of an ass (Jg. 15:9-17) and later died with his enemies by pulling down the two middle pillars of the house where thousands of Philistines were gathered (Jg. 16:23-31). **Jephthah,** though he made a rash vow, was nevertheless the victorious leader of the men of Gilead over the Ammonites (Jg. 11). The names of **David** and **Samuel** conclude the list, the former because he, like the judges, gained great victories for the Lord. Samuel is listed last, in keeping with the general practice of associating his name with **the prophets.** The prophets are not named, but many of the things that Elijah, Elisha, and the other prophets did are alluded to in what follows.

The men included in this list **through** their **faith conquered king-** 33 **doms.** What gave them their victories was their faith in God. Also through faith they **enforced justice,** meaning that their reigns as judges and kings were characterized by just and fair treatment (cf. 2 Sam. 8:15). Through faith, too, they **received** the fulfilment of certain divine **promises,** as is stated, for example, in Joshua 21:45: "Not one of all the good promises which the Lord had made to the house of Israel had failed" (cf. 1 Kg. 8:56).

Through faith men obtained personal deliverance from what seemed certain death. They **stopped the mouths of lions, quenched raging fire, and escaped the edge of the sword.** The first reference clearly is to Daniel, who was thrown into a den of lions and yet survived "because he had trusted in his God" (Dan. 6:23). Those who **quenched raging fire** 34 were Shadrach, Meshach, and Abednego, who refused to serve or bow down in worship to the Babylonian gods. Because of their faith (Dan. 3:28), they came out alive from the "burning fiery furnace" into which they had been cast. Men like David (1 Sam. 18:11; 19:10-12) and Elijah

---

29. Josephus (*Antiquities* 20.11.1) asks, "What more need be said?"—this as he comes to the conclusion of his *Antiquities,* which contains, in his words, "twenty books with sixty thousand lines."

(1 Kg. 19) and Jeremiah (Jer. 26) escaped the sword's fatal edge, and this by faith.

Through faith men have been lifted up and have gained unexpected strength: they have **won strength out of weakness,** have become **mighty in war,** and have **put foreign armies to flight.** Different occasions in Israel's history abundantly illustrate these statements. Hezekiah, near death, and Samson, in his blindness, gained physical renewal (Isa. 38:1-6; Jg. 16:28-31). David proved himself a mighty warrior against Goliath (1 Sam. 17). Time and again the Israelites routed foreign armies, in the belief that the battle was not theirs but God's (2 Chron. 20:15). And

35 faith has done even more: **Women received their dead by resurrection.** This is a clear reference to the widow of Zarephath and to the Shunammite woman, whose faith prevailed over death; and thus, through the instrumentality of Elijah and Elisha respectively, they received their sons back alive (1 Kg. 17:17-24; 2 Kg. 4:18-37).

These are some of the things that faith has been able to accomplish. What the author now begins to stress, as he looks back over the past and views the needs of his readers, is that the same sort of faith amidst adversity produces endurance. **Some were tortured, refusing to accept release, that they might rise again to a better life.** The Greek verb *tumpanizō* means "to stretch on the *tumpanon*" (literally, "drum"), which was some sort of instrument of torture. Apparently the victim was stretched on a frame, perhaps like a wheel, and beaten to death with sticks and rods. A punishment of this kind is recorded in 2 Maccabees 6:18-31. During the persecutions of Antiochus Epiphanes, Eleazar the scribe, at the age of ninety, preferred to be tortured on the rack *(tumpanon)* rather than eat pork. Another instance of severe torture, that of a mother and her seven sons, may be found in 2 Maccabees 7. They, and many others along with them, suffered martyrdom, **that they might rise again to a better life.** The way was open to them for escape, if they would but compromise; but they kept the faith, choosing life in the resurrection to continued life on earth at the expense of conscience. They chose a **better** resurrection—better than the resurrections alluded to in the beginning of the verse, better than a resurrection to life in this world only.

36 In addition to these, **Others suffered mocking and scourging**—not uncommon in those days, especially for God's unique people—**and even chains and imprisonment** (cf. 1 Kg. 22:24-28; Gen. 39:20; Jer. 20:2).

37 **They were stoned,** for example, Zechariah (2 Chron. 24:20-21; cf. Mt. 23:35); tradition has it that Jeremiah was stoned in Egypt. **They were sawn in two.** There is no record of this ancient mode of execution either in the Old Testament or in the Apocrypha; there is, however, a tradition that Isaiah met this terrible death under Manasseh, being

sawn in two by a wooden saw.[30] **They were killed with the sword,** for example, the prophets in the reign of Ahab (1 Kg. 19:10, 14) and Uriah in the reign of Jehoiakim (Jer. 26:20-23). **They went about in skins of sheep and goats, destitute, afflicted, ill-treated.** Driven away from their homes, they were forced to bear the hardships of vagabond life. Their clothing was rough and crude, like Elijah's "garment of haircloth" (2 Kg. 1:8). These people, "forlorn, oppressed, ill-treated" (MOF), lived as men of faith **of whom,** the author declares, **the world was not worthy.** They 38 were cast out by the world as though they were not worthy to live in it—and yet the world was, in fact, unworthy of them. Poor, distressed, and persecuted, they wandered **over deserts and mountains and** made their homes **in dens and caves of the earth.** The statement is general in nature, although once again specific reference seems to describe conditions during the second century B.C., when the Syrians sought to eradicate every trace of the Jewish religion (cf. 1 Macc. 2:28; 2 Macc. 5:27; 6:11; 10:6).

Concluding Statement on Faith (11:39-40)

Such is the lot of those who live by faith. A life lived in full faith offers no guarantee of comfort and ease in this world. This is what the author seeks to establish in the minds of his readers. And one thing more he wishes to establish, as he looks back over his honor list: that **all these, though well attested by their faith, did not receive what was** 39 **promised.** This has already been said of the patriarchs (v. 13), and now the statement is broadened to include all the faithful of the Old Testament. They lived in faith, they died in faith; but that of which their faith assured them, the things they hoped for, they never received. This being so, does this imply that faith is restricted in what it can achieve? By no means. It is only that **God had foreseen,** the author says 40 encouragingly, **something better for us, that apart from us they should not be made perfect.** Theirs was a time of waiting and anticipation, looking ahead to the coming of Christ. This, above all, was what was **better,** something reserved especially for the Christian era. The author plainly does not mean that the Christian attains a better life or better reward than the ancients, for all possess together the promised inheritance. But the saving work of Christ was not in their time, although they do partake of its benefits (9:15). To them belonged the promise; to the saints of the new age belongs the fulfilment. It is in the new age

---

30. The tradition is embodied in *The Ascension of Isaiah,* a pseudepigraph of composite character, also in Justin's *Dialogue with Trypho* 120, etc.

that the **better things** are provided—the **better** covenant, with complete forgiveness of sins, the better hope, and so on.

Thus the author has come again to the main thrust of the Epistle. It was because of faith that the men of old were attested to (v. 2), a faith that surrendered all. This was the glory of Israel's heritage, from the blood of Abel to the martyrdom of the Maccabean zealots. Yet even so, this was but a preparation, a scheme of preliminary measures that find their true meanings only in Christ. In Him alone there is hope. Why, then, should the readers of the Epistle forsake their only way of salvation, the only One through whom could be obtained the promises the fathers never quite realized? The correct answer to this question, logically deduced from Biblical proofs, was to the author the surest antidote for apostasy.

Additional Notes

Christians as pilgrims

V. 9. Of Abraham it is said, "By faith he sojourned in the land of promise, as in a foreign land. . . ." The Greek verb for "sojourned" is *paroikeō*. It is used to describe an alien who lives in a country without civil rights. The noun *paroikia* came to refer to a group of aliens who lived in a given community. (The English word "parish" is derived from it.) As applied to a Christian community, the term refers to a group of people who live in the world but whose ways and manners are not of the world.

It is the thought especially of Hebrews and 1 Peter that the church is composed of a group of sojourners. Peter writes that Christians should live the time of their "exile" or sojourn in fear (1 Pet. 1:17). He exhorts also that they as "aliens and exiles" abstain from fleshly passions (1 Pet. 2:11; cf. 1:1). In Hebrews 11:9ff. the pilgrim stance of the Christian is beautifully depicted. It is touched on again in 13:14 in the words, "For here we have no lasting city, but we seek the city which is to come."

With this may be compared the expressive statement in *The Epistle to Diognetus* (second or third cent.): "For the distinction between Christians and other men, is neither in country nor language nor customs. For they do not dwell in cities in some place of their own, nor do they use any strange variety of dialect, nor practice an extraordinary kind of life. . . . Yet while living in Greek and barbarian cities, according as each obtained his lot, and following the local customs, both in clothing and food and in the rest of life, they show forth the wonderful and confessedly strange character of the constitution of their own citizenship. They dwell in their own fatherlands, but as if sojourners in them;

they share all things as citizens, and suffer all things as strangers.... They pass their time upon the earth, but they have their citizenship in heaven" (5.1ff.). For further reference to Christian pilgrimage, see J. B. Lightfoot's erudite note on 1 Clement 1.1 *(The Apostolic Fathers,* pt. I, vol. 2, p. 5f.).

"Sarah herself"

V. 11. Sometimes, as here, the smallest of points presents great difficulties. The problems of this verse, briefly, are as follows:

1. The faith of Sarah. On the basis of Genesis, it would appear that Sarah is not a choice example of trust in God. Why, then, should she be numbered in the list of those with great faith?

2. The faith of Abraham. On the other hand, the Old Testament does attach much significance to the faith of Abraham, especially at the time when God promised that he, though childless, would have a multitude of descendants (Gen. 15:1-6). Paul, too, in this connection, stresses Abraham's faith: "He did not weaken in faith when he considered his own body, which was as good as dead ... or when he considered the barrenness of Sarah's womb" (Rom. 4:19ff.).

3. Continuity of thought. It is said that verse 11, with its reference to Sarah, breaks into the thought-sequence; for in verse 12 the subject is again the faith of Abraham. In fact, except for verse 11, the material in verses 8-19 forms one solid piece on Abraham.

4. Meanings of words. The biggest problem, however, concerns the Greek phrase *eis katabolēn spermatos.* It is generally translated "to conceive seed," but the fact is that the expression does not mean this. A literal translation would be "for the throwing down of seed"—not the reception of seed (female part) but the deposition of seed (male part) in the process of generation.

Several solutions have been proposed to solve these problems:

1. Some believe that the difficulties of the passage can be alleviated by excision of the words *kai autē Sarra* ("Sarah herself"), regarding them as a very early addition to verse 11. Zuntz, following Field and Windisch, has led a recent move in this direction.[31] He sees this not only as the best solution to the problem but thinks, additionally, that this can best account for the other minor textual variants in the verse. But this is conjectural on Zuntz's part, a conjecture which, it might be added, is supported by no text-witnesses.

2. Most interpreters believe that the text as it stands is genuine. They are united in their feeling that the difficulties listed above are not in themselves insuperable, that, for example, digressions do occur (esp. vv. 13-16) in the text of 8:19; and some feel that it is not unthinkable

---

31. Zuntz, p. 16, n. 4.

that Sarah's faith (which she must have had) be mentioned together with the faith of Abraham. After these points of agreement, however, different interpretations are again resorted to.

a. It is suggested that since the literal meaning of *eis katabolēn spermatos* seems inapplicable to a female, the expression should rather be translated "for the founding of a race." Thus, Sarah received strength from God for the establishment (through Isaac) of a posterity.

b. It is suggested that the words *autē Sarra* should be read differently, not in the nominative case ("Sarah herself") but in the dative ("along with Sarah"). The translation of the text thus would be: "By faith he [Abraham] also, along with Sarah, received power to beget a child when he was past age, since he counted him faithful who had promised. . . ."

Of these two interpretations, the first is quite unnatural and the second, although it numbers distinguished advocates on its side, suffers the disadvantage of appearing to be an ingenious contrivance rather than a straightforward explanation of the text. Other explanations, therefore, are preferred by other commentators.

c. It is suggested that the word *steira* "barren," (supported by P[46], D, Latin Vulgate, Syriac Peshitta, and others) was originally a part of the clause, that the full clause should read *kai autē Sarra steira*. If this clause is read as a concessive clause, the translation would read: "By faith, even though Sarah was barren, he [Abraham] received strength for procreation, though he was past the age." This makes Abraham the subject of verses 8-13 and puts Sarah in a subordinate role—with no question about her faith or lack of faith being raised.[32]

d. It is suggested that much of the difficulty of the expression *eis katabolēn spermatos* disappears if *eis* is taken in the sense of "as regards" or "with reference to," and that, if an ellipsis is understood, the usual translation "power to conceive" requires no alteration. In this case, then, the meaning of the text would be: "By faith Sarah herself received power with reference to Abraham's begetting of a child [or, the casting down of seed into her], and this even when she was past the age. . . ."

The many knots in the passage are difficult to untangle: (a) is apparently preferred by Hewitt and looked upon favorably by Héring; (b) is the choice of Michel and F. F. Bruce; (c) is convincingly argued for by Matthew Black and followed by the committee of the United

32. For a similar view that Abraham is the subject of v. 11, see TDNT, III, 621.

33. M. Black, "Critical and Exegetical Notes on Three New Testament Texts, Hebrews xi. 11, Jude 5, James i. 27," *Apophoreta: Festschrift für Ernst Haenchen* (Berlin, 1964), p. 39ff.; cf. Metzger, p. 672.

Bible Societies' Greek New Testament;[33] and (d) is the preference of Montefiore.

Ton monogenē, "only" or "only begotten"?

V. 17. The author refers to Isaac as Abraham's "only son" (ton monogenē, literally, "the only"). The KJV and ASV read here "only begotten son."

There has been much discussion in recent years as to the precise meaning of monogenēs. Is it best rendered "only" or "only begotten"? The RSV, as well as other newer translations, has been greatly criticized for its rendering "only Son" (as applied to Jesus in the Johannine passages where the term occurs) instead of "only begotten Son" (cf. Jn. 1:14, 18; 3:16, 18; 1 Jn. 4:9). It has been thought by some that "only Son" compromises what Scripture teaches elsewhere (Ps. 2:7; Heb. 1:5; see Additional Note on 1:6) on Jesus' being begotten, or in some way reflects on His virgin birth.

Monogenēs, even in an older lexicon like that of Thayer, is defined as "single of its kind, only."[34] The Liddell-Scott-Jones lexicon says of it, "'only member of a kin or kind'; therefore, 'only,' 'single,' 'unique.' "[35] Moulton and Milligan cite various examples of the use of monogenēs in the secular papyri. In their beginning statement on the term, they say: "Monogenēs is literally 'one of a kind,' 'only,' 'unique' (unicus), not 'only-begotten,' which would be monogennētos (unigenitus), and is common in the LXX in this sense (e.g. Judg 11[34], Ps 21 (22)[21], 24 (25)[16], Tob 3[15]). It is similarly used in the NT of 'only' sons and daughters (Lk 7[12], 8[42], 9[38]), and is so applied in a special sense to Christ in Jn 1[14, 18], 3[16, 18], 1 Jn 4[9], where the emphasis is on the thought that, as the 'only' Son of God, He has no equal and is able fully to reveal the Father."[36]

This statement could scarcely be improved upon, although Arndt and Gingrich point out that some prefer a somewhat heightened sense for monogenēs in John and 1 John, which results in a meaning similar to "first-born" (prōtotokos) in such passages as Romans 8:29, Hebrews 1:6, etc.[37] Nevertheless, Arndt-Gingrich defines monogenēs as "only"—"Also unique (in kind) of something that is the only example of its category."[38]

How is it, then, that the early English versions came to translate monogenēs as "only begotten"? First, it should be said that not all the early English translations read "only begotten." William Tyndale, whose

---

34. Thayer, p. 417.

35. Liddell-Scott-Jones, p. 1144.

36. Moulton-Milligan, p. 416f.

37. Büchsel (TDNT, IV, 739ff.) prefers this heightened meaning in John and I John.

38. Arndt-Gingrich, p. 529.

English translation of the New Testament was the first to be based on a Greek text, in his edition of 1534 translated *monogenēs* as "only" in John 3:16, 18.

Second, it should be noted that "only begotten" is due to the influence of the Latin Vulgate. Jerome produced the Latin Vulgate in the last years of the fourth century. His work was mainly a revision based on various old Latin copies extant at that time. The Old Latin Codex Vercellensis, for example, was written prior to this time and it read *unicus*, "only" in John 1:14, 18; 3:16, 18. Jerome, however, in these passages, changed *unicus* to *unigenitus*, "only begotten." The Latin Vulgate text prevailed in the Middle Ages and exerted considerable influence, especially on the early English translations.

It is interesting to notice that even the KJV translated *monogenēs* as "only" in Luke 7:12, 8:42, and 9:38. In these passages, too, the KJV was following the Latin Vulgate which rendered *monogenēs* here as *unicus*. In other words, in the Latin Vulgate and in the KJV, the word *monogenēs* is inconsistently rendered—sometimes as "only" and sometimes as "only begotten." If, however, the KJV in several instances translated *monogenēs* as "only," it is difficult to see why recent translations must be suspect because they also translate *monogenēs* as "only." The point at issue is not the deity of Jesus, nor is His deity diminished by translations (such as RSV, NEB, TEV, Moffatt, Goodspeed, Phillips, etc.) that read "only Son." As "only Son," He is the unique One, the Only One of His kind. Others may be "sons of God," but not Son in the sense that He is.

Hebrews 11:17 well illustrates the meaning of *monogenēs*. Isaac is called "the only son." He was not the "only begotten son" of Abraham, for Abraham begot other sons. Isaac was, however, the "only son" of promise, the "beloved" son of Abraham. *Monogenēs* ("only"), therefore, shades into the meaning of *agapētos* ("beloved").[39]

---

39. Moffatt, *Hebrews*, p. 176. Cf. F. F. Bruce, *Hebrews*, p. 308. For further references, see Dale Moody, "God's Only Son. The Translation of Jn. 3:16 in the R.S.V.," JBL 72 (1953), 213-19; an abridgment of this article appeared in *Bible Translator* 10 (1959), 145-47. Cf. B. F. Westcott, *The Epistles of St. John*, third ed. (London, 1892), p. 169ff.; F. Kattenbusch, "Only Begotten," DCG, II, pp. 281-2; F. C. Grant, " 'Only Begotten'—A Footnote to the New Revision," ATR 36 (1954), 284-87; R. L. Roberts, "The Rendering 'Only Begotten' in John 3:16," *Restoration Quarterly* 16 (1973), 2-22.

HEBREWS TWELVE

The Example of Jesus
(12:1-3)

The previous chapter on the heroes and heroines of faith is not, as is sometimes thought, a detached masterpiece of religious prose. Of course, it is not at all inconceivable that the author may have used its leading ideas on other occasions. But here in the Epistle it does not stand in isolation. Combining religious fervor and religious insight, it is a brilliant exhortation positioned in the middle of two grand sections of appeal (10:19-39 and ch. 12) for Christian endeavor. Thus this chapter now begins with, or rather continues, a challenge to its readers that they persevere in their faith to the end. **Therefore, since we are sur-** 1 **rounded by so great a cloud of witnesses, let us also lay aside every weight, and sin which clings so closely, and let us run with perseverance the race that is set before us.** The figure is that of the athletic contest, a frequent device in the writings of Paul (1 Cor. 9:24-27; Phil. 1:30; 1 Tim. 6:12; 2 Tim. 4:7, etc.[1] The word *agōn* refers to any kind of contest or struggle in which the competition is intense. Here, with the accompanying **let us run,** the reference clearly is to a race. The Christian race, as the context shows, is a marathon race, not a short sprint. Others have been on the track ahead of the present competitors—all those whose daring faith the author has eulogized. They have finished their part of the race and in relay fashion have passed on the baton to their successors. Having finished, they are now appropriately described as a **cloud** or host of witnesses. In what sense are they witnesses? Figuratively, of course, for certainly the author does not mean to suggest that those

---

1. See Victor C. Pfitzner, *Paul and the Agon Motif* (Leiden, 1967).

who have gone on are now literally looking down from heaven on earthly affairs. The term "witness" may be taken in one of two senses: either in the sense of one who sees as a "spectator" (as in 1 Tim. 6:12), or in the sense of one who bears witness to something—in this case to those who have borne witness to God and to the power of faith in their lives. The latter sense suggests that they are witnesses in terms of their exemplary lives. The author's precise thought is unclear, although the general idea is that these witnesses are watching as intent spectators the progress of the runners in the stadium. There they are in the stands. They surround the runners like a cloud, a multitude—the author having pointed time and again to their faith. They are urging and cheering the runners on to victory, inspiring them by their example and their presence.

Entering the Christian race requires preparation, a casting aside of every encumbrance and of every sin. The word for "weight" is *onkos*. It denotes "bulk" or "size" or "mass." In connection with an athlete it is often used to refer to any "excess weight" of the body; it is also used of any heavy article that might be carried or worn on the body. The metaphor is primarily that of the runner who throws off the weight of unnecessary things, like cumbrous clothing, although the thought of reducing weight by training and exercise is not far removed. The point is that the Christian must rid himself of anything that would impede him. He must strip himself down for the race of faith.

This means that sin, which so sorely hinders every Christian, must be thrown off. The King James text here reads, "the sin which doth so easily beset us"; but the concept of each individual person's having a "besetting sin" is not in the passage. It is sin in general that is meant:[2] sin, in any and all of its forms, which **clings so closely**, like a trailing garment that threatens to entwine about the runner's feet.

The negative preparations having been completed, the race itself is to be run with endurance (cf. 10:36). The tendency of some would be to faint along the way or to give up the race altogether. But the exhortation is to run the "appointed" or "prescribed" racecourse. This is the meaning of the adjective *prokeimenon* (**set before**). The term is used of food that is prepared and set before a person. It is used of a task that is set, and, concerning competitors, of a prize in a contest. The Christian is to run the appointed race no matter what the cost,

---

2. In this context nothing more is implied. Some commentators, however, see in this expression a further reference to the sin of apostasy, which was the one great danger facing the readers. But apostasy would not be a handicap in the race but would instead amount to a complete withdrawal from the race. Nor does the definite article *tēn* refer to any particular sin but to what is characteristic of sin—that it clings to men so tenaciously.

looking to Jesus the pioneer and perfecter of our faith. The successful 2
runner is not easily distracted; he must look neither at the crowds nor
at his competition. This is forcefully suggested by the author's word
for "look." The verb *aphoraō* means "to look away from all other things
to look at one."[3] So the Christian runner must have his eye set on
Jesus—"with no eyes for anyone or anything except Jesus." On Him
the Christian casts his steady gaze because He is the **pioneer** and
perfecter of faith.[4] The Greek term for **pioneer** is *archēgos* (see comment on 2:10), which often means "author" or "originator," but here
refers to one who takes the lead or sets the example. It was Jesus who
first taught the "great salvation" (2:3), and it was He who led the way
in it. He is the leader and inspiration for men's faith, the goal toward
which they strive as runners in the race. Thus the thought passes from
the encouragement of earthly examples to Jesus as the supreme example
who is to be imitated. And He is the example for men *because* He is
the **perfecter** of faith. That is, in Him faith has had its full expression,
its ultimate consummation. In Him faith has attained perfection, especially in His sufferings (cf. 5:7-10).[5]

How Jesus was the pioneer and perfecter of faith is further explained: **Who for the joy that was set before him endured the cross,
despising the shame.** As the Christian has before him the appointed
(*prokeimenon*) race, Jesus had before Him the appointed (*prokeimenēs*)
joy. That this **joy** is described as being **set before** Jesus argues against
the possible rendering of the clause, "who instead of the joy." (See
Additional Note.) In the case of the latter rendering the thought would
be that Jesus chose earthly agony instead of heavenly joy, but the
picture is rather of Christ's having to do an unpleasant task and of His
being able to do it because of the anticipated joy of being at the
Father's hand.

Death by crucifixion was a death reserved for slaves and criminals,
an experience unfit for civilized men. Of it Cicero had said: "Let the
very mention of the cross be far removed not only from a Roman
citizen's body, but from his mind, his eyes, his ears."[6] But Jesus endured

3. Cf. the statement of Epictetus (2.19.29), "looking to God in everything both
small and great."
4. Translations (such as the KJV, ASV, RSV) that render the Greek article with
the possessive pronoun "our" restrict the thought of the passage. It would seem
better to view the article simply as the regular construction with an abstract noun—
"the pioneer and perfecter of faith."
5. Delling associates Jesus as "perfecter of faith" with His function as priest, i.e.,
Jesus has given faith its "perfect basis by His high-priestly work" (TDNT, VIII, 86).
Spicq (II, p. 386) connects this phrase with faith as the objective guarantee of
things hoped for (11:1) and with Christ as the One who gives men through their
faith the certainty of victory.
6. *Pro Rabirio* 5.

it. He suffered as few men have been called upon to suffer. Indeed, crucifixion was torture. With hands and feet nailed to a cross, the victim was unable to move or protect himself from heat or cold or insects. Yet uppermost in the author's mind at this point is the indignity and degradation of it all: Jesus, he says, despised its bitter shame. What a contemptible sort of death it was—the victim, stripped of his clothing, unable to take care of his bodily needs. But Jesus did not shrink from doing what He knew to be the will of God. "It is one thing to be sensitive to disgrace and disparagement, another thing to let these hinder us from doing our duty. Jesus was sensitive to such emotions; he felt disgrace keenly. But instead of allowing these feelings to cling to his mind, he rose above them."[7]

This Jesus did in anticipation of His joy of exaltation; for now, the author says, He **is seated at the right hand of the throne of God.** The words are again a reminiscence of Psalm 110:1, only this time, in contrast to the others, the author uses the Greek perfect tense. His meaning is, therefore, that Jesus took His seat in the past and continues to the present to sit royally on the divine throne.

The Christian then, if he would run well, must look to Jesus, for
3 He is an example not only of faith but also of endurance. **Consider him who endured from sinners such hostility against himself,[8] so that you may not grow weary or fainthearted.** There is a definite stress on "endure" all through the passage. Jesus **endured** (vv. 2, 3); and the author says that his readers must likewise endure (v. 7), that they must persevere or endure in the race (v. 1). The exhortation in these lines may be put thus: "Consider Jesus. Compare His experiences with your own. He, too, lived in the flesh and was a companion in tribulation. He was violently opposed, His sayings were twisted, and His claims were ridiculed. Consider His sufferings and the manner in which He met them." The implication is strong that, if the readers of the Epistle make an accurate reckoning, they will not collapse on the track before the race is finished.

Discipline, the Proof of Sonship
(12:4-11)

If the readers have tallied correctly, they have found that their afflictions do not compare with the burdens of others before them.

---

7. Moffatt, *Hebrews,* p. 197.

8. The earliest extant MSS (P[13], P[46], Aleph) read *eis heautous (autous),* "against themselves." This reading, at first sight, makes little sense. However, the author's thought may be that sinners were really going against themselves by opposing Christ. Though difficult, the reading perhaps is to be preferred because of its difficulty, since scribes over the years would tend to smooth out the expression.

They had suffered persecution but, the author reminds them, **In your 4 struggle against sin you have not yet resisted to the point of shedding your blood.** The language of the athletic contest is continued, although **your struggle** (*antagōnizomenoi*) refers now not to the race but to the contest with sin. The question here is whether **resisted to the point of shedding your blood** is to be taken literally or figuratively. Is the author saying that they had not yet literally shed blood, or is he saying that they have not yet been dead serious in the Christian conflict? The previous verse supplies the answer. Christ endured great hostility, to the point of shedding His blood. As yet, they had not. Their test had not been of the severest type, for as yet none of their number had gone to death as martyrs for the sake of Christ.[9] The question implied again is, Why should they, when others have suffered so much, give in to the lesser strains on their faith?

The subject of suffering is an important one in the Epistle. The author has already shown that Jesus had to suffer as Messiah and high priest of His people (2:9ff.); and he has shown, further, that his readers must demonstrate courage in the face of conflict, for in a "very little while" the Coming One will come (10:35ff.). He now adds to his "philosophy on suffering" by arguing against the commonly accepted notion that suffering is a sign of divine disapproval. To the contrary, he reasons, suffering is essential and even valuable, for through it God reveals His care and establishes a meaningful relationship of father and son. The author asks, **have you forgotten the exhortation which 5 addresses you as sons?** It is of little consequence whether the words are translated as a declarative statement or as a question. In keeping with his purpose in writing a "word of exhortation" (13:22), the author finds an appropriate quotation in the Septuagint rendering of Proverbs 3:11-12: "**My son, do not regard lightly the discipline of the Lord, nor lose courage when you are punished by him.**" In the original admonition the speaker is the wise teacher who speaks for wisdom, while **son** refers to the student of the wise teacher. But the author sees the quotation as charged with meaning for his readers, warning them not to regard it lightly nor to miss the lesson that reproof is the universal lot of children. The quotation continues: "**For the Lord disciplines him whom he loves, 6 and chastises every son whom he receives**" (cf. Rev. 3:19). "Spare the rod and spoil the child" is not a proverb of Scripture, but the merits of "the rod of discipline" are clearly and frequently taught. "Do not withhold discipline from a child; if you beat him with a rod, he will not die" (Prov. 23:13; cf. 22:15; 29:15). Pain inflicted by a father is for

---

9. As to how this statement bears on the problem of the original readers of the Epistle, see p. 31.

232 • JESUS CHRIST TODAY

a purpose. So the author reasons that by means of trials and difficulties God trains His children in the way He wishes them to go, that rather than these difficulties serving to indicate God's displeasure, they are in reality a proof of His love. Hardship and pain, therefore, are not to be viewed in the abstract, as isolated, incoherent phenomena; on the contrary, they must be related to the totality of a creation governed by a heavenly Father. "To endure rightly, one must endure intelligently."[10]

Only here in the Epistle does the author speak of God as a father, and it is significant that such language appears in a section on suffering. A good father deals gently and understandingly with his children, and yet there are times when his generous nature gives way to straightforward correction and painful retribution. Thus the author reassures

7 his readers by telling them that **It is for discipline that you have to endure.** The proper education of a child includes physical discipline which, though unpleasant at the time, works for the development of character. **God is treating you as sons; for what son is there whom his father does not discipline?** If God is truly their Father, then he must treat them accordingly. "He who spares the rod hates his son, but he who loves him is diligent to discipline him" (Prov. 13:24; cf. Dt. 8:5).

8   No real son, then, is exempt from fatherly correction. **If you are left without discipline, in which all have participated, then you are illegitimate children and not sons.** The author takes for granted the ancient practice of assigning the illegitimate son no portion of the inheritance, and regards as obvious also that a lack of concern of the father to give correction is a sign of illegitimacy. Their sufferings, he maintains, are clear proofs of their sonship—if God did not bother to discipline them, they would not be His children.

Elaborating the parallel of earthly and heavenly discipline, a further

9 argument is presented: **Besides this, we have had earthly fathers to discipline us and we respected them. Shall we not much more be subject to the Father of spirits and live?** The reasoning is forceful. Earthly fathers administer discipline, and yet do they not have respect from their children? Do they not often have this respect even when their discipline is whimsical and spasmodic? If so, then how much more respect—and submission—is due to God,[11] who disciplines in wisdom

10. Moffatt, *Hebrews,* p. 201. Philo (*On the Preliminary Studies* 177), too, quotes Prov. 3 and applies it in much the same way as does the author of Hebrews. In another of his works (*The Worse Attacks the Better* 146) he argues that it is better that God correct His servants rather than leave them alone in sin. Likewise, Seneca contends that the hardened soldier knows that blood is the price of victory, so God hardens and disciplines those whom he loves (*On Providence* 4.7-8).

11. God is here termed "the Father of spirits." This is a unique designation, although the expression has behind it a distinct Biblical background. Gen. 2:7 relates that God created man by breathing into his nostrils "the breath of life." In Zech.

and love that men might truly live? **For they disciplined us for a short 10 time at their pleasure, but he disciplines us for our good, that we may share his holiness.** Earthly discipline is temporary, coming as it does only in the early years of life; and too often it is inconsistent simply because it originates with human parents whose discretion is necessarily imperfect. Earthly discipline confines itself to the sphere of earthly life; but heavenly discipline, which is never arbitrary, seeks to purge God's own from sin and secure for them a permanent participation in the divine life whose essential requirement is holiness (cf. v. 14).

God may lay upon Christians special stresses and strains that penetrate to the inner core of their faith, but all of these are for a purpose. This is in reality the central thread running through the paragraph, which is now summed up in one further observation. **For the moment 11 all discipline seems painful rather than pleasant.** Pain, of course, is not pleasant, especially when it is being experienced. But later, as one mentally retravels the path of those experiences, it no longer seems so deep or lasting. Pain, therefore, is a great instructor and achieves great results. (Christ learned by suffering [5:8].) So it is with God's chastisement of His children. **Later it yields the peaceful fruit of righteousness to those who have been trained by it.** Divine discipline "is not a stone flung down arbitrarily on human life, but a seed."[12] That seed, when sown, develops into the **fruit of righteousness** (cf. Js. 3:18), which, in sharp contrast to the gnawing anxieties which attend pain, is described as **peaceful.**

Exhortation to Encourage Others (12:12-17)

The Epistle only here and there sheds light on its first readers. Who they were and what precisely were their problems, can never be known with certainty. What is possible, however, is to extract from the text bits of information on the readers and to piece these bits together in some kind of pattern. The Epistle apparently is addressed to one particular Christian community. But there have been subtle hints all along to the effect that not everyone in the community was pressing ahead. This is evident in the author's emphatic tone in passages such

---

12:1 God is described as the One who "formed the spirit of man within him," and in Eccl. 12:7 it is said that "the spirit returns to God who gave it." Two passages in Numbers (16:22; 27:16) speak of God as "the God of the spirits of all flesh." (Cf. with "the Lord of spirits" found frequently in Enoch and in 2 Macc. 3:24.) By "the Father of spirits" is here meant, as can be seen when the phrase is contrasted with "earthly fathers," that God is especially responsible for man's spiritual being.

12. Moffatt, *Hebrews*, p. 205.

as 3:12: "Take care, brethren, lest there be in any of you..." (cf. 4:1; 6:11). "Some," as has been seen, had already forsaken the common assembly (10:25); but if one is allowed to read between the lines, this "some" does not mean "most," or even a bare majority. As a whole it would seem that the congregation of original readers was not in imminent danger of defecting. Many of them were still quite capable of standing on their own; and now the exhortation is that they should do so, not simply for their own good but for the good of their weak brothers who were at the point of exhaustion.

12   **Therefore,** the author says, **lift your drooping hands and strengthen your weak knees.** The exhortation is in the words of the Old Testament, from Isaiah 35:3. The listless hands and the paralyzed knees blend in making a picturesque metaphor for discouragement and despair. It is the coward who, with hands fallen to his side and feeble knees, gives up when the way is hard. And cowardice is contagious! Courage, however, can revive sinking hearts and renew progress on the Christian

13   way. **Make straight paths for your feet.** These words are a quotation from Proverbs 4:26a (LXX), the whole passage undoubtedly being on the mind of the author as he wrote: "Let your eyes look directly forward, and your gaze be straight before you. Take heed to the path of your feet, then all your ways will be sure. Do not swerve to the right or to the left; turn your foot away from evil" (Prov. 4:25-27). That is, they were to walk in a straight line, they were to live honestly and openly, without moral or spiritual inconsistencies in their lives. They were to be especially careful about their lives **so that what is lame might not be put out of joint but rather be healed.** It is quite clear here that not all of them had attained to the same spiritual level. While some were able to regain their strength, others were weak and fainting. This demanded extra efforts on the part of the strong (cf. Rom. 15:1), lest the lameness become dislocation. **Put out of joint** is the translation for *ektrapē*, a word that might as well mean "turn away" or "avoid," but here with **lame** must be understood as a technical term for "be dislocated." The admonition is that the strong are to move onward in a straight course and bear along with them their weak brothers who otherwise might be tempted to turn aside and abandon the Christian race.

14   **Strive for peace with all men** (cf. Ps. 34:14), **and for the holiness without which no one will see the Lord.** The translation **with all men** suggests that the exhortation is to maintain peace with non-Christians as well as with Christians, but the connection with the following verse does not support this interpretation. The author here is speaking of matters that must be put right within the community. Stagnation and decay were taking hold. There was lameness in the church. Thus every

tendency toward factiousness and disarray must be overcome with the forbearance of love. **Holiness** as used in the Epistle is primarily a ritual word (cf. "sanctified" in 10:10). It is the drawing near to God with a cleansed conscience on the basis of the sacrifice of Jesus (10:14, 22). As under the old covenant an unclean person could not enter a sacred enclosure to worship, so without holiness the ultimate vision of God is impossible (cf. Mt. 5:8). But here the thought turns on practical holiness and morality. It is similar to Paul's admonition to the Thessalonians: "For God has not called us for uncleanness, but in holiness" (1 Thess. 4:7).

Common interest in the welfare of the group is urged. **See to it 15 that no one fail to obtain the grace of God.** Later the author will have special instructions concerning the leaders of the congregation (13:17), but here he places the responsibility of oversight on every member of the church. Like elders in the church (cf. 1 Pet. 5:2), they, too, are to "watch" *(episkopountes)* over men's souls. They watch in order that there might not be any lost from their number. They are to be diligent to see that none fail to attain the rich provisions of God's grace (cf. 2 Cor. 6:1; Gal. 5:4). They are also to see to it **that no "root of bitterness" spring up and cause trouble.** The words are taken from the Book of Deuteronomy: "Beware lest there be among you a man or woman or family or tribe, whose heart turns away this day from the Lord our God to go and serve the gods of those nations; lest there be among you a root bearing poisonous and bitter fruit . . ." (Deut. 29:18). The passage, a warning against the evils of idolatry and apostasy, neatly fits the situation of the original readers of the Epistle. By **root of bitterness** is not meant a bitter root, but rather some sort of poisonous root that might bring destruction. Undoubtedly what is referred to here, as in Deuteronomy, is a person who might spring up among them and infect with malignant growth the vigor of the whole group. The results would be tragic, for indifference begets indifference and apostasy begets apostasy. The tone of the passage is like that of 3:12: "Take care, brethren, lest there be in any of you an evil, unbelieving heart, leading you to fall away from the living God." **By it the many** would **become defiled** and, therefore, would be unable to share the full fellowship of God spoken of in the previous verse.

In addition, it is necessary that they take care in reference to their own personal morality: **that no one be immoral or irreligious like Esau, 16 who sold his birthright for a single meal.** It is clear from what is said in the next chapter (13:4) that immorality, or fornication, was a problem for at least some in their number. Thus the term should be taken here in its normal, literal sense. There is a question whether both **immoral** and **irreligious** refer to Esau, or the latter term only. The clause is ambiguous in the Greek. But the Old Testament never represents Esau as an immoral person. Further, the author's description of Esau in the following lines suits a profane or **irreligious** person, but nothing more. It appears, then, that **immoral** is not to be connected with Esau.

As Genesis 25:29-34 relates, Esau was a worldly-minded individual who sold his birthright for a single meal. He was a man of low views who had little inclination for spiritual things. A man without inner depth or outlook for the future, he was the kind of person who is totally caught up in the day to day affairs of life. He regarded lightly his religious privileges as the first-born, through whom the honor of descent passed, and forfeited them—all on account of a sudden burst of appetite.

17 His loss, the author says, was irrevocable: **For you know that afterward, when he desired to inherit the blessing, he was rejected, for he found no chance to repent, though he sought it with tears.** The passage, as translated here, is not as clear as it could be. "Repentance" as ordinarily used in the Bible has a distinct religious connotation, denoting a change of attitude toward sin or even "conversion."[13] But this is not the meaning here, for nowhere does the Old Testament mention Esau's "repentance" in this sense. What Esau did seek, however, was a change in his unfortunate lot. He wanted the blessing that had already been pronounced on his brother Jacob; and when he realized that he could not receive it, he "lifted up his voice and wept" (Gen. 27:38). He wept because he could not change the blessing. Isaac had blessed Jacob and, in Isaac's own words, "Yes, and he shall be blessed" (Gen. 27:33). Esau could not change an act that had already transpired. It is in this sense that it is said that there was no **chance to repent** for Esau. The Epistle certainly is not dogmatizing on Esau's final destiny or even on his later years, which indeed did come to show a marked difference of attitude toward his brother.

Thus it is better to understand **repent** more generally, referring to any sort of a change of mind or decision. The thought of the passage is that Esau, after committing himself to a bad bargain, could not change its consequences—he found no chance to change it, though he sought to change it with tears.[14] The author, to be sure, has a practical lesson in view: his readers, too, by despising the Christian privileges conferred on them, can, like Esau, lose unalterably their inheritance.

---

13. See TDNT, IV, 999ff.

14. "Those tears of Esau, the sensuous, wild, impulsive man, almost like the cry of some 'trapped creature,' are among the most pathetic in the Bible" (Davidson, p. 242). The whole verse is well rendered by Montefiore: "You know that when he afterwards wanted to inherit the blessing, he was rejected (for he had no opportunity of getting the decision changed) although he sought it with tears." Cf. the translation of Knox, which is similar; cf. also R. T. Watkins, "The New English Bible and the Translation of Hebrews xii. 17," *ExpTimes* 73 (1961) 29-30.

Sinai and Zion
(12:18-24)

In this and the subsequent paragraph the author presents the grand finale to the exhortation begun in 10:19. What follows in chapter 13 is much like an appendix to the main work. The author thus far has pursued many ideas but always his objective has been the same: to stabilize his readers in their faith and to convince them that there is no alternative open to them except Christ. This objective is still with him as he places before his readers one final contrast between the two dispensations. The first, outward and physical by nature, accompanied by awful terrors, shut God away from men and made it plain that they could not draw near. The second, which is spiritual and eternal, brings men into heaven itself, to the realm of angels and good men made perfect, to God and to Christ, whose blood has opened the way. The privileges of the new era, therefore, are very great, which demand a reception and appreciation of these privileges and a life of true holiness. Why should they settle for a "mess of pottage" when they have received a heavenly calling?

For you have not come to what may be touched, a blazing fire, 18
and darkness, and gloom, and a tempest, and the sound of a trumpet. 19
Manifestations of God in the Old Testament are consistently associated with natural elements such as fire and clouds and darkness (Ex. 3:1-6; 40:34-38; 1 Kg. 8:10-13. At the giving of the law, these appalling phenomena were present. "Mount Sinai was wrapped in smoke, because the Lord descended upon it in fire; and the smoke of it went up like the smoke of a kiln, and the whole mountain quaked greatly. And as the sound of the trumpet grew louder and louder, Moses spoke, and God answered him in thunder" (Ex. 19:18-19).

Then, as the holy mountain "burned with fire to the heart of heaven" (Deut. 4:11), there was **a voice whose words made the hearers entreat that no further messages be spoken to them.** Deuteronomy 5:22ff. says that God spoke "out of the midst of the fire, the cloud, and the thick darkness, with a loud voice," and that the people were so afraid they implored Moses to mediate God's words to them (cf. Ex. 20:18-20). **For they could not endure the order that was given, "If even** 20
a beast touches the mountain, it shall be stoned." The sanctity of the mount was not to be violated by man or beast (Ex. 19:12-13). Such a command emphasizes the materialistic conception of holiness that was linked with the old covenant. God's presence was there on the mount. Nothing was to touch it. If any living thing did, even accidentally, it in turn was not to be touched. Any transgressor was to be stoned to

21 death,[15] no human hand was to be laid on it. **Indeed, so terrifying was the sight that Moses said, "I tremble with fear."** These precise words are not recorded of Moses in the Pentateuch. Possibly the author is drawing on a popular understanding of Moses' feelings since it is said that "all the people who were in the camp trembled" (Ex. 19:16). Deuteronomy 9:19 registers Moses' fear on a separate occasion (cf. Acts 7:32 for still another occasion).

The author's portrait of Sinai is grim and terrifying, accenting the awesome aspects of that revelation which came with the old dispensation. Over against this, however, stands the new covenant, the supreme evidence of God's grace among men. Here there is light instead of darkness, salvation in place of destruction. Christians now have a 22 privileged posture. **But you have come,** the author says, **to Mount Zion and to the city of the living God, the heavenly Jerusalem.** Zion was originally a stronghold of the Jebusites which was captured by David (2 Sam. 5:6-9); later, it came to stand for the enlarged city of Jerusalem, God's dwelling-place (Ps. 9:11; 76:2). It is the heavenly city built by God Himself (11:10), the place where the living God gathers with His people. It is called here **the heavenly Jerusalem,** in Revelation "the new Jerusalem" (Rev. 3:12; 21:2). Before this celestial order Christians stand, in contrast to the terrestrial Mount Sinai. The expression **you have come** (*proseléluthate*) is in the perfect tense and denotes their conversion to Christianity. When they came to Christ they came to Mount Zion. True, they did not come literally into the city, for, as the author later says, "We seek the city which is to come" (13:14). But in Christ and with the new covenant they share spiritually in the city. The language possesses an air of the Christian's glory and triumph.

The author next begins to enumerate the inhabitants of the heavenly 23 city, to which Christians have come: **to innumerable angels in festal gathering, and to the assembly of the first-born who are enrolled in heaven.** The passage is difficult, although not as difficult as it is made out to be by many interpreters. The different punctuations adopted by various translations should be noted carefully.[16] A multitude of angels is often depicted in Scripture as surrounding the throne of God. In Daniel's description of the "Ancient of Days" it is said, "A thousand thousands served him, and ten thousand times ten thousand stood before him" (Dan. 7:10; cf. Deut. 33:2). In Revelation, also, gathered around

15. The KJV, on the basis of a few late manuscripts, completes the quotation of Ex. 19:13 from the LXX by adding "or thrust through with a dart."

16. The punctuation of the RSV (supported by the Latin and Syriac versions) is probably to be preferred. This construes *panégurei* as a dative connected with "myriads of angels" in the preceding verse, with the resultant meaning "innumerable angels in festal gathering." But the constructions of the KJV, ASV, and NEB are quite possible and entail no radical difference in meaning.

the throne are many angels, "numbering myriads of myriads and thousands of thousands" (Rev. 5:11). The Epistle has already spoken of angels as "ministering spirits" for those who are to inherit salvation (1:14), and here it sees them as crowding about the throne in festal array for worship.

This much is clear. But what is meant by **the assembly of the first-born who are enrolled in heaven?** Some would say that the **first-born** are the angels because they were the first inhabitants of heaven. Against this, however, is the basic meaning and use of **first-born.** Elsewhere Scripture does not refer to the angels as **first-born;** and, furthermore, in the Epistle **first-born** seems to convey the idea of privilege and heirship (1:6; cf. 12:16). (See Additional Note on 1:6.) Besides, why would it be said of angels that they were **enrolled in heaven?** It might be said of them that they are **enrolled,** indicating that they are citizens of the eternal city; but why would it be said that they are **enrolled in heaven?** In the case of angels, to add the words **in heaven** would be superfluous. It would appear, therefore, that the whole expression can best be understood to refer to men. Other parts of Scripture are consistent with the view that it is men, not angels, "whose names are [written] in the book of life" (Phil. 4:3; cf. Lk. 10:20; Rev. 21:27).[17] **The assembly of the first-born,** then, must denote the church itself, made up of men on earth who, when they believe, have their names inscribed on the citizen roll in heaven.

To this heavenly community God's privileged children have come and in it hold membership. They also have come **to a judge who is God of all, and to the spirits of just men made perfect.** The familiar translations that read "God who is judge of all" are not exact. The main thought is that God is the God of all, of angels and men, of living and dead; and that as God He is the Judge to whom men must give account (cf. 4:13). The implication is that He is a God who is not to be regarded lightly. He is not a happy-go-lucky sort of God.

In the celestial world there are also **the spirits of just men made perfect.** This would seem to refer to the departed **spirits** (cf. 1 Pet. 3:18) who in this life were **just,** to all those who died in faith and have gone to their reward, whether they lived under the first or the second covenant. They are **made perfect** in the sense that they have reached their final destiny, made possible by the sacrifice of Christ.

Thus the heavenly city is comprised of select inhabitants. When a person becomes a Christian, he becomes at the same time a citizen of the heavenly city which is composed of innumerable angels, of members of the church on earth, and of the departed saints. He gains direct

---

17. Cf. TDNT, I, 619f.

24 access to the God of all and he comes, too, **to Jesus, the mediator of a new covenant, and to the sprinkled blood that speaks more graciously than the blood of Abel.** Jesus is placed last in the listing of the heavenly citizenry, as a climax, because it is His "single offering" that has made perfection possible (10:14) and because His blood brings men to God. In saying that He is Mediator of the new covenant and that His blood avails, the author is but reiterating his central message. **The sprinkled blood** (cf. 1 Pet. 1:2) is not a reference to the sprinkling of blood at the Passover but to the covenant blood, in this case the blood of Jesus that ratified the new covenant (cf. 9:18ff.; 10:22). It speaks "better things"—a key expression in the Epistle—because its message is gracious. The blood of Abel cried for vengeance against Abel's murderer, but the blood of Christ calls for forgiveness, cleanses the guilty conscience, and opens the way to heaven.

Listen to Him Who Speaks
(12:25-29)

One final appeal is now made. As Mount Sinai and Mount Zion stand in bold contrast, so does the character of their revelations. The one that was physical struck terror in those who witnessed its inauguration: it was spoken on earth. The other, gracious and reassuring, is spoken from heaven. The argument is from the lesser to the greater. (See Additional Note on 2:2.) If the first could not be rejected without retribution, then certainly the second cannot be.

25 **See** (*blepete* as in 3:12) **that you do not refuse him who is speaking.** The one who speaks is God, as in 1:1. The exhortation, as in 2:1, is to pay the closer attention to and hold on to the gospel message which alone can give life. The reasoning that follows is similar to that of 2:1-4 and 10:28-31. **For if they did not escape when they refused him who warned them on earth, much less shall we escape if we reject him who warns from heaven.** The first half of the sentence refers, of course, to the Israelites and to their refusal. But in what sense did they make refusal? And who was the one who **warned them on earth?** Perhaps the author means that it was Moses who warned on earth, but characteristically in the Epistle it is God who does the speaking. In any case the main point of contrast is not the contrast between speakers, between Moses who spoke from earth and Christ who speaks from heaven. It is rather a contrast between the two revelations themselves, the one given on earth—earthly—and the other coming from above. It is a contrast of kinds—between prophetic oracle and a Living Voice who continues to speak from heaven.[18]

---

18. For a similar contrast—that between the messages of John the Baptist and Jesus—see John 3:31-36.

But of what did the Israelite refusal consist? Though it is true that at Sinai the people refused to hear the voice of God,[19] it would seem that the author has in mind refusal on a larger scale. Instead of Israel's refusal on one occasion, he is probably thinking of their obstinate rejection of God's will over the centuries. They persisted in unbelief and disobedience, as a result of which they were denied entrance into God's rest (3:7ff.). "Every transgression or disobedience" done by them "received a just retribution" (2:2). Now, however, God speaks **from heaven;** and the sorry plight of the Israelite nation signifies the consequences of human apathy.

The antithesis between the two covenants is further developed: **His voice then** (God's voice at Sinai) **shook the earth** (cf. Ex. 19:18; **26** Ps. 68:8); **but now he has promised, "Yet once more I will shake not only the earth but also the heaven."** The words quoted are from Haggai 2:6. When first spoken, as the next verse in Haggai shows, they had reference to the reconstruction of the temple under Zerubbabel. God said that He would shake all the nations and make their treasures flow in, to fill the temple with splendor. The author of Hebrews, however, sees in these words a grander meaning, fully convinced that they point to the dissolution of the cosmic order at the Second Advent. When the law was given, the earth quaked; when Christ comes again, heaven and earth will be completely shaken.

This phrase, "Yet once more," indicates the removal of what is 27 shaken, as of what has been made. Yet once more shows that the shaking will be final, just as Christ died for sins once and will appear one more time (9:28). **As of what has been made** refers to all created things; they are all destined to decay. "They will perish . . . they will all grow old like a garment" (1:11). These things, because they are material and perishable, will be removed when heaven and earth are shaken, **in order that what cannot be shaken may remain.** The physical and unreal pass away so that the real and eternal, of which the heavenly kingdom (v. 28) and the new covenant (13:20) are a part, may remain.

Therefore, the author concludes, seeing that these things are not **28** to last, **let us be grateful for receiving a kingdom that cannot be shaken.** The heavenly kingdom is not subject to agitation or alteration. Believers belong to it and share its treasured privileges; they have passed from death to life and live in its realm. Still they await its full and final consummation. This accounts for the use of the present tense **receiving**— Christians are in the process of receiving the eternal kingdom.

God's grace shown in a special way should, on the part of all be-

---

19. The verb for "refuse" (*paraiteomai*) is the same as that used in v. 19. There the clause literally rendered reads, "those who heard refused not to be added to them a word," that is, "the hearers entreated that no further word be spoken to them."

lievers, evoke thankfulness. "Let us be grateful" (cf. 13:15), the author
says, **and thus let us offer to God acceptable worship, with reverence
and awe; for our God is a consuming fire.** Remembering the majesty
of God goes a long way toward checking digression and apostasy. He
must be approached with **reverence and awe.** The two terms (for the
first see the comments on 5:7 and the footnote on 11:7) express cautious
reverence and suggest an attitude of intense devotion on the part of
the worshiper. He is indeed a gracious God, but He is also "a devouring
fire, a jealous God" (Deut. 4:24). He is indeed a God of love, but too
often this description of Him is distorted and makes Him something He
is not and has never been. "True love does not confuse good and evil,
it does not fail to distinguish between truth and falsehood, it does not
say, 'Peace, Peace!' where there is no peace.... If man insists on sin,
if he deliberately chooses evil rather than good, if of set purpose he
turns his back on the proffered salvation, then God Himself is helpless
to save him."[20] With similar thoughts the author brings his finale to an
end, leaving his readers to ponder the stern side of God's nature and
what His moral goodness requires.

Chapter 11 can best be epitomized in the word "faith." "Faith"
occurs twenty-four times in this one chapter. In 11:1 it is a hook word,
going back to 10:39, and it also frames an inclusion with 11:39. It is
the heroic spirit of faith, exemplified by the men of old, that is so
urgently needed by the readers of the Epistle. Abraham, for example,
tore himself loose from his own family and ventured out in faith on
receiving the call of God. As it is the nature of faith to live in hope, he
looked toward the unseen realities of God's eternal city. Men of faith,
like Abraham and others, have a pilgrim outlook: God's people must
recognize that they are wanderers and foreigners in a strange land.
It is faith, then, that gives divine approval (11:2) and understanding
(11:3), that makes one acceptable (11:4) and pleasing to God (11:5-6),
that takes heed and acts (11:7), that journeys out on the basis of God's
word (11:8), that is patient in sojourning (11:9-10) and looks for the
better country (11:16), that chooses abuse rather than wealth or ease
(11:24-28), and so on. God is not ashamed of men of faith (11:16), and
the world is not worthy of them (11:38). Yet as great as these men
were, God has provided something better for Christians (11:40). Christians share in the age of fulfilment.

Chapter 12 continues the exhortations begun in the latter part of
chapter 10. The readers are to be stimulated by memories of their own
glorious past (10:32-39), by the faith of others who lived before them
(11:1-40), by the example of Jesus in suffering (12:1-3), by the good

20. Robinson, p. 194.

uses of discipline (12:5-11), and by the duties and privileges that belong to those who have received God's final revelation (12:12-29). As Christians they must strip themselves down for the race of faith. They must fix their gaze, as they run, on Jesus. He is the model of endurance and triumph. He endured the abuse and shame of crucifixion, and He is now sitting at the right hand of God. Too, God has purposes in suffering. Christians *are* His children, and all of His children He disciplines in order that they might share His holiness. Holiness is the very quality of life they should aim at, especially in view of their unrivaled Christian privileges. There is a kingdom that cannot be moved. Christians should be grateful for this and for their membership in the great spiritual society.

Additional Notes

"Who for the joy..."

V. 2. "Who for the joy that was set before him" is the rendering of the KJV, ASV, RSV, and other translations. The NEB translates similarly, "who, for the sake of the joy that lay ahead of him..."; it includes in a footnote the alternative translation, "who, in place of the joy that was open to him...."

The force of the clause turns on the meaning of the Greek preposition *anti* ("for"). *Anti* originally meant "over against" or "opposite," but it is not used in the New Testament in this sense. Often *anti* means "instead of," "in place of." "Archelaus reigned over Judea in place of [*anti*] his father Herod" (Mt. 2:22). "What father among you, if his son asks for a fish, will instead of [*anti*] a fish give him a serpent...?" (Lk. 11:11). Sometimes *anti* is used to show that one thing is equivalent to another—"An eye for [*anti*] an eye and a tooth for [*anti*] a tooth" (Mt. 5:38). Sometimes *anti* takes on the sense "in behalf of." So Jesus was to give Himself "as a ransom for [*anti*] many" (Mt. 20:28; Mk. 10:45). And there are other possible meanings for *anti* in the New Testament.

Here in 12:2, several alternatives have been suggested. (1) *Anti* as meaning "instead of." Jesus went to a cruel death instead of holding on to His joy, that is, Jesus chose suffering instead of continuing in His place of honor with the Father in eternity (cf. Phil. 2:5ff.). This view is preferred by Montefiore and also by Nigel Turner.[21] (2) *Anti* in the sense of "in exchange for," as perhaps in 12:16. Jesus endured the cross in exchange for the joy He would receive in ascending to "the right hand of the throne of God." (3) *Anti* almost in the sense of "in order

---

21. N. Turner, *Grammatical Insights into the New Testament* (Edinburgh, 1965), p. 172f. Turner's two-page note should be consulted.

to secure," as probably in 12:16. This is the explanation of Moffatt and of F. F. Bruce. It is the view that was adopted by A. T. Robertson: "In Heb. 12:2 the cross and the joy face each other in the mind of Jesus and he takes both, the cross in order to get the joy."[22]

---

22. A. T. Robertson, *A Grammar of the Greek New Testament in the Light of Historical Research* (Nashville, 1934), p. 574.

HEBREWS THIRTEEN

Various Exhortations
(13:1-6)

The chief task of the author is now ended. The remainder reads very much like an extended postscript to the main work. It is here that Hebrews assumes the manner and characteristics of a personal letter sent to a particular group of Christians from a Christian friend. The author does write as a friend. His salutations are warm. He knows and speaks of particular situations in which his readers have an interest. His exhortations and warnings are varied, but they are to the point and are given in rapid-fire order as a teacher might counsel his students on numerous subjects, not wishing to overlook a single pitfall that might prove fatal.

Thus the tone and atmosphere of chapter 13 are different from the rest of the Epistle. In fact, the difference is so distinct that a few scholars from time to time have denied that it (or portions of it) was ever a part of the original composition. But such views have more to do with "the curiosities of criticism" than with the generally accepted facts. The majority of scholars do not question the integrity of Hebrews 13. Its exhortations and themes, such as in 13:10-16, are too similar to the preceding twelve chapters for it to be an independent tract tacked on by some unknown person at the end.[1]

The final chapter of the Epistle begins with social and moral injunc-

---

1. This has been very well demonstrated by Floyd V. Filson, *"Yesterday": A Study of Hebrews in the Light of Chapter 13* in *Studies in Biblical Theology*, Second Series, vol. 4 (Naperville, Ill. 1967). For linguistic support of the view that chapter 13 and the rest of Hebrews have a common authorship, see C. R. Williams, "A Word-Study of Hebrews 13," JBL 30 (1911), 129-36. On the different theories connected with chapter 13, see Guthrie, p. 50ff.

tions. These moral instructions are sometimes referred to as "paraenesis." Paraenesis, generally speaking, is exhortation. More specifically, it is "moral instructions with a dash of exhortation."[2] Often the exhortations are in a series and relate to various matters. It is likely that a paraenetic tradition, that was delivered to converts, existed in the early church and was apostolic and normative.

The typical exhortations, as represented in Paul, in 1 Peter, and Hebrews 13, consist of lists of virtues and vices, instructions for different members of the household, warnings against sexual sins, teachings on brotherly love, hospitality, and so forth. Thus the author admonishes,
1 **Let brotherly love continue.** He does not say to his readers: "Have brotherly love," or "let it exist among you," but rather "let it continue." They had shown this love in the past by serving the saints and by having compassion on their brothers in affliction (6:10; 10:33-34). Now the exhortation is that they continue in love, lest their feelings for one another grow cold.

With brotherly love go two specific imperatives, the first of which
2 concerns hospitality. **Do not neglect to show hospitality to strangers, for thereby some have entertained angels unawares.** In the ancient world hospitality was regarded as a solemn duty. Among the Greeks Zeus himself, under the title of *Zeus Xenios* ("Zeus the patron of strangers"), defended the sacred tie between host and guest and rained down punishment from heaven against any breach of this tie. Philo, as he is relating Abraham's reception of the three unknown travelers, comments, "In a wise man's house no one is slow in showing kindness; but women and men, slaves and free, are full of zeal to do service to their guests."[3] Especially among Christians, due to their peculiar circumstances, hospitality became a religious obligation. Christians often were on the road. Many were displaced and scattered from their native surroundings because of persecution; not a few went out preaching the gospel from place to place. The public inns were too costly for most Christians, and they were generally places of low repute. Special courtesies, then, were to be extended to all: "Practice hospitality ungrudgingly to one another" (1 Pet. 4:9; cf. Rom. 12:13). It was a "loyal thing" for Christians to render service to strangers in their brotherhood, especially to those who had set out on their journey in God's service (3 Jn. 5-8).

Brotherly love shown in hospitality brings results. Some have, unknowingly, **entertained angels.** One thinks readily of the angelic

2. See A. M. Hunter, *Paul and His Predecessors*, revised ed. (Philadelphia, 1961), p. 52ff.
3. Philo, *On Abraham* 109.

visits to Abraham and Lot (Gen. 18—19), but the lesser-known visits to Gideon and Manoah should not be passed over (Jg. 6:11ff.; 13:2ff.). The reference to angels does not mean that Christians should practice hospitality with the express hope of entertaining angels. It is instead another way of saying that those who show hospitality to all often gain unexpected benefits from their guests. "You never know," the author says, "what hospitality might bring."

The second imperative of brotherly love is to **Remember those 3 who are in prison.** This they had already done, probably in the midst of some local persecution (10:34). Now the encouragement is to make this a general rule of life, caring for those in prison, **as though in prison with them.** The principle taught is that of the Golden Rule: they were to imagine themselves in prison and to treat their oppressed brothers as they would want to be treated (see Mt. 7:12). To take care of prisoners involves industry and initiative. Strangers might come to their doors for service, but those in prison have to be sought out and waited on. "I was in prison and you came to me," said Jesus (Mt. 25:36).

The same compassion must be extended to **those who are ill-treated,** says the author, **since you also are in the body. In the body** does not mean "in the body of Christ." Others were undergoing hardships in the name of Christ. The readers are to remember those who suffer, keeping in mind that they themselves are also mortals in the body and as bodily men are subject to the same hardships.

The next ethical injunction pertains to sexual purity. **Let marriage 4 be held in honor among all, and let the marriage bed be undefiled; for God will judge the immoral and adulterous. Among all** (*en pasin*) can be either masculine or neuter. If neuter, it is to be translated "in all respects," which means that marriage in all its aspects is to be held in high esteem. If masculine, it is to be translated "among all," which means that the marriage state must be esteemed highly by all Christians, especially those who are married. The latter rendering is the more likely one. The immoral and adulterous are mentioned separately because the Greek language distinguishes between the two. Adultery (*moicheia*) denotes unfaithfulness on the part of married persons; immorality (*porneia*) is more general in nature and includes all sorts of sexual vices and abnormalities. **The marriage bed** is a euphemism for the physical intimacy of married life. Whoever defiles it and severs the marital ties falls under God's judgment.

Following this warning against immorality there comes a warning against greed. **Keep your life free from love of money, and be content 5 with what you have.** The apostle Paul, as does the author, links together covetousness and sexual impurity (Eph. 5:3-5), probably because material prosperity induces sensuality. Both are extreme forms of selfishness, and one is just as devastating to spirituality as the other. Against the dangers of money and its wrong uses, many passages from the gospels and epistles speak out (Mk. 4:19; 10:23; Lk. 12:15-21; 1 Tim 6:9-10, 17-19). That Christians should be content with what they have is a clear reflection of Jesus' teachings (Mt. 6:24-34); the whole passage on riches and contentment with what one has is very similar to 1 Tim. 6:6-10. Paul said to Timothy: "We brought nothing into the world, and we cannot take anything out of the world; but if we have food and clothing, with these we shall be content" (1 Tim. 6:7-8).

A craving for more and more things is the result of fear, a fear of want and destitution. Covetousness is thus, in reality, a distrust of God and of His providence. Over against this fear is the sure promise that God will never leave weak mortals in the straits of trouble; **for he has said, "I will never fail you nor forsake you."** The words are, in effect,

6 from Joshua 1:5 (cf. Deut. 31:6, 8; 1 Chron. 28:20). **Hence we can confidently say, "The Lord is my helper, I will not be afraid; what can man do to me?"** These words are quoted from Psalm 118:6. Both citations of Scripture are calculated to give great assurance to the readers. When persecution should come upon them, they might lose their worldly possessions, but they would not be deserted. They might be threatened with physical injury, but no one could harm them if they were on the Lord's side. "The argument of our author is that instead of clinging to their possessions and setting their hearts on goods (10:34), which might still be taken from them by rapacious pagans, they must realize that by having God they have enough. He will never allow them to be utterly stripped of the necessaries of life. Instead of trying to refund themselves for what they had lost, let them be content with what is left to them and rely on God to preserve their modest all; he will neither drop nor desert them."[4]

Warning Against Strange Teachings *(13:7-16)*

A fresh thought now begins. The author exhorts his readers to remember their former teachers. They have passed from the human scene, but their example and teachings remain; and these must be held on to without compromise. Novel teachings, therefore, must be avoided; for it is the grace of God, not foods, that Christians must rely on.

7 **Remember your leaders, those who spoke to you the word of God; consider the outcome of their life, and imitate their faith.** The author has in mind those who first evangelized the community of his readers. Apparently they are the same as those who heard the Lord and conveyed

---

4. Moffatt, *Hebrews*, p. 230.

to others the message of the great salvation (2:3). That they were no longer alive is implied in the words **consider the outcome of their life.** The word translated **outcome** *(ekbasis)* literally means "way out" and then "issue" or "end." The reference, however, is not necessarily to martyrdom. The author may well be referring to the spirit in which they died rather than the means by which they died. In any case they died in faith. This the readers are to **consider** *(anatheōrountes).* The verb means "to look back on," "observe keenly and carefully"; it is the term used for the very opposite of a superficial examination. And remembering their leaders, they are to follow the example of their faith.

Jesus Christ is the same yesterday and today and for ever. The **8** statement, though succinct, is not abrupt. The connection to the preceding thought is that when their leaders first spoke to them the word of God, the subject of their preaching was Jesus Christ. The Jesus whom they preached is still the same Jesus; the gospel from heaven that announced Him is the same gospel. The terms **yesterday and today** do not refer to any specific periods of Jesus' life, as though **yesterday** stands for His earthly existence and **today** for His session in heaven. They express in beautiful language simply past and present time. Jesus has been in the past and is in the present unchangeable, and the author adds with exultant assurance that He will remain the same for all time and eternity, **for ever.** God says of Him: "Thou art the same, and thy years will never end" (1:12).

"The finality of the revelation in Jesus, sounded at the opening of the homily (1:1f.), resounds again here. He is never to be superseded; he never needs to be supplemented."[5] Any new doctrine is, therefore, an infringement on His inherent authority. Thus the warning: **Do not** **9** **be led away** (or swept away from the truth as with a flood) **by diverse and strange teachings.** It is clear, from what follows, that these teachings were in some way connected with foods. They were varied in character, an inconsistent mixture—in contrast to the unity of truth that had been taught. They were **strange** in that they were foreign to sound, apostolic teaching.

No further hint is given that would help identify these teachings, although the readers of the Epistle knew precisely what the author was striking against. It may be that (1) disputes existed in the community over various food regulations that were primarily Jewish in character. It may be that (2) allusion is being made to ascetic tendencies of the sort found at Colossae—"Do not handle, Do not taste, Do not touch" (Col. 2:21)—including restrictions of diet. Or it may be that (3) the novel teachings concern sacrificial meals of some kind. These are only

---

5. Moffatt, *Hebrews,* p. 232.

a few of the possible views,[6] but it is well to remember that the author apparently adverts to a belief that the eating of food (not abstinence from) in some way benefited the participants. In any case it would seem that the various Pauline instructions on foods reflect doctrinal aberrations of a similar kind (cf. Col. 2:16-23; Rom. 14:1ff.; 1 Cor. 8:1ff.). Like Paul, the author goes on to say that foods are of no value in bringing one near to God: **It is well that the heart be strengthened by grace, not by foods, which have not benefited their adherents.** Paul had written the Corinthians: "Food will not commend us to God. We are no worse off if we do not eat, and no better off if we do" (1 Cor. 8:8). Elsewhere he had said that "the kingdom of God does not mean food and drink but righteousness and peace and joy in the Holy Spirit" (Rom. 14:17). The point of significance here is the contrast between **grace** and **foods.** Food laws, whether negative or positive, cannot strengthen those who live by them. Such scruples regarding what to eat have been done away with in Christ.

So divine grace must be sought. Further, those who live under grace have rights and privileges that are unique. **We have an altar from which those who serve the tent have no right to eat.** One of the ancient charges laid against Christians was that their religion lacked substance because in it there were no sacrifices. Such a charge was unthinkable to the author. "We *do* have an altar,"[7] he says, "but it is different from—and superior to—any altar of Judaism. And it is an altar that is exclusive in character, for not everyone can share in it."

Two questions arise here: (1) What is the Christian altar? and (2) Who are **those who serve the tent?** In response to the first question a number of opinions have been given. Some have said that the altar stands for the Lord's Supper; others that it refers to Christ Himself, or to the mercy seat where atonement is made, or to the cross on which Christ made His sacrifice. The passage makes perfectly good sense, however, if the word **altar** is understood as a metonymy for **sacrifice,** with the meaning being that to partake of the altar is to partake of the sacrifice of Christ. According to Levitical procedures, those who served at the altar shared in the sacrificial offerings. Thus to eat of the altar was to eat of the sacrifice on the altar. This is the thought of the author. Christians have an altar because they have a sacrifice—the grand, once for all, self-offering of Christ.

It is inappropriate and out of context, therefore, to think that the

---

6. For a summation of other views, see Helmut Koester, "'Outside the Camp': Hebrews 13:9-14," HTR 55 (1962), 304f.

7. "We" means "we Christians," as so often in the Epistle. Compare the expression in 10:21: "...and since we [Christians] have a great high priest over the house of God."

Christian altar is the Lord's Supper. To the contrary, the point of these verses is that Christians have no sacrificial food to eat whatever. They have an altar, but it is not a literal one. "Inwardness is the dominating thought of the entire paragraph. God's grace in Jesus Christ works upon the soul; no external medium like food is required to bring us into fellowship with him. . . ."[8] How incongruous, then, if the author should be speaking of a literal eating at the Lord's table.

Assuming this interpretation to be correct, the second question relates to those who are excluded from the benefits of the Christian sacrifice. This might be any group that depends on fleshly externals for salvation. But the description of the author is quite specific—**those who serve the tent.** The tent denotes the earthly tabernacle in the wilderness, for the next verse clearly refers to the Day of Atonement described in the Pentateuch. **Those who serve the tent** would be the priests. (There is a touch of irony here. They serve the tent instead of the true God, who no longer is in the tent.) Yet the author has in mind not just the Levitical priests. His meaning is broader and extends to all who continued to keep the Old Testament ritual, or in other words, to all those that lived under the old covenant. They, he says, have no right to eat of the Christian altar. They cannot participate in the blessings of Christ's atoning sacrifice.

The proof of this is seen by the author in the Levitical legislation (cf. Lev. 16:27), which now he partially restates: **For the bodies of those** **11** **animals whose blood is brought into the sanctuary by the high priest as a sacrifice for sin are burned outside the camp.** The ceremony indicated is that of the Day of Atonement, for it was at this that the high priest officiated. On such an occasion the flesh of the animals sacrificed was not to be eaten. The priests who tended the altar normally ate of the sacrifices, but not on that day. Instead the animal bodies were carried outside the camp and burned.

There is, further, the analogy of place. As the animals were burned outside the camp, **so Jesus also suffered outside the gate in order to** **12** **sanctify the people through his own blood.** Crucifixion in ancient times took place outside the cities. Jesus died **outside the gate,** that is, outside the city of Jerusalem (Jn. 19:20). His blood, in contrast to that of animal victims (9:12), was the means of sanctification and the one acceptable sacrifice for sin (10:29; cf. 1:3; 10:10, 14).

Jesus, then, was condemned and thrust out of the city. The Jews refused Him and literally made Him an outcast. From this it follows

---

8. Moffatt, *Hebrews,* p. 234. The drift of the whole passage is likewise brilliantly epitomized by C. F. D. Moule, "Sanctuary and Sacrifice in the Church of the New Testament," JTS 1 (1950), 37-38. Cf. Vincent Taylor's discussion in his *The Atonement in New Testament Teaching,* 8th ed. (London, 1945), pp. 105-10.

that Christians are to have no part with the people or the system that
13 refused Him. **Therefore let us go forth to him outside the camp, bearing
abuse for him.** The exhortation is for the readers to break all ties with
Judaism. Since in the Old Testament **the camp** represented the religious
community of Israel, to go outside the camp means to make a clean
break with unbelieving Israel. The exhortation is that the readers
should sever all ties with Judaism. Its glory was past. Those who wanted
to share in the true sin offering must abandon the old religion. It is
difficult to see why these words would have been chosen if the Epistle
were addressed generally to Gentiles.

But to go away from the camp was not easy. Abuse would have
to be borne. The shame that was His (12:2) would have to be theirs.
As Moses "considered abuse suffered for the Christ greater wealth than
the treasures of Egypt" (11:26), they too must calculate wisely and be
14 willing to suffer reproach for His name. And why not? **For here** (on
earth) **we have no lasting city, but we seek the city which is to come.**
The link of thought is that if they as Christians, like Christ, must be
cast out, what does it matter? Nothing earthly is dear to Christians.
They are outcasts, homeless; but like Abraham they look "forward to
the city which has foundations, whose builder and maker is God"
(11:10). (See Additional Note on 11:9.)

The author now rounds off his paragraph with a further extension
of his sacrificial language. Christ has made the one great sacrifice. No
other offering for sin need ever be made. The Christian cannot be
strengthened by foods. The Christian altar is spiritual in nature, not
15 material. Thus the only sacrifices left to him are spiritual ones. **Through
him then let us continually offer up a sacrifice of praise to God, that is,
the fruit of lips that acknowledge his name.** **Through him** stands in the
emphatic position—it is through Christ as high priest that their offerings
are to be made and not through the stilted Levitical apparatus. These
offerings are not seasonal, but they are to be made **continually.** The
sacrifice to be offered by the Christian is **a sacrifice of praise,** which is
described as **the fruit of lips** (cf. Hos. 14:2). Whatever may come,
whether good or bad, the Christian owes God sacrifices of praise and
thanksgiving. The exhortation here is very much in keeping with the
spirit of the Psalms, expressed in such words as: "With a freewill
offering I will sacrifice to thee; I will give thanks to thy name, O Lord,
for it is good" (Ps. 54:6; cf. 50:14, 23).

Giving to God **the fruit of lips** is one aspect of Christian sacrifice,
16 but this in itself is not sufficient. **Do not neglect to do good and to share
what you have,** the author reminds his readers, **for such sacrifices are**

pleasing to God.[9] The practical side of Christianity must never be overlooked, for to do good to one's fellows is also a sacrifice of which God approves. This is the type of sacrifice Christianity requires—not the blood of bulls and goats. The two kinds of sacrifices mentioned here, the sacrifice of praise and the sacrifice of personal service, are closely connected. Genuine gratitude to God begets awareness of the needs of others.

Further Exhortations and Concluding Words (13:17-25)

In speaking previously to his readers about their leaders (v. 7), the author went on to warn against the dangers of new teachings. They were to remember the lives of their former leaders and hold on to their sound teachings. Now there comes an appeal for them to follow trustingly the direction of their present leadership. This appeal, too, is to be understood in the light of subversive elements within that threatened the security and unity of the local church. **Obey your leaders 17** (hēgoumenoi, as in vv. 7, 24) **and submit to them; for they are keeping watch over your souls, as men who will have to give account.** The command is to obey and to submit. The latter term seems to imply insubordination on the part of some who may have been separating themselves from the main group (cf. 10:25). Their strange teachings doubtless contributed to their withdrawal. But the leaders are to be yielded to; their views in regards to faith must be heeded.

The author is not, of course, suggesting a rubber-stamp endorsement of the views of all leaders. He is dealing with a particular historical situation, and in this he is equating the faith of the leaders— whom he knows—with the original apostolic faith. Submission to the leaders, the author feels, is reasonable, since they bear a solemn responsibility. They watch over men's souls, as carefully as shepherds pass sleepless nights—knowing that as God's stewards they must give account. **Let them do this joyfully, and not sadly, for that would be of no advantage to you.** The implication is that already some church leaders of the first century were experiencing grief in their tasks instead of joy. This was of no profit to a congregation. The local congregation, therefore, should be willing to put forth every effort to cooperate with its acknowledged leaders. It should seek to lessen the pain of leadership, not to add to it, thus enabling its leaders to do their work with joy rather than with regrets over those who have slipped back to ruin.

---

9. Moffatt (*Hebrews*, p. 237) notes that the three definitions of worship or religious service in the New Testament (here, Rom. 12:1-2 and Js. 1:27) are all inward and ethical. With this should be compared the picture of the Christian in his daily round as a priest who offers spiritual sacrifices (1 Pet. 2:5ff.).

The author now requests that he, too, be shown a special favor of
18 Christian concern. **Pray for us, for we are sure that we have a clear
conscience, desiring to act honorably in all things.** The us and we are
epistolary plurals referring to the author himself. This is made clear by
his further reference to a **clear conscience** and by his switch from the
plural to the singular "I" in the next verse. The author clearly feels that
he is acting in the best interests of his friends, though some perhaps
were suspicious of his intentions. He thus asks their prayers in his
behalf, a request often made in the Pauline epistles (Col. 4:3; 2 Thess.
3:1; Rom. 15:30).

Their prayers, the author believes, will be effective. So he is in-
19 sistent in his request: **I urge you the more earnestly to do this in order
that I may be restored to you the sooner.** The author formerly had lived
among the people to whom he addressed the Epistle, and had probably
been one of their teachers. He is separated from them now and desires
to return to them. Why he was away and why he could not come to
them immediately, are matters entirely unknown. Verse 23 seems to
indicate that he was not in prison and that his absence was only temporary in nature.

Greek letters written in the Hellenistic period followed a set form
at the beginning and the end. The concluding words of the Epistle are
in keeping with the accepted form, containing a prayer, final remarks,
and greetings from the author. As the author has asked the help of his
20 readers' prayers, so now he prays for them. **Now may the God of peace
who brought again from the dead our Lord Jesus, the great shepherd
21 of the sheep, by the blood of the eternal covenant, equip you with
everything good that you may do his will.** This is the only specific
reference to the resurrection of Jesus in the Epistle, although the repeated theme of Christ at God's right hand assumes it. The prayer is
directed to **the God of peace,** a descriptive phrase which is often found
at the close of Paul's letters (1 Thess. 5:23; 2 Thess. 3:16; Rom. 16:20;
etc.). There is here, perhaps, an allusion to local disharmony. In speaking
of Jesus as **the great shepherd,** the author blends together old and new.
Only here does he speak of Jesus in terms of a shepherd; but elsewhere
he has been careful to underscore Him as the great priest (or high
priest) of the Christian religion (4:14; 10:21). **The blood** of the covenant
is, of course, the blood of Christ by which the covenant was ratified.
It is closely linked with the resurrection because God accepted it as
the atoning sacrifice and thus raised Christ from the dead. It was His
blood that mediated the new covenant, here termed **the eternal covenant**
in contrast to the Mosaic covenant that passed away.

The controlling petition in the prayer is that the readers be equipped
with everything necessary to do God's will. The request echoes the

thought of 10:36. The author's wish is not that they may have everything, but that they may do the will of God. Yet it is God who supplies the essential grace, he says, **working in you that which is pleasing in his sight, through Jesus Christ.** God acts in men "to will and to work for his good pleasure" (Phil. 2:13); **to** Him, therefore, because He lives and works in believers, **be glory for ever and ever. Amen.** It seems best to understand the doxology as addressed to God the Father, since **the God of peace** is the subject of the prayer.

A postscript must still be added, which includes verses 22-25. There is no reason to think that these words were not a part of the original writing. If they had been appended by another hand in order to give the whole a Pauline-apostolic look, then surely the effort would have gone further and the product would not have been so enigmatic. The note has, however, an authentic appearance due to its simple and straightforward manner.

I appeal to you, brethren, bear with my word of exhortation, for I **22** **have written to you briefly.** Here now is the author's own description of his work; he calls it a **word of exhortation.** All through the Epistle his aim has been to admonish and to appeal to his Christian brothers. He knows full well that some have been resentful of his efforts. To them it might seem that he has said too much. But he is sure that he has written briefly, especially in view of the critical situation of his readers and the weighty subjects he has had to handle. He thus seeks a serious and kind reception for his letter.

A further personal note is given. **You should understand that our** **23** **brother Timothy has been released, with whom I shall see you if he comes soon.** Since the New Testament mentions only one Timothy, there is no reasonable doubt about the identity of this Timothy. He was a companion of and colaborer with Paul, a young man who was especially dear to him, who often was with Paul when he wrote his letters (1 and 2 Thessalonians, 2 Corinthians, Philippians, Colossians, Philemon) and often received personal instructions from him (1 and 2 Timothy). He seems also to have been a close associate of the author of Hebrews, for the author hopes that the two of them may be soon reunited with the readers. Timothy perhaps had been in prison; but if so, the circumstances of this imprisonment are unknown.[10]

---

10. The Greek term translated "has been released" is *apolelumenon.* It can have several meanings: (1) To "set free" or "release a prisoner" (Jn. 18:39; Acts 5:40; 16:35) or to "pardon someone" (Mt. 18:27; Lk. 6:37). (2) To "send away" or "dismiss," as in the case of man divorcing his wife (Mt. 1:19; 5:31; 19:3). (3) To "send away" or "dismiss" a crowd (Mt. 14:15, 22) or an assembly (Acts 19:41). In the passive the verb means to "be sent away," "leave," "depart"—to "be sent on a journey" (Acts 15:30, 33). Arndt-Gingrich (p. 96) prefers the latter with reference to Timothy, that he has left or departed, perhaps sent away on a mission;

At the last there come the usual greetings. In the ancient Greek letter the greeting was a set literary form and was used to establish the bonds of friendship.[11] The greeting might appear at the beginning or 24 end of the letter. **Greet all your leaders and all the saints. Those who come from Italy send you greetings.** Though greetings are customary, it is unusual that the people addressed be urged to greet their leaders. This might be an indication that the author is directing his letter to a smaller group within a larger one—either to a small group that was part of a church in a large city, or possibly to a small factious group that had withdrawn from the larger local church. At any rate they were to greet their leaders and obey and submit to them, as they were instructed to do in verse 17. If **Those who come from Italy** is the correct translation of the Greek phrase,[12] then the Epistle was written outside Italy and the Italians in the area were taking this opportunity to send their greetings to friends in their homeland. On the other hand, the phrase can mean "those who live in Italy." In this case the author would be writing from Italy and the residents of Italy would be sending greetings to their Christian friends abroad.

25 The Epistle ends with **Grace be with all of you. Amen.** A typical Greek letter would conclude with "farewell" (*errōsthe,* literally, "be strong"). Christians transformed the Greek secular letter in both its opening and closing formulas. This is the typical Christian conclusion, used frequently to bestow divine grace on those who read the apostolic messages.

So the author concludes his letter. He has had much to say (5:11). He has declared the fundamental truths of the Christian religion and he has grappled with the minds of men slow to believe, those who mentally and spiritually were adrift at sea. In chapter 13 he has given his final exhortations and appeal. He wants them to hold on to Christ at all costs. They are to remember the lives of those who first spoke the word of God to them. They are not to be carried away by strange teachings. Jesus Christ is the same yesterday, today, and forever. The author will await a face to face meeting with his friends to give them a further "word of exhortation."

---

although it allows the possibility of Timothy's having been released from an unknown imprisonment.

11. See Terence Y. Mullins, "Greetings as a New Testament Form," JBL 87 (1968), 418-26.

12. The Greek phrase is *hoi apo tēs Italias* and is as ambiguous in Greek as in English. Literally rendered the whole clause reads, "They of Italy greet you." This is the translation of the ASV. The NEB likewise resorts to a comfortable ambiguity: "Greetings to you from our Italian friends."

Index of Main Subjects

257

Index of Authors

Index of Scripture References

Old Testament

New Testament

4:6 — 48f., 97
4:7 — 37, 72, 99, 103
4:8 — 103
4:10 — 97
4:11 — 21, 48, 96f., 100, 128
4:11ff. — 89
4:12 — 29, 37, 65, 92, 98f., 103
4:12f. — 47
4:13 — 99, 103f., 239
4:13f. — 47
4:14 — 49, 80, 92, 100, 147, 169, 189f., 254
4:14ff. — 117, 188
4:14-7:28 — 39
4:14 - 10:18 — 38, 100
4:15 — 49, 76, 79, 83, 106
4:15-5:10 — 47
4:16 — 88, 100, 104, 146, 184, 188f., 193, 197, 208
5:1 — 47, 49, 80, 108
5:1ff. — 223
5:1-10 — 40, 48, 105
5:2 — 109, 149, 166, 193
5:3 — 41
5:5 — 39, 47, 53
5:5f. — 105
5:5-10 — 48
5:6 — 62, 137
5:6-10 — 47
5:7 — 114ff., 208, 242
5:7ff. — 81, 83, 114, 229
5:7-10 — 45, 114ff.
5:8 — 46, 54, 115, 233
5:8f. — 135, 149

5:9 — 37, 68, 76, 146, 173
5:10 — 39, 49, 62
5:11 — 32, 46, 129, 256
5:11f. — 54
5:11-14 — 31, 46
5:11-6:12 — 48
5:11-6:20 — 105
5:12 — 27, 117f., 120
5:12ff. — 196
5:14 — 76
6 — 196
6:1 — 76, 112, 171
6:1-6 — 36
6:2 — 37, 111
6:3 — 22
6:4 — 37, 91, 148
6:4ff. — 107, 113, 121
6:4-8 — 193, 196
6:5 — 72, 167
6:6 — 195
6:7 — 36
6:7f. — 46
6:9 — 27, 37
6:9f. — 44
6:9-12 — 196
6:10 — 31, 196f., 246
6:11 — 178, 190, 234
6:12 — 49, 63, 209
6:13 — 49
6:13f. — 144f.
6:13-20 — 190
6:17 — 63, 161, 173, 209
6:18 — 29, 178, 190
6:18f. — 143
6:19 — 46, 49
6:19f. — 41
6:20 — 39, 49, 62
7 — 108, 180
7:1 — 48f.
7:1ff. — 45

7:1-10 — 48
7:1-14 — 40
7:1-28 — 105
7:3 — 45, 48, 151
7:4 — 46, 48
7:7 — 37
7:8 — 35
7:9 — 48
7:11 — 39, 46, 48, 76
7:13 — 149
7:13f. — 155
7:15 — 39, 144, 149
7:16 — 149
7:17 — 149, 187
7:18 — 21, 158, 177
7:18ff. — 160
7:19 — 21, 37f., 48, 76, 149, 190
7:20 — 48
7:20ff. — 40
7:21 — 39
7:22 — 37, 130, 157
7:23 — 144, 187
7:23f. — 46
7:25 — 41, 68, 104, 108, 149, 176, 184, 208
7:26 —39, 100, 106, 149
7:27 — 37, 40f., 46, 154, 160, 170, 176, 194, 199
7:28 — 48, 54, 76
8 — 180, 187
8:1 — 39f., 56, 62, 108, 186
8:1-6 — 21
8:1-10:18 —39, 105
8:2 — 37, 108, 169, 176
8:3 — 40, 106, 187
8:3ff. — 108
8:4 — 39, 106
8:5 — 36, 164, 175, 183, 208